THE WINTER WAR

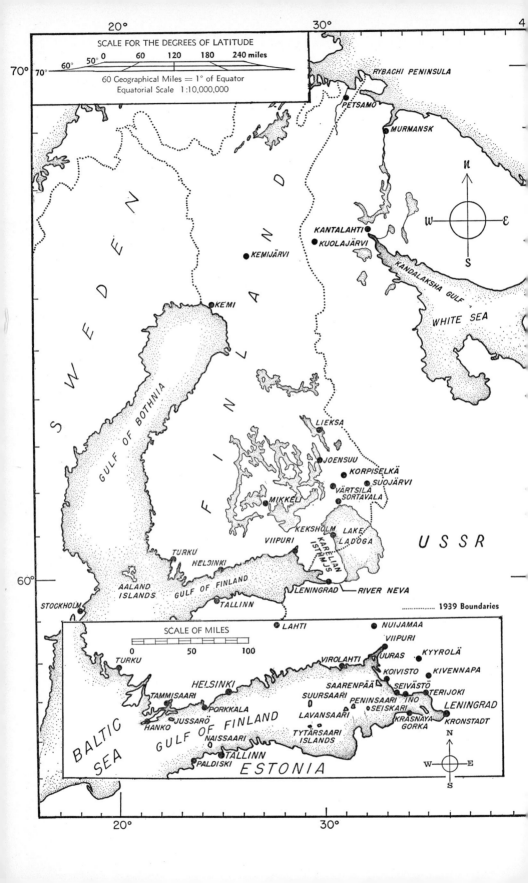

20°   30°   4

SCALE FOR THE DEGREES OF LATITUDE

60° 50° 0   60   120   180   240 miles
70° 70°

60 Geographical Miles = 1° of Equator
Equatorial Scale 1:10,000,000

RYBACHI PENINSULA

PETSAMO

MURMANSK

S W E D E N

F I N L A N D

KANTALAHTI
KUOLAJÄRVI

KEMIJÄRVI

KANDALAKSHA GULF

KEMI

WHITE SEA

GULF OF BOTHNIA

LIEKSA

JOENSUU

KORPISELKÄ
SUOJÄRVI
VÄRTSILÄ
SORTAVALA

MIKKELI

KEKSHOLM LAKE
LADOGA
VIIPURI

TURKU
HELSINKI

KARELIAN
ISTHMUS

U S S R

60°

AALAND
ISLANDS   GULF OF FINLAND

LENINGRAD   RIVER NEVA

STOCKHOLM

TALLINN

·········· 1939 Boundaries

LAHTI   NUIJAMAA

SCALE OF MILES   VIIPURI

0   50   100   VIROLAHTI UURAS KYYROLÄ

TURKU   KOIVISTO KIVENNAPA

SAARENPÄÄ SEIVÄSTÖ
HELSINKI   SUURSAARI   INO TERIJOKI
TAMMISAARI   PENINSAARI
PORKKALA   LAVANSAARI SEISKARI LENINGRAD
JUSSARÖ   KRASNAYA
HANKO   TYTÄRSAARI   GORKA KRONSTADT
NAISSAARI   ISLANDS
BALTIC
SEA   GULF OF FINLAND   N
TALLINN   W   E
PALDISKI   ESTONIA   S

20°   30°

𝔗HE WINTER WAR

FINLAND AGAINST RUSSIA 1939–1940

VÄINÖ TANNER *Former Foreign Minister of Finland*

STANFORD UNIVERSITY PRESS STANFORD, CALIFORNIA

First published in Finnish 1950

STANFORD UNIVERSITY PRESS, STANFORD,
CALIFORNIA / LONDON: OXFORD UNIVER-
SITY PRESS / © 1957 by the Board of Trustees of
the Leland Stanford Junior University / Printed in
the United States of America by Stanford University
Press / *Library of Congress Catalog Card Number:
57-5904*

FOREWORD

Seventeen years is a mere gleam in history. Yet, upon reassessing this brief span of years that divides us from the events described in this book, it becomes increasingly difficult to dissociate ourselves from them. Placed in proper historical perspective, the developments in 1939 assume a singular importance in recent history. One of these developments was the Winter War. By retracing the dramatic elements of this "Little War" one cannot escape the melancholy thought—How short is public memory! A generation is rising that has only hazy recollections, if any, of the episode; the umbilical cord between the present and the past is thus broken, and man is liable to continue his follies as before. The panorama of events moves with such dizzy speed that "current crises" obliterate the crises of yesterday, thereby turning the pattern of history into disjointed accidents. Who, for instance, can recall the seething public indignation that swept the United States when the Goliath of the East declared war on the David of the North? Who can remember the frenzied emotional outburst that seized the nation from coast to coast? In the end all the angry verbiage was incapable of triumphing over sheer force.

The lesson one could learn from this single episode seems essential, yet a new and thoughtful generation hardly remembers it. It is therefore understandable how the historian feels when he retraces the steps which the memoirs of Väinö Tanner, the distinguished citizen and statesman of Finland, present. His account of the Winter War must be considered as an important part of the history of the entire tragic era of our time. As former Minister of Foreign Affairs of Finland during the war months he is in a position to raise the curtain and throw a ray of light upon the stage of European affairs of recent date.

The author starts with the background of the war, when clouds of the oncoming crisis were rapidly gathering. Few were able to discern on the darkening horizon the approaching global conflict, and even those few were not sufficiently disturbed by it: they felt that as long as their own national interests were not immediately in peril there was no reason for alarm. The preliminary negotiations that followed, the three agonizing journeys the Finnish delegations made to the Kremlin, are vividly described and offer much food for contemplation. Throughout that period the impotent League of Nations at Geneva sat helplessly, and when, finally, it decided to expel the Soviet Union from the august body, its action hardly contributed to the desperate effort at enforcing a peaceful solution. Paper protests were futile, and the aid that reached embattled Finland during the ensuing weeks proved too little and too late; it only served to prolong the agony of the nation. It became increasingly clear that continued valor, though admired by the entire world, would spell national extinction. Finland had no choice but to bow her proud head and take the road to Canossa.

Finnish literature on the war is extensive; unfortunately, linguistic difficulties bar the student of history from familiarizing himself with it. Mr. Tanner's memoirs represent the first account in English. When I had the good fortune of meeting the author, he modestly offered the manuscript to me to examine and generously gave his permission to cite from it in my own work. After acquainting myself with its contents I urged him to prepare the work for publication in the United States. He hesitated for some time, and it took much persuasion on my part to win his consent. It now gives me great pleasure to contribute my modest token to a book that deserves a place of honor in postwar historical literature. It is my sincere hope that it will be widely read and that it will serve as an effective reminder of one vital lesson: that lasting peace can be enforced only when smaller nations can be assured of security based upon a moral order and on effective law enforcement.

ANATOLE G. MAZOUR

Stanford University
August, 1956

AUTHOR'S PREFACE

During the initial period of our country's independent existence, Finnish foreign policy was necessarily tentative until it found its proper course. At first the German orientation was the most powerful. When the First World War ended with a German defeat, the orientation became a Western European one. Yet before long an attitude of neutrality was observed to be the safest foreign policy for a small power. More than anything else it was the need to prevent the emergence of any conflict with our eastern neighbor, the Soviet Union, which influenced us to assume this stand. We worked on this basis throughout the 'twenties and likewise up to the end of the 'thirties. At the outbreak of the Second World War, Finland hastened to declare its neutrality in the hope that in this way it might avoid the misfortunes of war. Despite this step our country was drawn into the holocaust. The first stage was our engagement in the Winter War.

Many books have been written on Finland's Winter War. They have dealt with its military aspects—the course of events at the front, descriptions of battles and of heroic deeds. But the political background of the war has remained comparatively unfamiliar, at least to the general public. In its modest fashion, this book seeks to throw some light on that subject. It sets forth material on the negotiations before the war broke out, on the events which occurred during the writer's brief wartime term of office as Foreign Minister, and on the final conclusion of the peace. This report is based for the most part on notes which I made at the time, but, in addition to these, in certain passages I had recourse to contemporary documents, as for example in the opening part of the book, which deals with the preliminary negotiations.

As my notes can only describe events as I saw them, the book can of course not afford a full picture of the complex fabric of political incident during the period. If it nevertheless succeeds in conveying a correct understanding of the political activity of the Winter War period and perhaps also in furnishing material for future writers of history, its purpose will have been achieved.

V. T.

CONTENTS

THE WINTER WAR

CHAPTER 1

THE HORIZON DARKENS

One may perhaps consider that the first omen, in its fashion, of what was to come later consisted of a series of conversations which occurred in 1938 and which continued into the first half of 1939. The contact with the Soviet government that commenced at that time assumed a form exceptional in that it was conducted on behalf of the Soviet Union neither by a diplomatic minister nor by any other person holding a position of rank, but by the second secretary of the Soviet Legation in Helsinki, Boris Yartsev. This Mr. Yartsev had served at the Legation for several years and had built up a considerable circle of acquaintances in Helsinki, primarily in extreme leftist circles. He was a lively individual, pleasant in a way. One could easily discuss with him even the most delicate matters, as though he were a man who did not have to be particularly careful of what he said, unlike many people in his position. The story ran to the effect that he represented the GPU in the Legation— the state police of the USSR, in other words; the sort of official Soviet legations are supposed generally to have on their payrolls. His wife, a fine-looking woman past her first youth, was also quite well known in the capital since she represented the Russian tourist bureau, Intourist, and in that capacity organized pleasure and study trips to Russia.

In the early spring of 1938 this legation secretary, Yartsev, telephoned Foreign Minister Rudolf Holsti requesting with urgency an opportunity to speak to him personally. With characteristic courtesy Holsti consented to receive him, although strictly persons of Yartsev's station had no business with the Foreign Minister. The meeting was set for April 14, 1938. On keeping his appointment with Holsti, Yartsev asked whether he might discuss a couple of highly confidential matters. He had been in Moscow a few weeks before and had there received from his government exceptionally broad authority to discuss precisely with the Finnish Foreign Minister the improvement of relations between Finland and Russia. The conversations must be kept entirely secret. When Holsti expressed willingness to hear what he might have to propose and encouraged him to state his errand quite frankly, Yartsev started by referring to a question of the day which may be passed over here. Turning to the main matter, he launched into an extensive review of the general European political situation and of Finland's future position, as follows:

The Russian government wished to respect Finland's independence and territorial integrity, but Moscow was wholly convinced that Germany entertained such extensive plans of aggression against Russia that the objective of the extreme left wing of the German armies would be to effect a landing in Finland and thence to plunge their attack into Russia. At that time there would arise the question of what attitude Finland should assume toward these German intentions. If Germany were allowed to carry out these operations in Finland unopposed, Russia would not passively await the German arrival at Rajajoki but would throw its armed forces as far into Finland as possible, whereupon the battles between German and Russian forces would take place on Finnish territory.

If, instead, Finland were to oppose the German landings, Russia would offer Finland all possible economic and military assistance, binding itself to withdraw its forces from Finland after the war.

Mr. Yartsev further observed that Russia was prepared to offer Finland almost any concessions imaginable in the economic field. Russia had an almost limitless capacity to purchase our industrial products, among which he referred especially to cellulose, and also our agricultural products, chiefly for the population of Leningrad.

Mr. Yartsev said Moscow knew of German plans to the effect that if the Finnish government did not fall in with German aims, Fascist elements in Finland would then stage a revolt and form a government which would support German aspirations.

Finally Mr. Yartsev asked whether Holsti would be willing to negotiate on these matters only with him personally, as Derevyanski, the Soviet envoy in Helsinki, and Austrin, the other legation secretary, must by no means know of these conversations.

To this long exposition Holsti replied that it was part of his official function to receive any information or proposal of whatever description, but the President of the Republic determined the nation's foreign policy in its entirety. Consequently, without the President's authorization, he could not enter upon any regular discussions. Holsti also mentioned Finland's Scandinavian cooperation, the sole purpose of which, so far as Finland was concerned, was to preserve peace, and he assured Yartsev that the government's position was solid on domestic politics, since it represented three-quarters of the Diet, so that one could be quite sure the people would follow the government's pacific policy.

Holsti asked whether Mr. Yartsev, when he had spoken of a Russian offer of aid, had meant for instance the sale of arms to Finland; to which Yartsev answered that along with other forms of economic support this too could be considered as soon as Russia had guarantees that Finland would not help Germany in a war against Russia. On Holsti's then inquiring what he meant by guarantees, Yartsev replied that they could talk about this later, just as soon as there should be assurance that Finland wished to stay out of the war and to oppose the German invasion.

Here this interesting initial discussion closed. It had made plain the fact that the Soviet government apprehended the outbreak of war before long and that it wished to seek ways and means of securing its northern front. Clearly, it feared first and foremost an attack on the part of Germany. Yet the approach to the Finnish government had taken place in so strange a fashion that the members of the government who were aware of it, chiefly Foreign Minister Rudolf Holsti and Prime Minister A. K. Cajander, did not at first give it the attention it merited. I am not informed whether there was consultation with the other members of the foreign affairs committee of the Cabinet, Ministers Väinö Voionmaa and Uuno Hannula, during the initial phase of the conversations. In any case this opening move did not at first lead to continuing discussions. Presumably part of the reason for this was the fact that Mr. Yartsev had meanwhile left for Moscow and was thus for a time off the stage. On returning from Moscow, moreover, he visited Stockholm, where he discussed the Aaland Islands question with Foreign Minister Rickard Sandler and others.

MOSCOW'S AIMS BECOME APPARENT

As the matter made no progress for a month or two, unofficial persons took the initiative in getting discussions under way; for it turned out that although according to Mr. Yartsev the talks were to take place in utmost secrecy he had spoken of the matter to certain private persons (the Prime Minister's secretary Arvo Inkilä, General Aarne Sihvo, Mrs. Hella Wuolijoki, and perhaps others). With Inkilä in particular Mr. Yartsev had talked of his assignment much more frankly than with Holsti, and on this basis Inkilä tried to arrange a continuation of the exchanges. According to his advices, Mr. Yartsev did not consider that he could take a fresh initiative in the matter, but felt that it was now up to Finland to grasp the proffered hand. As Holsti had left for the League of Nations meetings at Geneva, Inkilä hoped that Prime Minister Cajander would receive Yartsev—on the condition, however, that the latter would then present his views and recommendations, regarding which complete uncertainty still reigned.

Cajander in fact consented to receive Mr. Yartsev on two occasions, the first toward the end of June, 1938, when they exchanged only uncommunicative observations of a general character, and the second on July 11. On that day a conversation took place between them which lasted an hour an a half. This time, too, the talk was initially about Germany's expansionism and the possibility that in a future war Germany would contrive to secure bases in Finland. Cajander regarded this as being outside the bounds of possibility, since the government would not permit so gross a violation of our neutrality and of our territorial integrity. When Yartsev asked whether Finland thought it could manage to protect its neutrality alone, Cajander replied that he who finds himself at war can rarely guarantee that he will keep his end up, come what may, but that Finland would certainly in any event do its best. He added that just as we would do all we could to prevent any foreign great power from exploiting Finland for its own purposes, we naturally assumed that the Soviet Union would also respect the inviolability of our territory.

At this juncture Mr. Yartsev repeated what he had already told Holsti, that if they might receive guarantees that the Germans would get no bases from Finland, the Russians for their part were prepared to underwrite Finland's inviolability.

Cajander touched upon the importance of stimulating trade and referred to the many earlier and unsuccessful trade agreement negotiations which had taken place. Mr. Yartsev acknowledged that trade was important, but before it could be put on the right track the political groundwork would have to be altogether clear, and in this light he still looked forward to the Finnish guarantees which he had mentioned. The two states must undertake a treaty; but the conversation brought no light as to its content.

At the end of the meeting Mr. Yartsev again insisted upon the absolute secrecy of the conversations. In taking his leave he remarked finally that Derevyanski, the Soviet envoy here, did indeed talk a great deal to various individuals, but that what he said was of no significance. He alone, Yartsev, had received his government's authorization to discuss these matters confidentially. Only after a general basis had been established might official entities develop the matter further.

At this point Cajander told me of the affair. Despite my position on the foreign affairs committee of the Cabinet I had until then been outside of it, ignorant of the phases described above. He was concerned that even after many encounters there was nothing clear about Yartsev's endeavors. Yartsev had spoken of guarantees only in general terms, but he had not revealed what character they might assume. Cajander considered it important to come to grips with concrete issues, and as in the Foreign Minister's absence no one else could continue the conversations, he hoped I would meet Mr. Yartsev and try to clear up where this was all heading. I agreed to this, and thus it happened that I met Mr. Yartsev for the first time on July 30, 1938.

The meeting, however, had no important results. Our conversation followed for the most part the same lines as Mr. Yartsev's earlier discussions, although I tried to shift the talk to a consideration of the development of commercial relations. Since there was no getting forward any other way, I asked him to present a detailed proposal. He promised to draft it and come back to the subject again.

Our next meeting took place on August 5. But Mr. Yartsev did not have with him the promised proposal, so the conversation mostly concerned other matters. I suggested that we confer on how quiet might best be preserved along the border and that we proceed to negotiate on working out a trade agreement. To this Mr. Yartsev replied that we might get somewhere this way as well, but he observed that other questions, above all political ones, were also involved in the subject. He proposed that the negotiations should commence in Moscow. I remarked that negotiation in Moscow would be awkward, first because it would attract more attention, and second because the Finnish negotiators would have to be in close touch with their government, for which reason perhaps Helsinki would be a more suitable place for negotiations. At length I brought up the Soviet attitude on certain cases in which the Peace of Tartu had clearly been violated, as for instance the interruption of transit traffic through the Neva and the detention of the steamship *Airisto* which had occurred a short time before.

Mr. Yartsev promised to take up these cases with his government and to try to bring them to a suitable conclusion. He also promised to inquire whether the negotiations might be held in Helsinki.

Even after this I had a couple of meetings with him, during the course of which the matter was by no means clarified. The first of these occurred on August 10, when Mr. Yartsev spoke of trivialities, not presenting his proposal this time either. When I reported this conversation to Cajander as had been my practice, the Prime Minister jotted down a brief reply which in his view ought to be delivered orally to Mr. Yartsev, despite the fact that the same ideas had already been expressed to him many times previously. The Prime Minister's proposed reply was of the following tenor:

While always adhering to the neutral policy of the northern countries, the government of Finland will at the same time permit no violation of Finnish territorial integrity nor consequently the acquisition by any great power of a foothold in Finland for an attack against the Soviet Union.

The government of the USSR, while undertaking to respect the territorial integrity of Finland at every point, will on the other hand not oppose Finland's proceeding even in time of peace to undertake in the Aaland Islands such military measures as the most perfect possible safeguarding of the integrity of Finnish territory and the neutrality of the Aaland Islands may require.

This reply was brought to Mr. Yartsev's knowledge on the following day, August 11. On that occasion he merely spoke once more of holding the negotiations in Moscow, considering this more advantageous than a meeting in Helsinki.

On August 18 Mr. Yartsev was for the first time ready to present something more precisely defined than his earlier general references to guarantees. Calling on me that day, he started right off by saying that Finland had presented a proposal under which it would "gain many advantages": a good trade treaty, the elimination of border incidents, the fortification of the Aaland Islands, etc. (Remarkable notion that these should bring advantage to Finland alone!) But what did Russia get? Nothing new for the present. The guarantees which had been hoped for were not promised.

Since he had been asked for a concrete proposal, he was now prepared to offer one. In slightly defective German he read off from his paper very much the following (I am quoting from my notes):

Moscow is ready to receive a Finnish trade delegation, but the limited character of the Finnish government's proposal in its political aspects gives reason to suspect that no results are obtainable on this basis. In order to attain the goal which is hoped for, Moscow thinks that if Finland approves Moscow's conditions the goal will be attained.

Russia's proposal is as follows:

1. If the Finnish government does not consider that it can enter upon a completely secret military agreement, Russia will be satisfied if it receives a written undertaking under which Finland stands prepared to ward off possible attacks and, to that end, to accept Russian military aid.

2. Aaland Islands. Much as fortification of the Aaland Islands is necessary to Finland from the point of view of security, just so necessary is the bastioning of Leningrad through fortification. Moscow can assent to fortification of the Aaland Islands if Russia is enabled to take part in their arming and if it is permitted to send its own observer to follow the work and subsequently to maintain surveillance over the use of the fortifications. Moscow wishes to emphasize that the activity of this observer would be entirely secret.

3. As a return favor for the foregoing, Moscow desires the consent of the Finnish government to erecting on Suursaari Island a fortified air and naval defense base.

On these conditions Russia is prepared:

1. To guarantee Finland's inviolability within the present Finnish boundaries, first and foremost the inviolability of its sea frontiers;

2. In event of need, to assist Finland by force of arms on advantageous terms;

3. To approve a trade treaty advantageous to Finland, which will benefit both agriculture and industry. (Here there was an insertion: Russia is ready to buy agricultural and industrial products, such as machinery, rubber, paper, and cellulose.) In short, Moscow is prepared to offer Finland an exceptionally advantageous trade treaty.

On my asking for a more detailed clarification of what Moscow meant by the "Russian military aid" it offered, Mr. Yartsev explained this did not mean the dispatch of Russian forces to Finland or any territorial concessions. Moscow did not wish to make the position of the Finnish government difficult through this offer. The main thing was the procurement of arms and the protection of the sea frontier.

When I remarked that the purchase of arms was a commercial matter which certainly could be thought over and which would depend on the quality and cost of the goods, Mr. Yartsev assured me that Moscow would sell arms on decidedly advantageous terms.

To my question as to what Moscow meant by Russia's "taking part in arming" the Aaland Islands upon their being fortified, Mr. Yartsev replied that it meant furnishing the necessary arms (cannon, etc.). It appeared not to mean financial assistance. But the Russian observer at the place of fortification was indispensable, so that Russia might know what was happening there and that the fortresses would not fall into German hands.

At length I said it was my view that this offer, the frankness of which the Finnish government was able to appreciate, could hardly meet with the government's approval. I nevertheless promised to pass it on to the Prime Minister.

To this Mr. Yartsev replied that Moscow had wanted to let Finland understand clearly what it hoped for, but that the formal side of the treaty could be worked out satisfactorily. It would be better to find out first whether a satisfactory agreement could be reached in the negotiations. If there was no surety for this, it would be better not to enter upon official negotiations. Their failure would be embarrassing to both parties.

I promised that I would at least let him know the Finnish government's point of view.

After nearly five months of conversations we had at last secured a fairly clear idea of what the Soviet Union was aiming at through these talks. The most important matter seemed to be the fortification of Suursaari as a bastion for Leningrad. In order to secure this concession the Soviet Union was prepared to assent to the fortification of the Aaland Islands as well (under its own surveillance, to be sure) and also to start trade negotiations, something which had been attempted several times hitherto and had proved fruitless. Compared to this, the talk of selling arms was of secondary importance; they could be had from many other quarters. But back of everything was a military treaty between the two countries. Finland was to give assurances that if there were a threat of war it would turn to the Soviet Union and ask its armed assistance. This would mean a defensive alliance, to which Finland, barred by the policy of neutrality it had adopted and by its Scandinavian outlook, would find it difficult to assent. Suursaari's status had been the subject of prolonged negotiations preparatory to the drafting of the Tartu peace treaty. At that time it had been the position of the Soviet Union that the island should remain unarmed, while on the contrary the Finnish government of the period demanded that the peace treaty should contain no limitations respecting this point. The importance both parties then attached to their respective contentions is shown by the fact that the whole peace treaty came close to being wrecked by this disagreement and that the Finnish government relinquished its position only at the eleventh hour. Now, instead, it was the Soviet Union which called for fortification of the island—but for its own purposes.

In any event, the position was now clear in so far that discussion of the matter could be undertaken within the government and there could be deliberation as to our attitude toward the propositions advanced. The outcome was that the government assumed a negative stand on the Soviet proposals, which Prime Minister Cajander phrased in the following terms:

The proposal tends to violate Finland's sovereignty and is in conflict with the policy of neutrality which Finland follows in common with the nations of Scandinavia.

I consider the principal significance of an expansion of trade relations as deriving from such expansion's being calculated to improve neighborly relations.

Improvement of relationships along the border would also be of advantage to both parties.

I transmitted this reply to Mr. Yartsev on August 29. He promised to report it to Moscow and to revert to the matter if he had anything new to say.

The matter did not rest here. The usual attacks against Finland began in the Russian press, and they were regarded as owing their origin to the Finnish government's negative attitude toward the Soviet proposal. Nor did Mr. Yartsev relax; he now said he required a more detailed answer than he had received. When he came to call on me again on August 15, we reviewed the proposals he had put forward, and I had to explain to him what the reply of the government to each particular point meant. I explained on this occasion that the government's response with respect to bases was negative; we were prepared to buy such arms as we might require, if the quality and price were right; as for the fortification of the Aalands and Suursaari, the government had rejected the proposals addressed to these subjects without making a counteroffer. Such a counteroffer, however, was what Mr. Yartsev wanted to receive.

For my part I considered the government's reply clear in every respect, but if Mr. Yartsev wanted to get a more closely reasoned answer with possible counteroffers, delivery of such a reply would have to wait until Minister Holsti should come back, since making expositions of this character did not fall within my field. Thus we agreed to await Holsti's return. This was my last encounter with Mr. Yartsev, and the whole subject dropped from view for a long time.

When Holsti returned at the beginning of October, Yartsev renewed his visits to him. He wanted to bring to a decision the questions "which we had taken up with our overcoats on and which were still in suspense, though it was time to put on overcoats again." Holsti had various meetings with him, during the course of which the matter was again mulled over in the old fashion. Toward the middle of October Holsti gave Yartsev an extensively analytical written answer in which was presented the government's attitude on the various points. On the fortification of the Aaland Islands Holsti now had occasion to remark that during their stay in Geneva he and the Swedish Foreign Minister, Rickard Sandler, had discussed the matter with the Soviet Commissar for Foreign Affairs, Litvinov, to whom they had made a report of the joint plans of Finland and Sweden regarding the islands. In Holsti's view it would be best to await the results of the diplomatic démarches with regard to the Aalands which would be made shortly to the signatories of the neutrality treaty affecting the islands as well as to the USSR.

A further explanatory talk took place between the two men on the basis of Holsti's written reply. In its course Yartsev said he was "an inexperienced young secretary," for which reason his duty had hitherto been that of using the most cautious language possible, but that now he wished permission to speak in the manner ordinary people use among themselves in discussing serious matters. Once more he described Finland's position in the war which might break out. Since Finland would then be unable to defend itself, it would be well advised to rely upon the military aid promised by the Soviet Union. The outlines of a military alliance became clearer in this conversation than they had been before. The future position of Suursaari was clarified as well: in the event of war the Soviet Union would assume responsibility for its defense.

Yartsev also had occasion to talk to the acting foreign minister, Väinö Voionmaa, who, upon Holsti's resigning from the government on November 16, 1938, conducted the business of the Foreign Ministry in an interim capacity. This encounter took place on November 21. Here there was repeated for the most part a conversation similar to those Yartsev had had with other members of the government. Yet before it was over the participants deliberated upon the way in which the subject could be carried forward. Yartsev proposed that a delegation be sent to Moscow to discuss the stimulation of trade and that a couple of political negotiators should be included in it. However, arrangements must be made in advance to make certain that these discussions would bear some fruit, for otherwise more harm than good would come of the whole thing. He judged that the affair could be straightened out with the Russian government in a matter of days. Without premeditation there came up on this occasion the thought of associating this subject with the tasks of the delegation which was to leave for Moscow on December 6, 1938, in order to dedicate the newly completed Finnish Legation building. Mr. Yartsev hoped that such a negotiating group as he suggested might start its trip even earlier. Minister Voionmaa promised to present these ideas to the government.

A further discussion did, in fact, then take place in Moscow, though on a decidedly modest scale. Voionmaa had told Mr. Yartsev that the talks begun in Helsinki could be continued in Moscow and that our envoy there, A. S. Yrjö-Koskinen, and the acting bureau chiefs Urho Toivola and Aaro Pakaslahti were authorized to represent the Finnish government in such negotiations. At the time the new Legation building was opened, Mr. Yartsev told Toivola that the accredited delegates would on the following day (December 7) have an opportunity to meet a high-ranking Soviet government official, whose name he did not however reveal. When the Finnish delegates came to the appointed place on the following day it turned out that Commissar for Foreign Trade Mikoyan was to receive them. At the same time, however, it was indicated that the Soviet Commissariat for Foreign Affairs had no knowledge of this discussion, for which reason Yrjö-Koskinen felt that his position as a diplomatic minister obliged him to stand aside from the meeting. Mr. Toivola and

Mr. Pakaslahti thus were the only Finns present at the meeting which took place in Mikoyan's office.

The Finnish delegates began by speaking of what might be done to encourage the development of trade relations, as was pertinent since they found themselves with the Commissar for Foreign Trade. Commissar Mikoyan expressed pleasure at having an opportunity to talk the matter over directly with representatives of the Finnish Foreign Ministry. He nevertheless remarked at once that before trade could be developed on any major scale certain political prerequisites would have to be met. From this point the conversation went forward on lines familiar through the exchanges which had taken place in Helsinki. The importance of Suursaari as a defensive outpost for Leningrad was conspicuously emphasized, and the Finnish negotiators received the impression that of the military questions touched upon, Suursaari was the most important to the Soviet Union. Toward the end of the two-hour discussion they returned again to trade matters. It was agreed that a number of persons representing Finnish commercial and industrial interests should that same evening have an opportunity to tell Mikoyan what Finland hoped for. Political questions were not to be discussed at that meeting. In Mikoyan's view the time to bring up political questions would come only after the necessary groundwork for them had been laid in matters affecting the encouragement of trade, the settlement of border questions, and other problems of current practical business.

Such a trade discussion did indeed take place that same evening in Mikoyan's office. On behalf of Finland there were present Yrjö-Koskinen; the Minister of Communications, Väinö Salovaara; and some representatives of Finnish trade and industry. To them, too, Mikoyan emphasized the importance of political relationships as a precondition to commercial interchange. Naturally, no decisions were reached.

This meeting may be considered as the final point reached in the first phase of the negotiations.

The second phase of the negotiations opened only several months later. On March 5, 1939, Litvinov, the Soviet Commissar for Foreign Affairs, asked Yrjö-Koskinen, the Finnish Minister at Moscow, to call on him and handed him a memorandum the principal content of which ran in the following fashion.

Two important questions, the encouragement of commercial relations and the fortification of the Aalands, still awaited solution. In order to create a favorable atmosphere for their satisfactory settlement the Soviet Union proposed that Finland should lease Suursaari, Lavansaari Island, the Tytärsaari Islands, and Seiskari Island to the Soviet Union for thirty years. The Soviet Union did not propose to fortify them but merely to use them as guard posts for the approaches to Leningrad. If the Finnish government agreed to this, relations would improve in great measure, and this would have a decidedly good effect on commercial relations. The Soviet Union hoped for a prompt Finnish reply.

It was possible to deliver the reply of the Finnish government to Litvinov as early as March 8. The government, whose foreign affairs portfolio had been assumed in December, 1938, by Eljas Erkko, declared that it could not consider leasing to a foreign power the islands referred to because they were inseparable parts of an area whose independence the Soviet Union had recognized and moreover confirmed through the peace treaty concluded at Tartu. The islands had been neutralized upon Soviet insistence, and no defense preparations had been initiated upon them. Finland would violate its neutrality by even undertaking to discuss the question.

Litvinov was greatly disappointed by the reply. As he put it, the Soviet Union had supposed that leasing the islands would not mean an abandonment of neutrality, as there was not even a thought of fortifying them. He now suggested that the islands, instead of being leased, be exchanged against a corresponding land area in eastern Karelia.

This new proposal met a negative Finnish response on March 13. Litvinov declared that he could not consider this reply as final either.

Thus this exchange of views took place remarkably fast, within a week's time.

Upon receiving Finland's last reply, referred to above, Litvinov had remarked that Ambassador Stein, accredited to Rome, who had earlier been the Soviet Minister in Helsinki, would come to talk these matters over further with the Finnish government. Mr. Stein did get in touch with Foreign Minister Erkko as early as March 11 and presented substantially the same views as Litvinov in Moscow to Yrjö-Koskinen. He also suggested the conclusion of a lease agreement for a period of time during which Finland should receive exploitation rights to forest areas in eastern Karelia.

Erkko replied that, since Finnish territory was inalienable under the constitution of the country, it was impossible to discuss the question. Germany, too, might demand some islands as observation posts, and to this Finland could never consent.

At Stein's request the government again considered the matter, and on March 20 its decision was brought to Litvinov's notice through Yrjö-Koskinen, who delivered the following oral note:

The Finnish government cannot negotiate regarding a matter which may in one manner or another involve the cession of parts of the territory of the state to another power. This negative reply is not to be understood in the sense that the Foreign Minister would be unwilling to continue an exchange of views with the purpose of reaching a solution to the questions raised by the Soviet Union regarding guarantees to its security.

Litvinov expressed his regret on the score of the negative reply and said that on the Russian side they now awaited concrete proposals of the Finns on the guarantees question. For its part Moscow had made such proposals in asking for the islands in the Gulf of Finland. Ambassador Stein made the same suggestion to Foreign Minister Erkko in Helsinki. But Erkko held fast to his position. He showed Stein the draft of a note which was to be delivered to the Soviet government and which contained an assurance of Finland's determination to defend its neutrality under all circumstances. Stein explained that the Soviet government would be unable to attach any value to documents of such a content if there was no move to undertake supplementary measures. On the same occasion he pointed out on the map the regions beyond our eastern frontier which the Soviet Union wished to cede in compensation for the islands, their area being in all 183 square kilometers.

Before leaving Finland, Ambassador Stein told Erkko that the Soviet Union could not accept Finland's negative reply, nor had it abandoned its demands upon the outer islands of the Gulf of Finland, since they were of great strategic significance to Soviet security. Consequently the problem remained open so far as the Soviet Union was concerned.

This was the last phase in these nearly year-long negotiations over guarantees to be given by Finland for the sake of strengthening Soviet security. Since in political respects the affair was not brought to a conclusion satisfactory to the Soviet Union, the trade treaty negotiations were also broken off. Nor did the Soviet Union give its assent to the fortification of the Aaland Islands, so that this matter fell through as well.

These negotiations showed that the Soviet Union tenaciously sought to have Finland assent to certain limitations on its right to make use of its territory and that Finland with equal tenacity opposed the suggestions put forward. Subsequently—when Finland was obliged, on the basis of the peace treaties made after the wars in which it was engaged, to cede much larger areas—criticism was directed against Finland's negative position of that time. Yet under the circumstances of that period a different approach to the case would hardly have been possible. There still existed trust in international law and in the binding character of signed and sealed treaties. It was not considered possible that a great power would seek by force to assume possession of territories which it had itself ceded to Finland through an express treaty. Under no circumstances would the Diet have been disposed to approve proposals of this sort if the government had presented them for its consideration. Moreover, it is uncertain whether concessions made at that stage would have prevented the presentation of fresh demands. Indeed, it is conspicuous that while the negotiations were under way the Soviet demands tended to increase and did not by any means come closer to the Finnish position, as might properly have been expected.

The demands made in these negotiations never came before the Diet for consideration. It may perhaps have been the government's duty to take this step, since these conversations had a decisive effect upon the country's future and in a way concerned matters of war and peace. The Soviet parties, however, emphasized at all times how indispensable it was that the conversations remain entirely confidential and secret. This consideration was once more underlined, for the last time, by Soviet Foreign Trade Commissar Mikoyan in the discussion which was held with him. The Finnish government did not consider that it could violate this requirement of confidential treatment, and for this reason it did not even approach the Diet Foreign Relations Committee.

Thus the Finnish government had rejected proposals put forward by the Soviet Union which would have led it astray from the path of neutrality which it followed. The following incident, which occurred in the spring of the same year (1939), showed that the same principle was followed also with respect to proposals received from other quarters.

Von Ribbentrop, the German Foreign Minister, had on April 28 suggested to the Finnish Minister in Berlin, Aarne Voionmaa, that the two countries conclude a nonaggression pact. Some days later the Legation received a draft text for such a pact. At the same time Germany had made similar suggestions to a number of other countries, including the three Scandinavian states. On the initiative of the Swedish government the foreign ministers of the North assembled at Stockholm to discuss these proposals. In a consultation on May 9 a resolution was approved in which it was stated that the northern countries wished to remain apart from all power groups which might possibly be formed in Europe. The foreign ministers emphasized the hope of the countries they represented that all states would respect their neutrality in the same manner as they in turn respected the inviolability of other countries.

The Finnish government replied to the German proposal on May 16, expressing its satisfaction in learning that Germany intended to respect Finland's inviolability and independence. As Finland aspired to remain outside all great power alignments and to avoid entanglement in possible wars, it considered the suggested treaty unnecessary, with all the more reason since it did not doubt Germany's interest in preserving the existing conditions in the countries of the North.

Sweden and Norway made similar negative replies to the German suggestion. Denmark, on the other hand, concluded a nonaggression pact with Germany. This did not stop Germany from invading Denmark just a year later.

WAR KNOCKS AT FINLAND'S DOOR

The negotiations affecting Finland's position, which have been described in the foregoing pages, were not detached phenomena; they were intimately connected with the general tension of European policy.

While these negotiations between Finland and the Soviet Union were under way, now in Helsinki and now in Moscow, European political skies were darkening rapidly. Hitler's Germany assumed a more menacing aspect than ever. In March, 1938, its forces had marched into Austria, where a completely National Socialist order was established. After ordering the affairs of that country to its taste, Germany disturbed the peace of the world with the Czechoslovak question. To begin with, it was merely a matter of the German populations in the western and northern parts of Czechoslovakia, the so-called Sudeten Germans, who under Henlein's leadership had made demands upon the Prague government. In a nerve-racking war of propaganda Germany declared that they were being oppressed and finally demanded that the area be attached to Germany. England and France intervened in the matter. British Prime Minister Neville Chamberlain made as many as three trips to Germany with his umbrella—to Berchtesgaden, to Godesberg, and finally to Munich—in order to deal with Hitler personally. At the last of these meetings, with French Premier Edouard Daladier also present, the ill-famed Munich agreement was made on September 30, 1938. The area inhabited by the Sudeten Germans was incorporated into Germany without a shot being fired, and Czechoslovakia lost its natural line of defense. On returning from this trip Chamberlain made the remark about "peace in our time," which has become famous. But the "appeasement" helped only for a brief time. Half a year later Germany called for the liquidation of all Czechoslovakia. After dramatic midnight conversations between Hitler and President Emil Hacha of Czechoslovakia, Germany on March 15, 1939, thrust into the core of Czechoslovakia with its Panzer divisions and made a German protectorate of Bohemia and Moravia. It was then realized that the outbreak of war was only a matter of time.

When the Munich agreement was made the Soviet Union was left out entirely. Its opinion was not asked, and the settlement naturally gave rise to ill-feeling there. But as the threat of war increased, the great powers realized that the Soviet Union would occupy an important position in it. They began to present it with proposals aimed at a military alliance. The Soviet Union was now in a good position; it might expect advantageous offers from both parties. As early as March, 1939, France and England initiated negotiations with the Soviet Union regarding collaboration against Germany. Not much news about these negotiations carried on in Moscow leaked out. So much was learned, however: that the Soviet Union required the prospective treaty to assume a form under which certain smaller powers specified by name, among them Finland, should be given guarantees of the Allied great powers to cover the contingency of their becoming the victims of an attack. "Indirect aggression" was also to be considered an attack. By this was meant the assumption by these states of a pro-German stand. As such "guarantees" would have afforded a chance for intervention in the domestic affairs of these small states, even to the point of giving them military aid without their asking for it (i.e., to proceed to occupy them), this provision gave rise to great uneasiness in Finland as well as elsewhere. Approaches were made to the Western powers to inform them that such a treaty of guarantee would not be acceptable. In the end, no treaty of alliance between the Western powers and the Soviet Union was concluded, and it is possible that it was precisely this question of guarantees which was one of the causes for the breakdown of the negotiations. Nothing, however, was revealed even subsequntly as to the particulars of these negotiations.

During this period there occurred a change in the management of Soviet foreign affairs. Molotov took over the Foreign Affairs Commissariat in Litvinov's stead. This was taken to mean a shift in the foreign policy of the Soviet Union.

At the same time as the Western powers were taking part in these negotiations in Moscow, the Soviet Union was negotiating with Germany. However, the world did not get the slightest hint of these dealings. The first approach took place as early as the end of May, 1939, but the negotiations got under way regularly only at the beginning of August. It came as a great surprise when the world learned on August 23, 1939, that Germany and the Soviet Union had signed a pact of nonaggression and conciliation procedure. I chanced at the time to be in Oslo, where the collaboration committee of the Labor parties of the North was holding its meeting. The initial attitude toward the publication of the news was almost ironical. The former sworn enemies, the Communist Soviet Union and National Socialist Germany, as allies! There was indeed occasion for much raillery, and there was no notion of what a fateful treaty this was. Even while we were returning to Stockholm by train I was talking to Gustav Möller, who was then Swedish Minister of Trade, and we found no reasonable explanation for this astonishing step. In Finland the publication of the treaty did not at first cause concern. Quite on the contrary, it was imagined that the continuation of peace so far as Finland was concerned was now assured, since its two powerful neighbors had concluded an alliance.

Yet it was not a week before it became clear what the purpose of the treaty was. The treaty opened for Germany the opportunity to start the war it had planned against Poland without having to fear a war on two fronts. The issue was a dispute over so small a matter as the Danzig corridor. The Western powers had guaranteed Poland's inviolability, and on that account Poland was inflexible. On September 1 the German armies swarmed over the Polish border. On September 3 England and France declared war on Germany, without however being able to help Poland in any way. Polish resistance was crushed in a matter of weeks.

Upon the outbreak of war the Finnish government at once, on September 1, issued a neutrality declaration, asserting that it intended to follow a policy of complete impartiality during the war. It was issued on Finland's behalf individually and again jointly with the other countries of the North. Thus Finland had declared with all possible clarity that it wished to remain out of the war.

The Soviet Union remained neutral for a couple of weeks; then, on September 17, it attacked defeated Poland and conquered its eastern part. On the same day Foreign Affairs Commissar Molotov handed Yrjö-Koskinen, the Finnish Minister in Moscow, a notification to the effect that in its relations with Finland the Soviet Union would follow a policy of neutrality. On this account Foreign Minister Erkko on the following day announced through the Finnish News Agency that this notice had been received in Finland "with great satisfaction" and that "it was in harmony with the spirit of the pacific and friendly conversations which Finland had had with the Soviet Commissariat for Foreign Affairs."

Thus, so far as Finland was concerned, everything seemed to be in order, and the country might hope to avoid war.

In evidence of the atmosphere of great trust which permeated Finnish life even in the late summer of 1939 there may be mentioned the fact that I had prepared for presentation to the Diet a budget bill for the coming year drafted in an altogether normal fashion. The government had been confident that peace would continue to be preserved in Europe, and that the war of nerves which had been going on for a full year had been mere saber rattling. When I delivered my budget speech in the Diet on September 8, however, the situation had completely changed. In my speech I noted that, by reason of the war which had broken out and because of the falling off of foreign trade, state revenues would considerably diminish, and therefore expenditures must be reduced as well, but that I hoped that this reduction could nevertheless be carried out in agreement with the government. Thereupon the opposition brought its heavy guns to bear upon the government and accused it of incompetence in drawing up its budget. The government had not taken into account the fact that war was at our gates—as if the moment of its outbreak could have been determined with certainty in advance! It was easy to reply that if the opposition had been aware of this it had done wrongly in not advising the government of it beforehand. But after this the budget bill had to be gone over again. Together with J. W. Minni, the Councilor in charge of the budget at the Treasury, I devoted almost two weeks to reviewing the budget point by point, and we were successful in pruning some 700 million marks of expenses out of it. These proposals for reductions were delivered to the Finance Committee of the Diet for its consideration. In order to make up for dwindling customs revenues the government was furthermore obliged to present proposals for increases in duties and other taxes and for new taxation.

The same spirit of confidence, not to say unconcern, was shown with respect to the intensification of our defense preparations. As long ago as 1935, to be sure, a basic procurement program had been approved for the defense establishment, which was intended to fill up the worst gaps in the equipment of the army. Under this program a total of 1,158 million marks was to be used, beginning in 1938, for basic army procurement. But soon it became apparent that the sum would be insufficient, for which reason in 1937 a new basic procurement committee was set up to complete the program. On the recommendation of the government the Diet in May, 1938, approved a new basic procurement program under which there was to be earmarked a total sum of 2,710 million marks over the years 1938 to 1944 for basic procurement and other defense needs. Of this sum 460 million marks were to fall to the share of 1938; to 1939–43, annually, 400 million; and to 1944, 250 million. The project became law. Of the sums thus appropriated, however, only a very small amount had been used by September, 1939, so that the army lacked many absolute requisites at a time when they were really needed.

Yet in other respects there had been an endeavor to take the uncertain political situation into account. Thus in the spring of 1939 the Diet passed many laws which took cognizance of a possible outbreak of war. Among them may be mentioned the national security law, the obligatory labor law, the civil defense law, and the law for intensification of defense preparedness in time of war.

But let us go back to developments in the field of foreign policy.

Hardly had the Polish war been decided when the Soviet Union went into action farther north as well. It urged the governments of the Baltic states to send their foreign ministers to Moscow for negotiations, and the result of the negotiations was that these countries, each in turn, made treaties of friendship and reciprocal aid with the Soviet Union. Estonia made such a treaty on September 28, 1939, granting naval and air bases to the Soviet Union at the same time. Latvia made a treaty on October 5 and Lithuania on October 11. Through that treaty Lithuania got the long-sought city of Vilna which the Soviet Union had just taken from Poland, but in return Lithuania had to grant military bases to the Soviet Union.

The demands presented to the Baltic countries, and the prompt submission of the latter, occasioned great uneasiness in Finland. There was reason to believe Finland would not escape the same sort of demands; for the Soviet Union now had its hands free to act, after making its treaty of alliance with Germany, and the other great powers were bogged down in war. Nor was it necessary to wait long before there was a rapping at Finland's door. On October 5 Foreign Affairs Commissar Molotov called in Yrjö-Koskinen, the Finnish Minister in Moscow, and told him that the Soviet Union had taken note of the Finnish government's indication of its desire to develop the relations between the countries, political as well as economic. Since the international situation had changed owing to the war, the Soviet government now wished to proceed to an exchange of views with the government of Finland regarding certain "concrete political questions." He expressed the hope that the Finnish Foreign Minister would come to Moscow to discuss them or that the government would accredit some other person for that purpose. On Yrjö-Koskinen's asking whether the Commissar could go into further detail as to what concrete questions he particularly meant, Molotov made no answer but added that the Soviet government hoped that the conversations might be begun as soon as possible, for which reason he requested an answer, if possible, within the next few days.

When word of this pronouncement reached the government on the following day (October 6), it naturally aroused concern, particularly since no information on the "concrete political questions" had been secured. The newspaper-reading public was also worried on perusing the following uncommunicative item on October 7:

As Foreign Minister Erkko said in the statement he gave the Finnish News Agency on September 18, there have been negotiations between Finland and the Soviet Union through diplomatic channels on various matters of a political and economic character. The Soviet Union has now inquired whether the Finnish government would be disposed to send a special representative to Moscow to discuss the matters of current interest, and the Finnish government is at present deliberating upon the subject.

It was plain from the start that there was no alternative to accepting the invitation. It was decided to deal with the matter by making the most careful preparations possible on the basis of such indeterminate knowledge, without paying attention to the Russians' request for speed. Soon, however, it became apparent that the Soviet Union did indeed regard the matter as urgent. By October 7 Molotov was pressing for an answer. On the following day Derevyanski, the Soviet Minister in Helsinki, called on Erkko to say that he had an important communication to make. He said that Moscow was "boiling over" because no reply had been received yet, that Finland's attitude toward the invitation was different from that of the Baltic countries, and that this might work to the detriment of progress in the matter. Erkko replied that he did not know how the Baltic countries had acted but that the Finnish government had not lagged in preparing and dispatching its answer; rather, it had considered the matter in the normal course of business. It became clear from the conversation that the Soviet Union would bring up much the same sort of matters as with the Baltic countries. The Soviet Union wished to establish in the Baltic region a state of affairs calculated to protect it and its neighbors against falling victims to the war.

Molotov had expressed the wish that the Foreign Minister might by preference go to Moscow. But Erkko was reluctant to go, for the reason that, as he put it in talking to some foreign journalists, "the Foreign Minister's place is with his government." At this point they began to consider State Councilor J. K. Paasikivi, who was Minister in Stockholm at the time. He undertook to go, and thus began his activity—which he later was to resume—in the field of problems affecting Russo-Finnish relations.

It also was necessary to prepare instructions for the delegation which was to be sent. Since there was no really precise knowledge of the demands which would be presented — no more than a guess as to the direction they would take — the instructions were formulated in vague terms. According to its general directives, the delegation was to note that the problems between Finland and the Soviet Union had been settled and ordered by the treaty of peace between the two countries; in addition, the nonaggression pact the two countries had entered upon formed the basis of their political relationships. The aim and object of Finland's foreign policy had been the maintenance of friendly relations with all its neighbors. Finland had been and continued to be in the closest relationship of cooperation with the other countries of the North, which found themselves in the same position as itself, its goal being two objectives of a fundamental character—the consolidation of peace and an unconditional striving to remain clear of all disputes. Finland represented no danger to any other country. In testimony of its will to adhere to the policy of neutrality it had adopted, Finland had scrupulously publicized its decision that it would also defend its neutrality by force of arms. Hereby Finland wished to show that it would not allow itself to be used against anybody.

These general observations obliged the negotiators to maintain from the start a negative attitude toward such proposals as might have a disturbing effect upon Finland's political position as described or upon Finland's policy of neutrality. If the Soviet Union should make proposals affecting Finland's territorial inviolability or sovereignty, the negotiators were to declare that none of them was authorized to make promises that would violate the national constitution, but that according to the parliamentary system prevailing in Finland it fell to the government and the Diet to approve or reject such undertakings as the Soviet Union proposed.

In the detailed instructions associated with these general principles, various problems which might come up during the negotiations were dealt with. The negotiators were not authorized even to discuss the concession of military bases or suggestions regarding boundary changes on the Karelian Isthmus. On the other hand, the cession of some of the islands in the Finnish Gulf against territorial compensation elsewhere might be considered. A treaty of reciprocal aid between Finland and the Soviet Union was also out of the question.

At one o'clock in the morning of October 9 it was announced to Moscow that Finland would send J. K. Paasikivi as its representative. And on October 9 the President of the Republic confirmed the instructions to be given to the negotiators.

As there was a possibility of a surprise attack, new age classes of the reserve were called up for "extra refresher courses" on the following day, October 10. This amounted to partial mobilization.

Other measures were taken as well. Interior Minister Kekkonen on

October 10 delivered an address in which, drawing the attention of his fellow citizens to the gravity of the situation, he urged city dwellers to move to less exposed localities. On the same day there was a practice air raid warning and blackout in Helsinki.

These events had a considerable influence on public opinion. The people realized that they were all threatened by the same peril. The conflict of opinions which had continued to split the nation in the wake of the July elections now was forgotten as we faced these grave matters. The basis of the government was likewise broadened to a degree, when on October 13 two representatives of the Swedish People's Party entered Cajander's Agrarian-Social Democrat government — Dr. J. O. Söderhjelm as Minister of Justice and Baron Ernst von Born as Minister without Portfolio. Later, when the situation became yet more grave, the basis of the government was broadened still further.

When I spoke at the Workers' House in Helsinki on October 8 on the occasion of the fortieth anniversary of the Social Democratic party, I dealt for the most part with the questions of the day. I wished to emphasize in this circle, too, the need for unanimity. Among my remarks were the following:

In any event it is important in these days that our people be of one mind. The differences of views which have hitherto characterized our public life had best be set aside for the time being. In the last analysis they are small matters when our country's independence and its future existence may come to be at stake. When danger threatens from without we cannot afford such differences.

CHAPTER 2

THE FIRST TRIP TO MOSCOW

Paasikivi left on his Moscow journey the evening of October 9. In his briefcase he carried the instructions confirmed by the President. Johan Nykopp, department head in the Foreign Ministry, and Colonel Aladár Paasonen accompanied him as aides. They reached their destination on the eleventh. No discussions, however, took place on that day.

The first contact with the Soviet negotiators took place in the office of the Commissar for Foreign Affairs in the Kremlin on October 12 at 5:00 P.M. For Finland there were present Paasikivi, Yrjö-Koskinen, Nykopp, and Paasonen; for the Soviet Union, Stalin, Molotov, Potemkin, and Derevyanski. The Finnish negotiators now received an oral statement as to what the Soviet Union expected of Finland. The Russians made reference to the state of war in Europe and asserted that the vital interests of the Soviet Union required that no enemy should have access to the Gulf of Finland. On the south of the Gulf the Soviet Union was secured by the treaty with Estonia, but there was no such surety on the north. It was suggested that Finland agree to conclude a local treaty of reciprocal aid relating to the security of the Gulf of Finland. There was talk of the necessity for a military base on the Finnish coast, in which connection Hanko was mentioned as a possible site. In Petsamo Finland was called upon to cede the Rybachi Peninsula as far as Maattivuono. In order to protect Leningrad, the boundary between the nations should be moved to the line Kuolemajärvi-Kyyrölä-Muolaa-Lipola. Finland must also cede islands in the Gulf of Finland, among them Suursaari and Koivisto. By way of compensation for the areas whose cession was sought, the Soviet Union would make available territory in eastern Karelia, an area many times larger than the ceded districts. In order to avoid difficulties, the Soviet representatives wished not to take up the matter of the Aaland Islands in this connection.

The Finnish representatives said they were unconditionally opposed to the conclusion of a reciprocal aid treaty and commented on the demands for territorial concessions to the effect that Finland could not abjure the inviolability of Finnish territory.

When the first conversation was over, Paasikivi wired the government in Helsinki word of the Soviet demands, requesting further instructions. In reply he received by cable fresh directives, the main import of which was as follows:

Finland could not assent to any treaty of assistance and could not grant any bases. The Rybachi Peninsula was important to Finland because Petsamo was Finland's only ice-free harbor, and to develop it Finland had made great sacrifices. For this reason it had been Finland's intention to ask for the half of the Rybachi Peninsula which belonged to the Soviet Union as compensation for possible concessions on its part. An endeavor should be made to consider Suursaari as a question apart, to be taken up after the outcome of the conversations on the outer islands of the Gulf of Finland. Cession of Saarenpää on Koivisto was out of the question. As for Somero and Narvi islands, they were important to Finnish maritime traffic but were without military significance to the Soviet Union. The new boundary on the Karelian Isthmus proposed by the Soviet Union was impossible from the Finnish point of view, since it would place Finland in a situation of jeopardy.

STALIN STATES HIS MINIMUM DEMANDS

The next meeting with the Russian negotiators was arranged for October 14. In the meanwhile Paasikivi had received from Helsinki the additional instructions he had requested. The session began at 4:30 and ended at 7:00.

Paasikivi began by reading a memorandum drafted by Colonel Paasonen which strove to show that no peril threatened the Gulf of Finland. Under the terms of this memorandum, he said, he was prepared to discuss those islands which lay closest to the Soviet shore, namely Seiskari, Lavansaari, and Peninsaari. The Soviet Union might, against compensation, integrate them into its defense system.

The offer was held to be so trifling as not to be worth the trouble of discussing it. In the view of the Russians the boundary between the states was too close to the city of Leningrad, only thirty-two kilometers away. Russia already had cannon which carried fifty to sixty kilometers; Finland could secure similar ones, and then Leningrad would be within artillery range. Yet they did not wish to speak so much of military details as of the political significance of the situation. The great war now in progress required that they obtain complete security. If they were to take into consideration the views of the military command, they would have to call for the boundary existing at the time of Peter the Great. (This boundary, later established through the peace treaty, was thus under consideration even at this early stage.)

Paasikivi: The line your military command has in mind would be quite impossible on economic grounds alone.

Stalin: Soldiers never think in economic terms.

As Stalin's more extensive remarks give the best picture of the background of the demands, it will be well to set forth their substance. He spoke roughly as follows:*

"It is not the fault of either of us that geographical circumstances are as they are. We must be able to bar entrance to the Gulf of Finland. If the channel to Leningrad did not run along your coast, we would not have the slightest occasion to bring the matter up. Your memorandum is one-sided and overoptimistic. We must bear in mind also the worst possible eventualities. Tsarist Russia had the Porkkala and Naissaari fortresses with their twelve-inch guns, and the Tallinn naval base as well. At that time it was impossible for an enemy to come through the breach. We do not ask either for Porkkala or for Naissaari, as they are too near the capitals of Finland and Estonia. On the other hand, an effective seal can be created between Hanko and Paldiski.

"It is a law of naval strategy that passage into the Gulf of Finland can be blocked by the cross fire of batteries on both shores as far out as the mouth of the Gulf. Your memorandum supposes that an enemy cannot penetrate into the Gulf. But once a hostile fleet is in the Gulf, the Gulf can no longer be defended.

"You ask what power might attack us. England or Germany. We are on good terms with Germany now, but everything in this world may change. Yudenich attacked through the Gulf of Finland and later the British did the same. This can happen again. If you are afraid to give us bases on the mainland, we can dig a canal across Hanko Neck, and then our base won't be on Finnish mainland territory. As things stand now, both England and Germany can send large naval units into the Gulf of Finland. I doubt whether you would be able to avoid an incident in that case. England is pressuring Sweden for bases right now. Germany is doing likewise. When the war between those two is over, the victor's fleet will come into the Gulf.

"You ask, why do we want Koivisto? I'll tell you why. I asked Ribbentrop why Germany went to war with Poland. He replied, 'We had to move the Polish border farther from Berlin.' Before the war the distance from Poznan to Berlin was about two hundred kilometers. Now the border has been moved three hundred kilometers farther east. We ask that the distance from Leningrad to the line should be seventy kilometers. That is our minimum demand, and you must not think we are

* According to the notes made by the Finnish interpreter who attended the discussion.

prepared to reduce it bit by bit. We can't move Leningrad, so the line has to move. Regarding Koivisto, you must bear in mind that if sixteen-inch guns were placed there they could entirely prevent movements of our fleet in the inmost extremity of the Gulf. We ask for 2,700 square kilometers and offer more than 5,500 in exchange. Does any other great power do that? No. We are the only ones that simple."

When the Finnish representatives, in accordance with their instructions, emphasized that no part of Finland's mainland territory could be alienated, the Soviet representatives observed — additionally to what Stalin had said, perhaps in jest, about cutting a canal through Hanko Neck —that such cessions had been made before. Russia had sold Alaska to the United States, and Spain had ceded Gibraltar to England.

Paasikivi made the principal statements on behalf of the Finnish negotiators. He kept strictly within the bounds of the instructions he had received and argued on juridical grounds. It was of importance to Finland that there should not be separated from its territory portions which might subsequently be converted into military bases of a great power. Not to speak of opinion at home, there would be great suspicion in Sweden, Norway, and Denmark if there were foreign forces on our territory. This would not be in keeping with our neutrality. And we wished to remain neutral.

Stalin also took up the circumstance that Finland had mobilized and had evacuated its cities. They, too, had sent forces to the border. This could not last long without risk of danger. It was necessary to come to a decision. At the time this statement was not accorded sufficient attention. Later, viewed in connection with the shooting at Mainila, it took on an ominous look.

As many new facts and problems had come up in the conversation, Paasikivi declared that he must go to Helsinki to consult with the government. It was agreed that the negotiations should be continued around October 20 or 21. The Russians promised they would deliver their proposals in writing before the Finns left.

In a further meeting, held at 9:30 that same evening, the Finnish representatives received the Soviet proposals in the form of a written memorandum. As subsequent conversations were based upon this important document, there is occasion to transcribe it here in its entirety. It read as follows:

The principal concern of the Soviet Union in its negotiations with Finland relates to two problems:

(a) Guaranteeing the safety of Leningrad;

(b) Assurance that Finland will, on a basis of friendly relationships, come to maintain a close association with the Soviet Union. Both points are indispensable in order to safeguard the Soviet shore of the Gulf of Finland and also the Estonian portion of that shore, the independence of which the Soviet Union has guaranteed, against the attack of a foreign enemy.

In order to carry out this undertaking it is necessary:

1. That the Soviet Union be enabled to close the mouth of the Gulf of Finland through artillery fire from both shores, so that hostile naval and merchant vessels may be barred from the waters of the Gulf of Finland;

2. That the Soviet Union be enabled to prevent the access of an enemy to those islands of the Gulf of Finland which lie along the channels west and northwest of Leningrad;

3. That the Finnish boundary on the Karelian Isthmus, which is now at thirty-two kilometers from Leningrad (that is to say, within reach of shells from long-range cannon), be moved somewhat further north and northwest.

Separately there arises the question of the Rybachi Peninsula at Petsamo, where the boundary is ineptly and artificially drawn and where it should be corrected in accordance with the attached map.

Proceeding on the basis of the foregoing proposals, it is necessary to settle the following questions, in common harmony and for the common advantage:

1. Lease to the Soviet government for a period of thirty years of the port of Hanko and of the surrounding area over a radius of five to six nautical miles to the south and east, and of three nautical miles to the west and north, for the establishment of a naval base, armed with coastal defense guns, which would be capable through artillery fire, together with the base at Paldiski on the south shore, of cutting off access to the Gulf of Finland. For the protection of the naval base Finland is to permit the Soviet Union to maintain the following personnel at the port of Hanko:

1 regiment of infantry
2 anti-aircraft batteries
2 air force regiments
1 tank battalion

—in all not over five thousand men.

2. The right of Soviet naval forces to use Lappohja Bay as an anchorage.

3. Cession of the following areas to the Soviet Union against compensatory territory:

The islands of Suursaari, Lavansaari, Tytärsaari, and Koivisto, the part of the Karelian Isthmus from the village of Lipola to the southern edge of the city of Koivisto, the western parts of the Rybachi Peninsula; in all 2,761 square kilometers in accordance with the attached map.

4. In return for the areas referred to under Point 3, the Soviet Union will cede to the Republic of Finland Soviet territory in the regions of Repola and Porajärvi to the extent of 5,529 square kilometers, in accordance with the attached map.

5. Reinforcement of the nonaggression pact now in effect between the Soviet Union and Finland, by adding a stipulation to the effect that the contracting par-

ties bind themselves to refrain from participation in such groupings or alliances of powers as may be directly or indirectly hostile to the other contracting party.

6. Destruction by both parties of the fortified areas situated along the Finnish-Soviet border on the Karelian Isthmus, leaving ordinary border guard forces along the line.

7. The Soviet Union will not oppose Finland's arming the Aaland Islands through the use of its own forces, on the condition that no foreign power, Sweden included, shall have a hand in their fortification.

As will be observed, the point on the reciprocal aid treaty was left out of the memorandum, and its place was taken by the proposed addition to the nonaggression pact referred to under Point 5.

On the basis of the memorandum thus received, a further brief conversation took place, in which the Finns sought, for the most part, to obtain explanations of several points in the memorandum.

To conclude, the following views were exchanged:*

Paasikivi: We have to submit all questions of this sort to the Diet for its approval. Furthermore, almost all the matters dealt with in the memorandum must be decided upon as questions of constitutional import, which means that they require a five-sixths majority.

Stalin: You are sure to get ninety-nine percent support.

Paasikivi: The Hanko Neck concession and the cession of the area on the Isthmus are exceptionally difficult matters.

Stalin: It's nothing, really. Look at Hitler. The Poznan frontier was too close to Berlin for him, and he took an extra three hundred kilometers.

Paasikivi: We want to continue in peace and remain apart from all incidents.

Stalin: That's impossible.

Puusonen: How do these proposals of yours fit in with your famous slogan, "We do not want a crumb of foreign territory, but neither do we want to cede an inch of our own territory to anyone"?

Stalin: I'll tell you. In Poland we took no foreign territory. And now this is a case of exchange. So we will expect you back on the twentieth or twenty-first.

Molotov: We'll sign the agreement on the twentieth and give you a dinner the next day.

Paasikivi: When we come back will depend on the government.

The meeting broke up at 10:00 P.M.

The Finnish negotiators left on their return journey the following day (October 15) and reached Helsinki on the morning of October 16.

* From the Finnish interpreter's notes.

MOSCOW'S DEMANDS EXAMINED IN HELSINKI

That same day (October 16) a small discussion group within the Council of State was organized by reason of the demands presented in Moscow. Those present were the Council members Prime Minister Cajander, Foreign Minister Erkko, Defense Minister Niukkanen, and myself, as it was incumbent primarily on us as members of the Cabinet foreign affairs committee to follow the course of these negotiations. The military were represented by Marshal Mannerheim; by the commander in chief of the armed forces, Lieutenant General Österman; and by the chief of the general staff, Lieutenant General Oesch. The other participants were the ministers Paasikivi and Yrjö-Koskinen, Colonel Paasonen, and Chief of Bureau Nykopp.

To begin with, Paasikivi gave a clarifying exposition of the demands presented by the Russians and of the discussions that had followed. Thus far the Finnish negotiators had assumed a negative attitude toward all Russian demands save that for cession of certain islands in the Gulf of Finland. If we persisted in that attitude, it was useless to continue the negotiations. In that event there would be three possibilities before us: (1) war would break out; (2) nothing would happen; or (3) the Russians would drop their demands. The Russians had asked three specific questions, and these must either be answered yes or no, or a compromise proposal must be offered. The next time we would have to give our final answer.

Foreign Minister Erkko was strongly opposed to further concessions. Hanko could in no case be ceded, nor could the boundary on the Isthmus be shifted. Cession of the islands might be discussed. As Paasikivi had not brought with him from the Russians the map relating to Hanko, Erkko reached the conclusion that they had evidently dropped that demand.

Defense Minister Niukkanen associated himself with Erkko's stand. No Diet could accept the Russian demands.

Minister Yrjö-Koskinen judged that if we could satisfy the legitimate defense requirements of the Russians, as others had acknowledged them, war would not break out.

On Prime Minister Cajander's asking whether the marshal and the general staff could prepare a counteroffer, Marshal Mannerheim took the floor to remark that if Russia would be satisfied with a frontier at seventy kilometers from Leningrad, the military could make a counteroffer. If it were admitted that a heavily armed great power might invoke legitimate rights and request frontier rectifications, there was perhaps reason to suppose that Russia might obtain the fortress of Ino, which was as valuable as Hanko. With the batteries of Ino and of Krasnaya Gorka opposite, Russia could cut off access to Kronstadt. Between Hanko and Ino there was indeed the difference that closing the Gulf of Finland at its mouth was more advantageous to the Russians. As for Hanko and the Isthmus, he was of the same opinion as Erkko.

General Oesch observed that the present border was the shortest line possible and that it was exceptionally advantageous to us from the point of view of military geography. If the line were moved in the fashion proposed by the Russians, its length would be doubled and the border region would afford an aggressor a greatly superior point of departure for an attack. Finland's whole defense line would have to be moved deeper, and a considerable part of our line of fortifications, which was, to be sure, not entirely completed, would remain on the other side of the frontier.

I said that I was of the same opinion as the military representatives in considering that it was not up to the Russians to defend the Finnish coast. The inmost extremity of the Gulf of Finland was, however, another matter. The islands in the eastern part of the Gulf being 150 kilometers distant from Leningrad, they should suffice for Leningrad's security. There was no loss of honor in talking about them. One might also discuss ceding the Ino area and the protective strip surrounding it, likewise a Russian demand for minor border rectifications on the Isthmus. The Finnish people would surely understand if we should negotiate on the basis I suggested. Hanko, on the other hand, was out of the question.

Yrjö-Koskinen remarked that it would be important to learn Sweden's position. Would Sweden furnish effective aid if we got into trouble? He judged that a declaration to that effect would carry great weight in Moscow.

Paasikivi remarked that the earlier representations of the Scandinavian countries on our behalf had evidently made no particular impression.

Prime Minister Cajander did not state his own opinion but confined himself to guiding the discussion.

We decided to wait for the statement and the possible counteroffer to be drafted by the military officials.

During the following days it was not possible to carry the matter forward in Helsinki. A meeting of the heads of state of the countries of the North had been arranged for October 18–19 in Stockholm, and President Kallio together with Minister Erkko took part in this "congress of kings" on behalf of Finland. This meeting of the chiefs of state— three kings and one president—was brilliantly staged. There is no need to say much of its fruits. The Finnish delegates went to Stockholm presumably with the intention of introducing the subject of Finland's position into the conversations. This had not been agreed upon previously in Helsinki, and no information on the matter was revealed after the Finnish representatives had returned. It was only much later that I happened to hear from the Swedish Prime Minister, Hansson, that the matter had been taken up with him. President Kallio had not felt that he could speak of it, as he feared a negative response. Erkko, on the other hand, had inquired whether aid might possibly be expected from Sweden. He had received an unconditionally negative reply. Unfortunately, not even the Cabinet learned of Sweden's stand before the negotiations were resumed. When Erkko was asked about Sweden's attitude before the Foreign Relations Committee of the Diet, he gave a guarded answer. A clear answer might possibly have influenced the Diet's attitude.

At home the negotiations which had been undertaken with the Soviet Union began to attract attention and to arouse uneasiness. Although no word of the Russian demands had become public, they were nevertheless being guessed at, and there was talk about them. Delegations began to call on the Council of State expressing their intransigent opposition to the demands. The Prime Minister received, among others, a large delegation representing all parishes of the Isthmus, who firmly demanded the rejection of even the least cession of Isthmus territory.

One day about that time, Paasikivi and Yrjö-Koskinen stopped by to see me at the Finance Ministry. They were worried and said that they had come to talk about the negotiations which were under way. As old Finnish nationalists, they remarked jokingly, they had had plenty of experience with the need to make concessions in the face of adversity during the Tsar's time; they still were of the opinion that the negotiations must produce results even at the cost of concessions. But neither of them was willing to cede Hanko.

Only after President Kallio and Foreign Minister Erkko had returned from Stockholm was it possible to start on preparations for another round of negotiations in Moscow. The Council of State was called into private session in Prime Minister Cajander's office on October 20. On this occasion the whole Cabinet was made acquainted with the Soviet demands, which were discussed in preliminary fashion. As a result of this conversation Erkko was given the task of drafting a written reply to be handed to the Russians and also of drawing up fresh instructions to be given the negotiators.

Erkko completed his draft the next day (October 21), whereupon the Council of State met to examine it. In the draft reply as well as in the instructions there was this time a slightly more yielding attitude than in the first instructions. We were prepared, as before, to cede the islands.

We were willing to discuss Suursaari too, with certain reservations. We were also a little more prepared to yield to the demand for a shift of the border on the Isthmus. According to Erkko's draft reply and to the instructions, the border would have run from the part of Rajajoki east of Haapala to the Gulf of Finland at a point east of Kellomäki church. In this wise it would have straightened out the so-called Kuokkala bend, which the Russians had asked for as far back as the peace negotiations at Tartu and which had long been the subject of discussion there. The reply concerning a lease of Hanko and Lappohja harbors was rigidly negative as before. Nothing was said of the Rybachi Peninsula at Petsamo.

The reply was in fact finally phrased in the terms of Erkko's draft.

When the written reply to be handed the Russians had been completed, we went on to consider the special instructions to be given the negotiators. They were to contain directives on how far the negotiators might go in the sense of concessions if the reply which was about to be presented were not satisfactory to the Russians. The proposal Erkko had prepared instructed the negotiators to refuse any concession on Hanko and Lappohja. Of Suursaari only the southern half might be offered, although as a last resort all of Suursaari might be offered to keep Hanko out of jeopardy. There was to be no yielding on the Rybachi Peninsula. All reciprocal aid treaties were to be refused. Regarding the boundary on the Isthmus three alternatives were mentioned. Alternative A: The Kuokkala bend might be straightened, and thus the border would be moved to forty-five kilometers, instead of thirty-two, from Leningrad. This would be sufficient to eliminate the theoretical possibility, advanced by the Russians, that Leningrad might be subjected to artillery fire from Finland. Alternative B: Ino could be ceded as an isolated fortress. This would ward off all peril from seaward. Alternative C: If the Russians should demand that Ino be attached directly to their own territory, this might be done by means of a connecting strip lying between the line Ino-Vammeljoki-Lintulanjoki-Jäppinen and the Gulf of Finland.

Only the alternatives regarding the Isthmus were discussed at this time. Niukkanen was prepared to cede Ino, since it was of no significance for Finland. On the other hand Erkko, Von Fieandt, and Kekkonen opposed this cession. So did Voionmaa, as it would constitute a repulsive servitude. Kekkonen conceded to the negotiators the authority to straighten the Kuokkala bend, but no more. If that did not satisfy the Russians, the negotiators must seek fresh instructions.

As a majority of the Cabinet set itself in opposition to a grant of broader powers, there remained in the instructions only the authority relating to the elimination of the Kuokkala bend.

This discussion had lasted rather long, from 12:30 to 3:30. In the official session which was held immediately thereafter the President took part as well. He said that with respect to the Isthmus he favored the powers proposed under the first of the above-mentioned alternatives. In his opinion only the southern part of Suursaari might be ceded, and of the Rybachi Peninsula the northern part. In the President's view, before the negotiations should start there should be called to the attention of the Russians the border violations which had been occurring. (Russian planes were flying over our side of the line with increasing frequency.)

The President then confirmed the instructions which had been drawn up.

In speaking of the impending trip, Paasikivi had required that some one of the members of the Council should be sent with him; otherwise he declined to go himself. He went on to demand that I be his travel companion. This was presumably because we had worked together often before.

The suggestion found support among the members of the Council. As my friends from my own party also joined in supporting the proposal, I felt it my duty to assent. On Erkko's suggestion the President in fact named me as second negotiator along with Paasikivi.

As the precautionary measures of the defense establishment were eating up money, an appeal to the people was necessary. In its session of October 21 the Council decided to raise a domestic loan of 500 million marks for application to these expenses. It was successful beyond expectations. Before the end of November the loan had been oversubscribed by 200 million marks. It was at this stage, also, that gifts began to pour in on the government and the defense establishment as well as on the Red Cross and other aid groups. Warm clothes were collected for the reservists. A number of industrial plants and business firms began to pay wages to their personnel who were in the reserves, ordinarily half pay, with supplements based on the number of children. The will to undertake sacrifices was great.

CHAPTER 3

THE SECOND TRIP TO MOSCOW

In being chosen one of the Moscow negotiators I had come to be associated with an undertaking of responsibility, in which we had to endeavor to defend Finland's rights in the face of demands which sought to prejudice them. I was sensible of how much we should have to answer for and, at the same time, of how weak was the position which the Finnish representatives would occupy in carrying out their task.

We departed on October 21 in the train that left at 6:30 P.M. Besides the official negotiators, Paasikivi and myself, there came also our Moscow envoy, Yrjö-Koskinen, and Colonel Aladár Paasonen and Johan Nykopp. The interest of the public in our journey was evidenced by the thousands of people who came to the Helsinki station to see us off with testimonials of flowers and singing. The members of the Cabinet who had come, and all our friends, wished us luck and success in our mission. The same sort of interest was shown at many stations along the way. At Riihimäki station a great crowd of people had gathered who greeted us with song. After that we went to bed. But at Lahti the greetings were renewed. As Paasikivi was unwilling to get up, I put my winter overcoat over my pajamas and went out on the platform of the car to thank them for their greetings and their good wishes. We were the object of the last of such greetings only at Terijoki.

Our trip was slow on account of troop movements, as the reserve refresher courses were just under way. For this reason we reached Viipuri quite late, on October 22 at 7:30 A.M. From there on our progress was still slower, and in particular at Rajajoki and Valkeasaari there were long stops for border formalities. At Valkeasaari our younger companions exchanged money for us, bringing us the rubles we would need to use. On account of all the delays we reached Leningrad at five in the afternoon.

It was with considerable curiosity that I looked over old Petersburg—which I had earlier often visited, the last time twenty-two years before—since even after the Russian Revolution it remained impossible for ordinary citizens to cross the border. The Finland Station seemed to be much as it had been before. On our arrival some officials were at the station to bid us welcome. Our baggage was delivered to porters they had secured and was thus taken out to automobiles waiting in front of the station. Conspicuous were the swarms of people milling about the station, far greater than I remembered from any of my earlier visits. Evidently word of our coming had spread, as a considerable crowd had gathered in front of the station to watch our arrival.

We were taken by car to the Astoria Hotel in the center of town, where foreign guests coming to the city are usually lodged. It was a respectable old hotel, but now it looked pretty dilapidated. It appeared that at the moment it was housing some kind of trade congress from all over the country; the participants were swarming everywhere in the lobby and the corridors. We were assigned to a handsomely furnished luxury suite on the top floor. But this time we did not manage to take much advantage of it, as we felt very hungry, and moreover we were desirous of seeing the city before the train left. We ate in an imposing restaurant on the main floor, where for a reasonable price we secured special Russian dishes. The wines, too, were of domestic manufacture. After eating we went off for a walk through the city to look at its evening life. There were plenty of people in the streets. Our attention was especially drawn by the long queues of people standing in front of the stores, particularly the food stores. To judge from this, the shortage of foodstuffs was considerable. One queue was longer than the rest—I should say over a hundred yards long. I went to where it started with the idea of finding out what they were queued up for. There I was surprised to find a little booth thrown together out of planks where the evening newspaper, the Leningrad *Pravda*, was being sold. Seemingly reader interest was very great. But I learned from one of the Russians that when paper required for domestic needs was unobtainable, they bought newspapers partly to meet that need.

On this occasion we did not have much time at our disposal to see the town, since we had to catch the night train which was to take us to Moscow. The train was the famous "Krasnaya Zvezda" ("Red Star") in which there were assigned for our use comfortable first-class compartments. As I had never before traveled in the interior of Russia, I should have been very glad to examine the landscape, but there was no opportunity for that by night. In the morning I was up and about early, looking out the window at the communities we passed. At least those regions I saw at that time appeared level, low, and for the most part unforested.

At 10:10 on the following morning (October 23) we were at the October Station in Moscow, where the personnel of our own Legation and the chiefs of mission of the three Scandinavian countries were present to meet us. Chief of Protocol Barkov bade us welcome on behalf of the government. Derevyanski, the Soviet Minister to Helsinki, was also present. We were taken in automobiles through the surging life of the Moscow streets to the new Finnish Legation building. The speed of the cars was wild, and the escort automobiles ahead of us shrieked quite dreadfully if pedestrians happened to block our progress. At the Legation the Minister's wife, Mrs. Yrjö-Koskinen, received us hospitably, assigning a room for the use of each of us. The Legation building, which had been completed only the year before, appeared roomy but very impractical.

We spent a fair part of the day getting our papers into final order. Among other matters they had to be translated into Russian, a job which the officers of the Legation rapidly accomplished. It occurred to me to visit the great agricultural exhibition then showing in Moscow, which had been opened in the last few days. Nykopp and I made the trip together. It was worth seeing. In the extensive exhibition grounds a separate large hall had been built for each of the many Soviet republics of the Union, and these showed in conspicuous fashion the ways of living in the various parts of this gigantic community, and above all the level of their agricultural development. On their walls, to be sure, were the conventional statistics and graphs, from which those interested might secure a more detailed grounding in Soviet conditions. In brief, the exhibition was extremely interesting and instructive. On the outer wall of one of the buildings we found, set up in large letters, Stalin's famous dictum to which reference has been made before: "We do not want an inch of foreign territory, but neither do we want to cede an inch of our own territory to anyone." For our own part we could only reflect on what the import of this slogan might be.

On this excursion I made my first acquaintance with the ways in which foreigners in Russia are helped and at the same time watched. Every day a couple of automobiles were parked in front of the Legation building, and when we set out in a Legation car one of these autos followed us. The GPU men in these cars were a great help, because they acted as guides and explained to us the peculiarities of each of the exhibition buildings. In the throng we happened to get separated from them for a while, but when we came out of the exhibition grounds we found them by our car faithfully awaiting our return.

Our first meeting with the representatives of the Soviet government took place at six o'clock in the evening of that same day. Paasikivi and I left by car for the Kremlin, with the GPU car faithfully at our heels. At the gates of the Kremlin we were stopped, and the guards at the portal examined the interior of our car by flashlight. After this we were requested to continue onward behind an escort car. This guidance was necessary in the huge labyrinthine courtyard because of the darkness. The machine stopped before the entrance to a large building. Here the commandant of the Kremlin received us, first courteously introducing himself. He led us to the elevator, which took us up about one story. Here before us was a long narrow corridor, through one of whose doors we passed. We found ourselves in a room where a secretary sat at a desk with a battery of at least ten telephones before him. As we had arrived a few minutes before the time set, we had a chance to take a glance at the room and at the man working there. He was constantly answering telephone calls and replying briefly to inquiries. At exactly 6:00 P.M. a door to the next room opened and we were asked to enter. We came into a fairly large room at the far end of which was a large writing desk. Along one side of the room was a longer table with chairs at either side. Here we were received by Marshal Stalin and Soviet Foreign Affairs Commissar Molotov. We were asked to take seats at the long table, and our hosts seated themselves at the opposite side.

When preliminary courtesies had been exchanged, Paasikivi read in Russian a memorandum which had been drafted in Helsinki. It affirmed, to begin with, that Finland wished to remain on terms of friendship and trust with the Soviet Union and was accordingly willing to deliberate upon means to satisfy Soviet wishes with a view to the defense position of Leningrad. A prerequisite, however, was that Finland's own security views should also be taken into consideration. Through good will on both sides the needs of the Soviet Union might be satisfied without offense to Finland's security and neutrality.

Assuming that the Finnish Diet for its part would also approve the stand of the Cabinet, the Finnish government was prepared to accept the following arrangements:

Finland was disposed to cede to the Soviet Union the following islands in the Gulf of Finland: Seiskari, Peninsaari, Lavansaari, and both the Tytärsaari islands. In addition, the Finnish government was disposed to discuss arrangements on Suursaari, the advantages of both countries being taken into account.

Finland was receptive to such boundary rectifications on the Isthmus as would eliminate the so-called Kuokkala bend. The boundary would then run from Rajajoki at a point east of Haapala straight to the Gulf at a point east of Kellomäki church, thus moving it thirteen kilometers to the westward.

Finland could not entertain the idea of ceding Hanko harbor and the area surrounding it, nor Lappohja Bay, as it was obliged to maintain the inviolability of the territory.

With respect to the proposal of the Soviet government, that the nonaggression pact between the two states should be amplified, it was asserted that the Finnish government would on certain conditions be disposed to clarify the treaty in question.

The Finnish government accepted with satisfaction the declaration of the Soviet government that it would not oppose the fortification of the Aaland Islands, and it asserted further that this fortification would be undertaken through its own resources and at its own expense, the obligations pertaining to neutralization under the 1921 treaty at the same time being taken into consideration.

In addition to the memorandum referred to, Paasikivi read another which set forth a protest against border violations which had occurred in the preceding weeks, particularly against aircraft flying across the border. Little attention, however, was paid to this on the other side of the table.

After the reading of these documents the discussion began. At its start I asked whether I might use either German or English, as my Russian was on the weak side. To this Molotov replied dryly with the single word, *Nyet*. As Paasikivi's Russian turned out to be pretty rusty, we were on this account technically at a disadvantage during the conversation.

Coming down to business, Stalin said that Finland was offering too little. He emphasized several times the fact that the Soviet demands were "minimal," and that for this reason there was no use in bargaining over them. There followed next an extensive exposition of why the Soviet Union had had to make demands upon Finland. According to this version, the war which had started in Europe might become a world war and last a long time. As it went on, some great power might undertake to attack Leningrad through the Gulf and via Finland. In order to ward off such an attack, the Soviet Union was forced to acquire the means to close the Gulf at its very mouth. The bases which had come into Soviet hands on the Estonian shore did not offer sufficient assurance, since Finnish territorial waters were beyond artillery range from Paldiski. For this reason Hanko was indispensable to them, for it lay opposite Paldiski.

According to their statement, for the same purpose—the defense of Leningrad—they also needed the islands in the Gulf which they had demanded. A more extensive discussion developed regarding the territories sought on the Karelian Isthmus. The Finnish offer respecting the rectification of the Kuokkala bend was rejected out of hand. In their view the area offered was too confined, since to deploy their forces the Russians would need much more room. Wishing to make more attractive suggestions, Stalin drew freehand on the general staff map on the table new lines along which the boundary should run. It was clear that he was well versed in the geography of the area. All these new boundary suggestions had the defect that their terminal point was north of Koivisto. We on the other hand had no authority to approve any of these new proposals.

There was some discussion of the demands relating to Petsamo. We felt we could promise to examine the cession of the northern part of the Rybachi Peninsula.

In the middle of things Stalin suddenly asked what we had to say about the areas the Soviet Union had offered in exchange, pointing out on the map the parts of Repola and Porajärvi parishes proposed as compensation. We replied that the question of compensation was something to bother about later, after we should first have seen whether we could reach agreement regarding the areas they had demanded.

Upon our asking why they made any demands of this nature at all, when the boundary between the two states had been settled in great harmony as recently as the Peace of Tartu, it came to light that they seriously entertained the possibility that Russia would become involved in warfare in the vicinity of the Gulf of Finland and perhaps also on the shores of the Arctic Ocean, for which reason they required a rectification of the frontier at Petsamo too. Stalin and Molotov several times referred to England and France as possible attackers. Stalin also recalled many times that during the First World War the British fleet had frequented Koivisto and had made torpedo boat raids from there into Petersburg harbor, sinking vessels. Beneath it all, however, one sensed that it was Germany they feared. The name of that state, too, came into the discussions as a possible attacker. At this we observed that such a possibility was very slight, since a nonaggression pact—actually an alliance—had just been concluded between Germany and the Soviet Union, so that an attack from that quarter ought not to be in the cards. In our view, furthermore, France and England would by no means be able to enter the Baltic in the course of this war.

In support of Finland's position we referred continually to the treaty of peace made at Tartu and also to the nonaggression pact made in 1932 on Soviet initiative and reaffirmed in 1936—a pact which allowed of no denunciation before 1945. These observations were of no avail; they were barely listened to. In the opinion of the Soviet negotiators these treaties had been made under entirely different circumstances.

After we had sat and talked for a couple of hours, Stalin and Molotov asked us once more to consider their demands regarding Hanko and the Isthmus. We said that their proposals on both points were unacceptable and asked them to consider the views set forth in the Finnish memorandum.

Stalin rejected this suggestion out of hand, asserting that Finland offered too little. He repeated that the Russian proposals were rock bottom.

As each side had thus determined that it was impossible to accept the proposals of the other, and as the discussion was thus in a way ended, we expressed our regret at the result and took our leave. There was no reference at the moment to a further meeting or to any other continuation of the discussion.

Molotov seemed astounded at our departure. He said as though by the way, "Is it your intention to provoke a conflict?"

To this Paasikivi replied, "We want no such thing, but you seem to."

Stalin on the other hand merely smiled in his usual enigmatic fashion.

At 8:00 P.M., after a two hours' session, we left the building. On departing we had the impression that the conversations had been broken off. At least, we would have been unable to take the initiative for their renewal.

At the Legation we took counsel together with Minister Yrjö-Koskinen regarding the situation which had developed, and deliberated on what steps we should now take. We drafted a cable to Helsinki in which we reported our results, and asked permission to return home. We further decided to order tickets for the next evening's train. In this way we would let the other party understand that we really regarded the negotiations as having been broken off.

But we had not managed to do anything before the phone rang at about 9:00 P.M. and Molotov's secretary asked us to come to a further meeting that same evening at 10:30. Thus the other party had taken steps to resume the negotiations. The thought sprang to mind that now we should receive an ultimatum. We agreed upon what we should do under different sets of circumstances.

The first invitation, however, was canceled later by phone and the meeting was set for 11:00 P.M. We observed, by the way, that this was a quite usual hour for talks at the Kremlin. Stalin in particular was accustomed to work beyond midnight, a habit which involved great fatigue for those used to the customs of another world and who got up early in the morning.

When we drove to the Kremlin at 11:00 the trip was made in the same fashion as the first time.

This time our hosts were again Stalin and Molotov. Our business got under way as though no interruption had occurred, and the conversation continued on the basis of the written exposition we had presented. As a written reply thereto Molotov read a memorandum he had drafted in the meantime and in which the defense needs of Leningrad were emphasized anew, although the Russians were prepared to reduce their original demands to a slight extent. They still insisted on obtaining Hanko, but they promised to keep there land forces of only four thousand (in place of the original five thousand) "until the termination of the British-French-German war in Europe." The other forces would remain for thirty years—in other words, until the end of the lease period. The Finnish proposal concerning the Isthmus did not satisfy them, but here, too, the Soviet Union presented a demand slightly altered from the original one, running somewhat along the lines Stalin had earlier sketched out on the map. The terminal point was again Koivisto.

We expressed as our attitude the belief that these new proposals would not be acceptable either. Having regard for the nature of the case we were, however, prepared to report them to Helsinki.

Molotov: How much time will that take?

Paasikivi: About four days. How can we get in touch with Helsinki from here?

Molotov: Send them a telegram.

Tanner: It would be necessary also to consult the Diet, which is not yet by any means informed regarding the whole matter. We cannot say exactly how much time this may require. We will give our answer the minute we are ready.

This satisfied the others, and we again left the conference room with the map we had received.

At the Legation we again discussed the position. We considered that cabling would produce no result in so great a matter; consequently we would have to depart for Helsinki and report. We cabled Helsinki regarding this decision and the course of the negotiations. We broke up at 2:00 A.M.

The next morning (October 24) Paasikivi came to my room, on edge after a bad night's sleep. He put our position thus: We had lived twenty years in the lap of an illusion. We had thought we could freely determine our own fate. We had chosen neutrality and a Scandinavian orientation as the line of our foreign policy. But now the truth was coming out. Our geographical position bound us to Russia. Was that so terrible? In the Tsar's times the Russian garrisons had not proved much bother in our domestic affairs; they would hardly do so now. The demands which had been presented settled our Scandinavian orientation and our relations with Germany. Now we ought to fight, but we could not. Finland could not undertake a war. If it broke out, we would lose it, and in that case the result would be much worse than any we should reach through accommodation. The infection of Bolshevism would spread into Finland, and it would lead us to final ruin. Now the decisive factor was whether Sweden would come to our aid. Per Albin (Hansson) must now give the final answer to this question.

Paasikivi was now prepared to recommend that the Soviet Union be granted a base in the west, in which connection he had in mind the cession of Jussarö. As for the line to be recommended on the Isthmus, he had in mind withdrawal to the maximum limit suggested by Mannerheim.

At Paasikivi's suggestion I promised to write a personal letter to Prime Minister Per Albin Hansson in Sweden, inquiring what Sweden's attitude would be toward Finland's case. We outlined the letter together.

As the day was free, I wished to make use of it by acquainting myself a little with Moscow, which I had not visited before. I got the use of a Legation car and went off to town with Nykopp to look at its most notable sights. We made a pretty extensive tour of it. When we reached the famous Red Square, on the long side I noticed Lenin's imposing tomb and before it a queue of perhaps a thousand people who were evidently awaiting admission. As we know, the tomb is a place of pilgrimage which every true-believing Bolshevik ought to visit. We drove up before the tomb and asked the guard at the barrier whether we might go in and look. But an officer who came up explained that it would be opened only about an hour hence, even though the queue was already considerable. So we turned away, explaining that we had not time to wait so long. At that moment the GPU men in the car which had been following us made their way forward and asked us to wait a moment. One of them went inside to say something. At once he returned and said we might go in immediately. We were thus specially favored.

We passed through the door and went down the stairs to the lower room, where Lenin lay embalmed in a glass case on a bier in the middle of the fairly large chamber. Ordinarily the stream of visitors may only file past this case and must leave at once. But we were allowed to remain by the case as long as we wished. We inspected Lenin's embalmed body and his waxlike face. He was just as he had been when I had seen him alive, save that his face seemed to have shrunk, as sometimes apparently happens in the embalming process. I remarked on this to the guide who was accompanying us and mentioned that I had met Lenin a couple of times in the old days, but that his head had been much bigger. Here I observed, however, that I was touching upon a ticklish matter. To be sure, they looked at me with respect as one who had met the man and shaken him by the hand. But they did not care for this observation. In any event the exchange of remarks terminated at once.

On leaving the mausoleum we continued our tour of the city.

On the same day (October 24) we left Moscow, again on the "Red Star," for Leningrad, where we were to spend the following day. We took advantage of it to visit Pushkin Village (the former Tsarskoye Selo). We chose our program according to a suggestion of Intourist and were conducted by its guides. There we visited several of the former imperial palaces. The rooms of the last Emperor and his wife left the impression that this ruler had been a good family man. The furnishings of the rooms, especially those of the nursery, contributed to this impression.

In the evening of October 25 we left Leningrad for Helsinki by train. The station platform was entirely roped off, and a guard of some thirty men stood before the train.

FINLAND APPEALS TO SWEDEN

Upon our reaching Helsinki I sent off to Prime Minister Per Albin Hansson the letter we had drafted in Moscow. Karl-August Fagerholm, a member of the Cabinet, who was just departing for Stockholm, took it to its destination. It ran as follows:

HELSINKI, October 26, 1939

BROTHER:

A grave matter occasions this letter to you—the gravest I have ever had to deal with.

You know that the Soviet Union has approached us with a series of demands. Stalin and Molotov fear that the war now under way may become extended and may be a prolonged one. They say they anticipate that in the closing phase of the war some great power [Germany] will attack the Soviet Union through the Gulf of Finland and possibly through Finland itself. On this account they wish in good time to place obstacles in the way of such an attack. For this reason they have forced Estonia, for one, to give them naval and other bases. Of these Paldiski dominates the southern part of the mouth of the Gulf of Finland. Yet this does not suffice for them. In order to close the Gulf at its mouth they require of us first the right to lease Hanko Cape for thirty years as a base. There they would set up batteries, and fleet and air stations. The area demanded is forty-five square kilometers in extent, thus nearly half of the entire cape. Four thousand Russian troops would man the area. For a naval station they demand the harbor of Lappohja on the south side of the same cape.

Their second demand involves the cession of various islands in the Gulf of Finland against compensation. The islands in question are Seiskari, Lavansaari, Peninsaari, and both the Tytärsaaris. On these artillery batteries would be erected. Thus these islands would form a second line of defense for the Gulf of Finland.

The third demand involves a boundary shift on the Karelian Isthmus. The present line is quite close to Leningrad, the shortest distance being thirty-two kilometers. The frontier is in their view dangerously near. Accordingly they have sketched out a new line, which runs considerably farther away and leaves the whole coast all the way to Koivisto in Soviet hands. On this shore there would be set up fortifications for the protection of Kronstadt.

The fourth demand involves the cession of a certain area in Petsamo. It would occasion the passage of the entire Rybachi Peninsula into their possession.

Fifth, they called for the conclusion of a treaty of aid between the Soviet Union and Finland. By reason of our negative stand they have more recently abandoned this demand.

Our position with regard to the demands made upon us is as follows:

Since we can do nothing about our geography, we are prepared to take cognizance of "legitimate" Soviet defense needs. Thus we are ready to cede to the Soviet Union the islands listed under Point 2. In any event we should be quite unable to defend them. We will also find a solution for the Petsamo territory referred to in Point 4 in some fashion or other. That point will perhaps disturb Norway first and foremost.

Regarding the question under Point 3, it is impossible for us to go so far to meet the Russians as they require, but we believe we can arrange the matter in such a way that the distance from the border to Leningrad will be about sixty kilometers, if that will settle the question. But even this would be very painful, since the territory which would be ceded is densely populated. In addition to which, border forts have of late been built in quantity throughout that area. Fortunately, the cession of this territory could be arranged under the guise of an "exchange of territories," which would save our face. The Russians are, in fact, disposed to release twice as much land in eastern Karelia.

Demand No. 1 is the hardest—the cession of Hanko Cape to the Soviet Union. For this involves the question of the Soviet Union's establishing itself on Finnish mainland territory, and far west to boot. From there the Soviet Union not only could control the Baltic but would also constitute a standing threat to Finland. At the same time the Soviet Union would there represent a threat to Sweden.

Disagreements are thus still so great that we do not believe we can reconcile them through additional concessions. But what may the consequences be if we refuse? The gentlemen of the Kremlin are stiff and declare that their demands are minimal, neither to be haggled over nor to be discussed. Consequently there exists a possibility that the consequence may be—war.

Have we any chance of avoiding war with the steamroller of the East?—that is the problem of the moment.

Earlier, when we imagined the possibility that we might become involved in war with the Soviet Union, we always had the idea it would happen under a different set of circumstances—that Russia would simultaneously be busy elsewhere. Under such circumstances we had thought we would be able to offer effective opposition. This time Russia has its hands entirely free. What is more, all the "police" of Europe are busy in other quarters. None of them would have the time to give even a thought to Finland's fate, still less could they assist us in even the most insignificant fashion—otherwise than through sympathizing newspaper editorials. Such, however, would presumably carry no great weight with the gentlemen of the Kremlin.

If we become involved in war—and that eventuality is possible if we refuse to accept the demands—we must take into account the possibility that we may lose the war. A small country against a great power which means to have its way—it is too ill-matched a game.

Then a lost war would be still worse than yielding to the demands in time. It would mean the devastation of the country, its alliance with the Soviet Union, maybe the establishment of a Bolshevist order in Finland.

I am writing down the draft for this letter during the negotiations in Moscow and after they have once been broken off only to be resumed again. I write to ask you a difficult question of conscience:

Is there any chance that Sweden, particularly since Hanko Cape is at issue, will intervene in this matter by giving Finland effective military assistance?

I think I know Swedish opinion on this subject. Consequently I am also aware that my question is a difficult one.

Finland is now living through moments which will decide its fate far into the future. If we yield to the demands, it will become difficult to maintain our Scandinavian orientation and our absolute independence. In this case we would be drawn into the Soviet sphere of influence. If we lose a war, the consequences will be even more disastrous. And in that event Sweden's position, too, will change markedly.

You will forgive me that I trouble you with so long a letter. I am not asking for anything. I do not even call for a reply if giving it would cause you difficulty. But if you have any chance of helping us, discussion will be necessary. In that event, however, Moscow will have to know of it before a final decision is reached.

I should like to emphasize further that for the time being the Soviet demands must be regarded as confidential. For the moment we have not informed the Finnish people of them, as we have not wished to make the negotiations more difficult through public discussion.

Faithfully yours,
VÄINÖ TANNER

Prime Minister Hansson answered this letter promptly—the very next day:

STOCKHOLM, October 27, 1939

BROTHER:

Your letter, which Fagerholm gave me personally yesterday evening, brought upon me that state of depression which arises when a person finds himself obliged to say something different from what he would wish to say.

My reply consists in the main of a repetition of what I felt it my duty to declare to Foreign Minister Erkko regarding our position over here the last time we met in Stockholm.

It has not been possible to reach any decision regarding Sweden's position, to begin with because such a decision has not been required as yet. I have, however, made certain inquiries, bearing primarily upon the chances of Sweden's taking part in protecting the neutrality of the Aaland Islands. In making these soundings it has naturally been necessary to take into account the consequences which would be entailed by Sweden's making an appearance in the Aalands. Indeed, it has been necessary to deliberate as to whether we are prepared to allow ourselves to be drawn into armed conflict.

It has been necessary to limit these soundings to conversations within a severely circumscribed group. On this account I have talked only with the party leaders. I have not considered it wise to carry the discussions to the Riksdag groups in their entirety, nor to the Riksdag itself. I have surely no need to give my reasons for this.

The result of these inquiries may be put most briefly by saying that the strongly preponderant opinion is to the effect that Sweden should take no steps which might involve the country in any incident. This stand, natural to a small country, is perhaps especially in favor among a people that has enjoyed the blessings of peace as long as Sweden has, and that has become accustomed to regarding its position as pretty well protected from the storms which sweep over the world. A secondary consideration, though one indeed not without influence in our analysis of our situation, is that our vigilance must be directed toward more quarters than one.

The conclusion has been that Sweden should not, by making an appearance in the Aaland Islands or in another fashion, expose itself to the danger of becoming involved in conflict with the Soviet Union. Here, then, is also the answer to the question you have asked: "Is there any chance that Sweden, particularly since Hanko Cape is at issue, will intervene in this matter by giving Finland effective military assistance?" You must not reckon with any such possibility.

We do not fail to perceive that Sweden's interests too will be endangered by reason of the altered relationships which might arise through unreconciled differences between Finland and the Soviet Union. But we are not now prepared to reach conclusions. It is bitter to have to say this, but any pretense would be out of place here.

We are considering what we might be able to do through diplomatic channels during the negotiations, and how we might be able to help Finland without direct involvement if an open conflict should break out. More I cannot say.

How cordially the thoughts of us here in Sweden are with Finland, especially during these days, you know so well that there is no need for me to say it.

Your faithful friend,

P. ALBIN HANSSON

In the same courier post with Hansson's letter, I received Fagerholm's impressions of the situation in Stockholm. He had met several of the members of the Swedish Cabinet: in addition to Prime Minister Hansson, Defense Minister Per Edvin Sköld, Foreign Minister Rickard Sandler, Minister of Education Arthur Engberg, and Minister for Social Affairs Gustav Möller, not to mention private persons.

On reading my letter Hansson had become very grave and had promised to call the Cabinet together to discuss it. He had not, however, wished to offer in advance any grounds for optimism. On delivering his answer the following day, Hansson had supplemented orally the thoughts in his letter and had said that apparently agreement could be reached with the Soviet Union on the other points but that the Hanko question seemed a difficult one to settle. If war should break out between Finland and the Soviet Union, it was conceivable that the Swedish Cabinet would be re-formed. Whether this would occasion a more active stand on Sweden's part was a matter on which Hansson did not wish to give an opinion, but the parties of the right certainly hoped so, as we were aware.

As for arms, Sweden had already furnished Finland with weapons, of which it had little enough for itself. Their shipment would be continued so far as possible. Upon the possible outbreak of war the position would indeed be altered according to the requirements of Sweden's neutral stand, but he considered it probable that Sweden would continue to do everything that might properly be expected of it. The transit of arms through Sweden should be possible to manage. If Norway could arrange it, Sweden could too. But what about Norway? With reference to foodstuffs, Sweden could very likely promise grain. In a pinch the Swedes could cut their own consumption.

Hansson had said that personally he would like to do a great deal more, but "I have to deal with a complacent people which wants to be left in peace." What form public opinion would assume if Finland were really to become involved in a war was another matter. It might even happen that acts of force would in that case bring understanding.

In talking to Sköld and Sandler, Fagerholm had observed that they favored a more active line than Prime Minister Hansson. The opposition of the Riksdag party groups was powerful, but then they had not been given detailed information. The Folkparti (the Liberal People's Party) was firmly opposed to any involvement in Finnish affairs, as was the Agrarian Party. The right had a more positive attitude toward Finland, but there was opposition there, too. The same might be said of the Social Democratic Party. Common to all party groups was the fact that the opponents of an active policy were determined and sure of their own minds, while our friends were uncertain and tentative, partly owing to the fact that they did not know what sort of demands had been put to Finland. Another difficulty was that the Swedes feared Germany would invade Skåne if Sweden took a position at Finland's side.

This was the way Sköld described the situation. He was personally a warm friend of Finland, but he felt that he could not work against the general line of the Cabinet. He had, however, been prepared to arrange for us considerable aid in the form of armaments if it should be needed.

Sandler, with whom Fagerholm had spent a whole evening, had been deeply concerned by the situation. He was ready to act to Finland's advantage in every possible manner and had planned to approach the American Minister to Stockholm, Frederick A. Sterling, the next day, urging him to appeal to his government to take vigorous steps in Moscow on Finland's behalf. He had also planned to approach the Italian Minister with the same idea. He would not approach England and France, since they might press Finland to make further concessions; it was to their advantage not to become involved in war with the Soviet Union, which might happen if peace in the North were to be breached.

Sandler had also promised in Sweden's name to take more forceful steps than hitherto in Moscow on behalf of Finland. When Fagerholm asked what chance there was of that when Sweden was not prepared to take any conclusive step, Sandler had answered that the Russians were bluffers and so Sweden could permit itself the pleasure of a little bluff, too. Sandler had seemed convinced that the Soviet Union would not start a war. There was moreover a chance that the matter might be settled even after the Russians had begun a war.

In accordance with his promise, Sandler did discuss the Finnish case with Sterling, the American Minister at Stockholm. Sterling had been much interested in the problem and had promised to act as Sandler suggested.

In this connection it is worth while pointing out that when the Swedish Cabinet was reorganized in the beginning of December, after the Soviet Union attacked Finland, Sandler was left out of it. He did not accept the policy which Hansson, at the head of the new government, had decided to follow with respect to Finland. At that time Christian Günther was named Foreign Minister in Sandler's place.

FINLAND REEXAMINES ITS STAND

We had arrived at Helsinki on October 26 at 8:35 A.M., and at 10:00 we went to call on President Kyösti Kallio. Prime Minister Cajander and Foreign Minister Erkko were also there. We reported the course taken by the Moscow negotiations. The President and the Prime Minister were astounded by the Russian demands, which they considered impossible to meet.

At 4:00 P.M. on the same day the members of the Council of State met in private session, where a report was again made.

At 11:00 P.M. there assembled in the Prime Minister's office, in addition to Cajander, Foreign Minister Erkko, Defense Minister Niukkanen, Marshal Mannerheim, and myself. Paasikivi was not present. The meeting had been delayed till so late in the evening because of the "Nation's Security" ceremony, which had been held just before.

The purpose of this meeting was to talk over the possibility of defending our country if war could not be avoided. Marshal Mannerheim's opinion was that Finland was theoretically in no position to fight a war: the equipment of the army was deficient, with ammunition to suffice for two weeks at the most. He hoped it would be possible to find a solution through which war could be avoided.

Niukkanen was of a decidedly different opinion. In his view Finland could very well hold out at least six months. The fortifications on the Isthmus would prove such as to withstand enemy attacks.

Further discussion concerned the subject matter of the answer to be given to the Soviet Union. Erkko had already jotted down a draft, which, as it was far from perfect, he was asked to draft afresh.

We broke up at 1:00 A.M.

The following day (October 27) I spent in my office, mostly attending to current business. At 8:30 P.M. the foreign affairs committee met at the Prime Minister's quarters. Paasikivi was present this time.

For the meeting Erkko had prepared a new reply. This was, however, not yet in final form. We revised it together, and Erkko promised to get the fresh text ready for the following day. The session ended at 9:30.

The Council of State assembled with its full complement on the next day, October 28, to examine the counterproposal Erkko had drafted.

During the discussion numerous objections to the proposal were again raised. Erkko undertook to rewrite once again the points objected to. It was curious, by the way, how nervous the Foreign Ministry was about getting delicate matters of this sort down on paper. My recollection is that we had to request a fresh draft of this reply no less than eight times.

At 3:00 P.M. we got in touch with the Diet on the matter for the first time. This was brought about by inviting the Speaker of the Diet, Väinö Hakkila, and the chairmen of the Diet groups of the various parties— Vilho Annala, Ragnar Furuhjelm, Sulo Heiniö, Mauno Pekkala, Pekka Pennanen, and Juho E. Pilppula—to take part in a joint session with the Council of State. Our purpose was to give them detailed information regarding the demands presented and the negotiations which had taken place.

Erkko rendered an extensive and factual report on the course of the matter. On this occasion no discussion took place. Those present were also informed of the new counterproposal as it then stood.

It was agreed that the party group chairmen should consult with the preparatory committees of their groups, after which we should assemble again. All who were apprised of the matter should be sworn to secrecy.

I agreed with Mauno Pekkala, the chairman of the Social Democratic group, that the group's preparatory committee should not be assembled in its entirety but only its most reliable members. The members of the party board should also be invited to the meeting.

This joint meeting of the Diet group's preparatory committee and of the party board was held in the Diet building on the following day (October 29) at 11:00 A.M. Fourteen persons were present.

I began by giving about an hour's presentation of the course of the negotiations to date. During the discussion which followed upon my report, all who spoke were in general satisfied with the manner in which the matter had thus far been handled.

As for the demands made by the Soviet Union, it was unanimously agreed that the cession of Hanko could under no circumstances be considered. It was greatly desired, however, that we avoid war, if only agreement could be reached with honor.

The upshot of the discussion was that: (1) the conduct of the negotiations to date had been satisfactory; (2) the government's new counterproposal was deemed good; (3) suggestions might be made for minor changes if peace could be preserved in this way.

During the discussion, reassuring reports regarding the state of public opinion in the country were offered.

On the same day (October 29) at 3:00 P.M. a further session of the Council of State was held, at which, in addition to the members of the Cabinet, there were again present Diet Speaker Väinö Hakkila and the party group chairmen named above, as well as Paasikivi. On this occasion we heard the reports of the chairmen regarding their conversations with their committees.

Pilppula, chairman of the Agrarian Diet group, said that the committee of the Agrarian League Diet group applauded the action of the government. In its opinion, the Moscow negotiations had proceeded satisfactorily.

Cessions of territory might become inevitable, he went on, but only as areas to be balanced against others given in exchange. The southern extremity of Suursaari might be ceded. As for the Isthmus, every square kilometer of it was precious. The Agrarian League nevertheless would assent to the government's proposed concessions on this point. A still different line could be made the subject of negotiations in order to avoid war if during the course of the negotiations this should become indispensable.

Petsamo, the Agrarian League held, was not vital to the country. In event of need, anything up to the whole area might be ceded if the Isthmus could be saved.

With respect to Repola and Porajärvi, the Agrarian Diet group thought that it might prove expensive to Finland to raise them to the level of the living standard which prevailed in the rest of the country.

The negotiations should not be broken off under any circumstances. They should be continued, as every day was of great significance in building up our armament.

In no event could cession of Hanko be negotiated.

Pekkala, chairman of the Social Democratic Diet group, relayed the group committee's recommendation that the government's counterproposal should be approved. If no agreement could be reached on this basis, the negotiations should nevertheless not be broken off.

Pennanen, chairman of the Coalition Party Diet group, spoke for his group, which had met the day before. It regretted having to determine its attitude on such an important matter in so brief a time. There was a general desire to have opportunity for further consideration of the matter.

Pennanen said the committee's opinion was that there was no profit in assuming an unconditionally negative attitude. Our country's defense preparedness was not as good as it ought to be, and there was no assurance as to the outcome of a war, if it should break out.

With respect to the demands, he declared that so far as they affected the islands, the five smaller islands might be ceded without further ado. The Diet group had its doubts regarding cession of the northern end of Suursaari, but that too might be surrendered in an emergency. The demands affecting Petsamo aroused no great concern.

On the other hand, the Isthmus was a sore point. Not all of them had been able to give an opinion as to how far to go with concessions there. Some, among them the speaker, felt that sacrifices must be made here too, although there could be no talk of such far-reaching demands as the Russians had presented. However, they supported the government's counterproposal.

Furuhjelm, chairman of the Swedish People's Party Diet group, said his group committee approved the trend of the government's counterproposal. For his own part, he was sure the group as a whole would approve it. An endeavor must, however, be made to avoid war. The government's counterproposal need not be the last word.

Annala, chairman of the Diet group of the Patriotic People's Movement (IKL), said that his group committee could not conceal its bitterness over the necessity to proceed as the government's proposal indicated. But the military command counseled it, since our defenses had been neglected.

In the group's view, the islands might be ceded against territorial compensation. The greatest doubts regarding territorial cessions arose in connection with the Isthmus. But as a start had been made along the path of negotiation, an endeavor should be made to give consideration to the views presented from the Soviet side.

It was easier to assent to cessions occurring in Petsamo if these would help our case farther south.

The IKL group particularly applauded the negotiators for the skill and address which they had exhibited in these exchanges. The group hoped that further proceedings would follow the same lines.

Heiniö, chairman of the Progressive Party group in the Diet, said his group approved the government's stand.

An effort should be made to prolong the negotiations so that our armament preparation might continue and our foreign policy might be clarified. For this reason negotiations should not be broken off.

Hakkila, the Speaker of the Diet, associated himself with the attitude Pekkala had expressed. He rejoiced over the fact that a united attitude had been presented by all the Diet groups and that the Diet stood solidly behind the government.

After the official presentations of their views by the groups, the discussion continued.

Annala observed that the territory to be given Finland as compensation ought to be of satisfactory extent. A compensation double in area was not enough, in his opinion. One could not measure in square kilometers an area which the other party could fortify in its entirety against our country.

Prime Minister Cajander: The Council of State has heard Marshal Mannerheim's opinion regarding the strategic aspect of the compensation offer. He cannot suggest a better compensation than Repola and Porajärvi. Their attachment to Finland would improve the line. All our waters would then run toward Finland.

Foreign Minister Erkko declared that the general staff was preparing various alternatives.

Von Born: As the government has been encouraged on many sides to continue the negotiations, I should like to ask how far we should go in making concessions. What would be our extreme line on the Isthmus?

Annala: There can be no talk of Hanko. But on the Isthmus some other line should be possible. We should not go to war on that account.

Pilppula: There can be no question of Hanko. Its cession would bring with it the use for Soviet purposes of the railroads of all southern Finland. On the Isthmus the line under Alternative C* would be about the extreme limit.

The Prime Minister wished to put it on record as a summary of the discussion that Finland should not break off negotiations over minor matters. If no agreement could be reached on the major issues, the business might be allowed to come to a head.

Pennanen remarked that his group had studied only the government's proposal, not the Russian demands. His own view was that the cession of Hanko and Koivisto was out of the question.

Heikkinen was of opinion that the government should hold rigidly to its own proposal. It might have Alternative C in its back pocket.

Pekkala inquired whether, if the Russians persisted in their demands, the negotiations should be broken off. To this, Von Born replied that he had given no opinion of his own but merely inquired where the extreme line might run in the views of the rest.

Pekkala: If a crisis arises despite all we can do, the matter must be handled in such fashion that the Diet may have its say.

Cajander: In the worst event it can presumably be handled so that, at most, negotiations will be broken off.

Paasikivi: It is possible that the Soviet Union will not give up its demand upon Hanko. Then it will be necessary to deliberate precisely with regard to how the conversations are to be brought to an end. If Russia sees that we do not want to break off negotiations, we will be in a weak position. Here, too, the situation is difficult. At that juncture it would be necessary to consult the Foreign Minister as to how to proceed.

In conclusion, Paasikivi asked when the new trip should be undertaken—on Monday or on Tuesday?

Erkko: If Finland takes a firm, rigid stand on Hanko, the Russians will give it up. The Soviet Union will keep after it to the last, as it could be used to squeeze out other concessions, but the Soviet Union would not let matters come to a break. Its chargé d'affaires here has called urgently today to inquire whether Finland planned to break off the negotiations, and he was gratified to hear that we intended to continue them.

To conclude, Prime Minister Cajander thanked those present for the information they had furnished.

Later on the same day, at 7:00 P.M., there was a session of the Council of State, in which Paasikivi also participated. There the draft reply was reviewed. Many further changes were made in it.

* See page 34 above.

The next day (October 30) Cajander, Erkko, and I met at 10:30 A.M. to go over the draft reply once more. After this it was considered to be in final form.

In the evening there was a meeting of the Social Democratic Diet group. There Pekkala, the chairman of the group, delivered a generalized report on the discussions within the Council of State. It gave rise neither to discussion nor to decisions.

In a session held on the last day of October, the President confirmed the new instructions to be given to the negotiators.

CHAPTER 4

THE THIRD TRIP TO MOSCOW

All preparations having thus been completed, we were quite clear as to the thinking which prevailed in Diet circles; it was again time to depart for Moscow. A great deal more time had been expended than Molotov had expected at our last parting. Instead of the four days he had figured on, at least twelve days had been required before the conversations could be continued.

Our group was the same as the last time, save that State Councilor Rafael Hakkarainen had now been added as interpreter.

Again there was a great crowd of people at the station to see us off. Friends and acquaintances wished us luck. Both Cajander and Erkko placed in my hand letters which contained final directives and encouraging assurances. Erkko said he knew Russia would not go to war over our problem. His letter was so illustrative of the point of view of our Foreign Minister that it is transcribed here:

In all haste I set down a few considerations before your departure:

1. The Russians do not want a conflict. Nor will they risk a fiasco before the eyes of the whole world when they have waiting for them a ready-made agreement: the islands of the Gulf and a defense ring around Petersburg. The Russian press has been quite silent right along, showing that they do not wish to imperil the negotiations and what has already been won.

2. It should be borne in mind that [their claim to] Hanko is the top trump in their hand, as they know how little we like it. By exploiting it they can squeeze out of us what they will, and they will give it up only at the very end. *We must not budge on Hanko or on any other locality in that neighborhood*; since if we do, our plight is plain, and Scandinavia is out. All the great powers without exception have warned us. We must hold fast.

3. I am satisfied that the new frontier on the Isthmus will follow the natural line. We ought to save Kivennapa and Koivisto. In order to save the Saarenpää battery at Koivisto we should be able to consider moving it elsewhere.

4. If we should be so fortunate as to reach an agreement, I should be grateful if you would ask the Russians whether they have anything against our reporting publicly to the Diet, and thus to the people as a whole, what their original demands were in their entirety. Otherwise it will become very difficult to handle the matter.

5. I continue to be preoccupied regarding the Rybachi Peninsula. Yielding there means the beginning of the end for Petsamo.

6. If you have time it might be good if you could inquire there with respect to the following matters:

    (a) A trade agreement (Yrjö-Koskinen has the papers);

    (b) Border-jumpers, and their return;

    (c) Fishing rights;

    (d) Transit through the Neva.

I wish you a good trip and good health. My thoughts shall be with you.

Best of luck,
ELJAS ERKKO

P.S. Hope P. does not lose heart.

I have remained ignorant as to what grounds Erkko had for his conviction. In any event he acted on it.

Prime Minister Cajander's letter set forth what Diet representative Antti Kukkonen, who had just come back from a trip to Sweden, had reported concerning the impressions he had picked up there. Kukkonen said he had come back with pretty considerable successes. The chairman of the Farmers' Party, Bramstorp, had assured him that his party was prepared to go much further on behalf of Finland than Finland seemed to think. Bramstorp had further said something to the effect that the Farmers' Party was ready to go just as far as any other party one might name. Regarding the terms of the USSR, Bramstorp had been of the opinion that Finland should not give up any port on the mainland, but he too had recommended cession of the islands. Evidently, Kukkonen believed, what had happened in the Baltic countries had altered the views of the Farmers' Party.

Kukkonen had also reported that the Swedish Cabinet had considered the Finnish question unofficially in its session of October 30, coming to the conclusion that a continuation of the present situation would cost Finland dear, for which reason Finland must be supported.

Cajander further remarked in his letter that President Kallio had telephoned him and firmly opposed the cession of Ino. This negative stand on Ino the President had justified on the ground that the Russians would then demand an extensive hinterland to serve as a protective belt for Ino.

THE SOVIET DEMANDS MADE PUBLIC

During the trip crowds had again gathered at most of the larger stations. There were songs and speeches at Kerava, Riihimäki, Viipuri, and Terijoki. Particularly at the two last-named places the greetings were most emotional, but at the same time worried.

We arrived at Viipuri the next morning (November 1) at 6:33 A.M. I went straight to the station restaurant to get something to eat. Here the station master, Mr. Saukkonen, sought me out to deliver a telegram and a later verbal message which had come for me from Erkko. The wire said that in a speech of the evening before Molotov had set forth in detail all the demands the Soviet Union had made upon Finland. The speech had been very harsh. By virtue of this the situation had, in Erkko's opinion, changed, and we were urged to break off our trip and to return to Helsinki on the next train to consult with the government again.

The wire had been dispatched at 2:10 A.M. The subsequent telephone message was to inform us that the wire was obsolete. I was asked to telephone Erkko from Viipuri.

At the station I bought the morning papers, which carried extensive reports of Molotov's speech. *Kansan Työ* in addition speculated that the negotiations would be broken off. I hurried to the sleeping car to wake Paasikivi. Then we went off together to the telephone in the station master's room.

Over the telephone Erkko told us that on learning of Molotov's speech he had wanted to let us know of it at once. After consulting with the Prime Minister he had sent the wire calling us back home. But at 3:00 A.M. the whole Cabinet had been convened. The upshot of the discussion which had taken place among them was that the majority wanted to leave it up to us whether the trip should be continued—indeed a remarkable way for a government to decide a weighty matter. It meant that the responsibility was shifted to our shoulders.

I told Erkko that our first reaction was to continue the trip, despite everything. We had already considerably exceeded the time limit within which they had expected us to return. But we promised to think the matter over more thoroughly, and we agreed I should telephone again from Rajajoki before we crossed the line.

We had a long discussion on the train regarding the changed situation. Molotov's act in publicly disclosing the matter, down to details, in the midst of the negotiations struck us as very strange. In Finland we had constantly striven to preserve the strictest secrecy so that injured feelings might not affect the course of the matter. Even the Diet members had been sworn to silence. And now the opposing party had exposed the case to the whole world! The purpose was of course to make of the demands a *fait accompli* which we could no longer evade. Despite Moscow's incorrect behavior we were unquestioningly of the opinion that the trip should be continued. By reason of public opinion at home and abroad, and not least by reason of Russian opinion, we could not break it off. If we were to do that, it would be taken as vacillation and perhaps as retreat. It would make a great to-do, in any event.

During the conversation Paasikivi was so exasperated that he accused Erkko of bungling. He criticized Erkko for threatening to resign from the government if more concessions were agreed to than he personally was willing to make. In Paasikivi's view that was a very comfortable way of divesting oneself of responsibility. It would result in the same blame-tossing as in the years of the oppression under the Tsar.

I felt myself in a position to give assurance that the Cabinet would hold together through the present crisis and that Erkko's talk of resigning was just a remark made in the heat of the moment.

When we reached Rajajoki the telephone circuit to Helsinki was already open, with Erkko at the other end. I reported the upshot of our deliberations: the preponderance of our thought was in favor of going ahead with the trip. Erkko said that the Cabinet approved this, and he wished us a good journey.

So we went ahead with the trip. Subsequently, this turned out to be a mistake. We ought, in fact, to have gone back and received broader authority from the government.

This time we reached Leningrad earlier than on our former journey, at 2:30 P.M. Thus we had plenty of time at our disposal before the night train left. Nor did we dally long in our headquarters in the Astoria Hotel. We strolled a little about the town, dropped in at the Finnish Consulate, visited an old church, etc. We observed that although they managed to keep the main thoroughfares in reasonable repair, the side streets were in quite impossible shape.

On returning to the hotel we wanted to enjoy once more the delicacies of the Russian table. We sat down in a part of the dining room where there were at first no other guests. But before long the tables around us filled up with nondescript young men. In passing, I might remark that while walking in the streets of the city we had noted the same sort of men behind us. Thus we were clearly under close surveillance. Since under such circumstances it was not exactly convenient to talk about business and, least of all, about that great affair we had been sent to conduct, our conversation developed into an exchange of anecdotes. Many a good story came out at the table, one of which helped us to ascertain that about us were people who spoke or at least understood Finnish. This was a story I told, and I had heard it sitting one evening in Vienna with Karl Renner, since then President of Austria, and Karl Seitz, the former Mayor of Vienna. The story ran something like this:

When the Austrian Bundeskanzler Dollfuss was murdered in 1934, he was succeeded in that office by Kurt von Schuschnigg, who later landed in a concentration camp through Hitler's agency. While Chancellor he lost his wife in an automobile accident and lived on as a widower. Mrs. Dollfuss was also still a widow, living on a state pension.

As Austria's finances were in chronic ill health, there dawned upon the Finance Minister a brilliant idea: Schuschnigg should marry Mrs. Dollfuss. This would kill two birds with one stone: the bereaved would get a companion and be happier, and the state would save the pension it paid Mrs. Dollfuss. This proposal was received with satisfaction in the Cabinet, and the only one who had doubts about it was Schuschnigg. But he was brought to agree to think the matter over. As a result, some time later he went off on a trip to visit Mrs. Dollfuss.

He presented his case eloquently, but Mrs. Dollfuss was at first not willing to think of the matter. She said she had become so used to her late husband that she would find it very hard to become accustomed to another sort of man. Her husband and Schuschnigg were very different in appearence. "My husband was short, he wore his hair brushed standing on end, and he was a trifle pop-eyed," she said; "but you are tall, your hair is combed flat against your head, and your eyes are in the usual place. No, I couldn't get used to you."

With this statement Schuschnigg had to go back to the Cabinet and report that his trip had been a failure. They greatly lamented the shipwreck of this good plan, and the Finance Minister in particular was upset. As they went on debating, they thought that a certain rabbi, famed for his wisdom, who lived in the city, might be able to give good advice. (Of course, in Austria a good story has to have a rabbi.) There was nothing for it but that Schuschnigg must go and consult the rabbi.

The rabbi thought over the problem, paused for a moment, and then said, "Hold a free general election."

"An election?" Schuschnigg asked. "What's that got to do with this?"

The Jew stuck to his advice, and said again, "Hold a free election. When you have done it and seen the result, you'll see what a little man you are, how your hair will be standing on end, and how your eyes will be popping out of your head."

When I came to the punch line, many of the men at the nearby tables burst out laughing. They could not maintain their characters as mere Russian-speakers but revealed that they knew Finnish too.

Once more we continued our journey to Moscow on the night train, arriving there on schedule at 10:10 A.M. The same persons were at the station to meet us as the time before. Barkov, the Chief of Protocol, asked us to be present that evening at a session of the Supreme Soviet of the USSR.

At the station I fell into conversation for the most part with the Swedish Minister, Winther. He said that he was trying to get an appointment with Molotov that same day to present Sweden's *démarche* in Finland's case. He promised to tell me later whether he had been received and what the result was of the interview. (Molotov did not receive him.) Winther also said that Aleksandra Kollontai, the Soviet Minister in Stockholm, was in Moscow in order to report on Swedish opinion. Mme. Kollontai had been attending many meetings, had even spent whole nights at the Kremlin. After these meetings she had been very tired. The following day the Kremlin's Scandinavian desk man had been very sour with Winther, who interpreted this as a good omen for our cause. Winther had also encountered the American Ambassador, Laurence Steinhardt, who had expressed the opinion to him that the Finnish business would end in an acceptable agreement. He had not, however, been able to cite any facts, merely the general frame of mind in the Kremlin.

At the Legation, where we stopped this time as well, they were very happy that we had come back to continue the negotiations. Our hostess, in particular, who had at all times solicitously looked to our comfort, showed her joy. Here it was feared that the negotiations had already been broken off as a result of Molotov's speech.

As soon as we reached the residence, a wire from Erkko was handed to me in which we were exhorted to hold fast. The wire, sent from Helsinki on November 1 at 10:15 P.M., read as follows:

Molotov's speech is regarded here as a tactical maneuver to frighten us. The same tactics were used successfully against Estonia. We are calm. The Russians must be shown a firm front. They are shaken to a degree by the impression made by the speech.

Despite the cable, we thought it best to revise slightly the text of the written answer approved by the President which had been handed us on our departure. To be ready for all eventualities, we eliminated the words stating that these concessions were Finland's "final limit." This we did on our own responsibility, but we reported it later to Helsinki.

A VISIT TO THE SUPREME SOVIET

On the first day no discussions could be arranged because the Supreme Soviet of the USSR was at the time convened in extraordinary session. The meeting had already been going on for a couple of days. The first day the general political situation had been reviewed, with the emphasis on foreign policy. It was then that Molotov had delivered the speech referred to above, discussing the negotiations with Finland. On the second day the western Ukraine, which had been seized by the Soviet Union during the Polish war, was formally received into the Union as part of the Ukrainian Soviet Socialist Republic. Western Belorussia was to undergo a similar process on the day of our arrival.

As we had no other business and as it would moreover be interesting to observe this most recent parliamentary form, Paasikivi and I decided to take advantage of the invitation we had received and attend the session.

The Supreme Soviet met in the Kremlin in an unbelievably enormous, beautiful, and brightly illuminated—almost glaringly illuminated —chamber. The ventilation in the chamber was splendid; although two thousand persons were gathered, no deterioration of the atmosphere was perceptible. Both houses were in attendance: the All-Union Soviet and the Soviet of Nationalities, numbering together some twelve hundred persons. The houses sat each on its own side of a central aisle. On a balcony at the end of the hall were about eight hundred spectators, and invited guests were in loges along the walls. On the platform at the front of the hall sat both executive boards: to the left of the Speaker the Cabinet, and to his right the Party Board. Kalinin, Zhdanov, and Budenny, sitting with the Party Board on the platform, attracted much attention. Stalin had quite withdrawn into a corner and did not seem to be much concerned with the meeting. Coming over to sit by Zhdanov, he seemed to find something amusing to talk about, judging from the fact that they were enjoying themselves very much. Both were smoking one cigarette after another, although smoking was clearly forbidden. On the Cabinet benches sat Molotov, Voroshilov, Mikoyan, Kaganovich, Beria, and others. Potemkin, Losovski, and other well-known figures who at the moment belonged to neither executive body sat on the benches with the representatives. Litvinov read newspapers, of which there was quite a heap before him, without paying the least attention to what was going on. The papers he had finished with he threw on the floor.

Photographers were constantly bustling about the floor, passing from row to row and photographing the representatives. The pictures would surely serve as a valuable memento of this important occasion.

The reception of western Belorussia into the Union was impressively staged. The delegates, some fifty persons, were brought from a room to one side, bearing their banners, to the front of the hall, where they stood beneath the Speaker's lectern. Speeches followed by several of them, and finally a speech by a member of the government. All the speeches were cut to the same pattern: paeans to the Soviet Union and complaints about the oppression formerly practiced by Poland. The *pièce de résistance* was a hysterical speech by a peasant woman. In all the speeches three men were exalted: Voroshilov, Molotov, and "the great leader of peoples, father Stalin." Every time one of these names was mentioned, the representatives stood up and clapped. It was amusing to see that the speakers broke off what they were saying and clapped too. Indeed, the recipients of these tributes joined in the applause as well. The clapping stopped only when the Speaker rang his bell. Then everybody sat down at once.

From our loge I tried to examine the representatives also. As far as could be judged from where we sat above them, they did not seem to be manual laborers. All of them seemed to have well-cared-for hands; clearly, most of them were party functionaries. The hall was full of a variety of dress and of racial features.

In the diplomatic loges there were on this occasion only the Mongols of Tannu-Tuva, the Estonian and Lithuanian ministers, and ourselves, representing Finland. "Quelle collection!" said Paasikivi.

The voting procedure of the Supreme Soviet was very remarkable to us. Each chamber voted separately by a show of hands. When a bill was presented for approval, the question was asked who supported it. Everybody's hand went up. Next was asked who opposed it. Naturally no one raised a hand then. Thus there came into being the law incorporating the western parts of the Ukraine and of Belorussia into the Soviet Union.

To one familiar with the procedures of Western European parliaments, the working methods of the Supreme Soviet seemed rather odd. The hand-clapping ceremony in particular impressed one as being very theatrical.

During an intermission we withdrew to a room at one side to partake of some refreshment. There was an abundance of various cold dishes and good wines on the tables. Here Chief of Protocol Barkov explained to us the fundamental laws of the Soviet Union and the working methods of the Supreme Soviet, as well as its voting procedures.

On this day a wire received from the Tass news bureau in Helsinki was published in the Moscow press, to the effect that the Finnish papers still opposed making an agreement with the Soviet Union. It is characteristic, wrote the correspondent, that in the opinion of these papers the proposals revealed by Molotov upon the continuation of the negotiations between the two countries might affect the course of the discussions. *Suomen Sosialidemokraatti* (the organ of the Finnish Social Democratic Party) said in its leading editorial that Finland did not want to be drawn into a great power bloc but must preserve unconditional neutrality. "We wish to establish friendly relations with our eastern neighbor, and we are prepared to assent to certain undertakings if we can be convinced that they are indispensable and if they do not violate Finland's neutrality." The paper expressed the hope that the negotiations between the Soviet Union and Finland might conclude successfully.

During the evening Paasikivi was very low in spirits and a prey to a mood of defeatism. He almost got me on edge as well. The omens were bad, he grumbled.

The next morning (November 3) the Estonian Minister, A. Rei, came to call, as we had agreed at the Supreme Soviet meeting the evening before. We talked of our trip, but for the most part about the recently concluded treaty between Estonia and the Soviet Union. Even at this date the agreement had proved disadvantageous to Estonia. Perhaps the treaty might have been a better one if Estonia had had time to think it over more thoroughly. But Estonia put its trust in Stalin's promise that Estonia's internal affairs would be left inviolate and that sovietization would under no circumstances be considered. Not even the trade agreement, made at the same time, was working properly. The prices set for Soviet goods were too high, and those paid for Estonian produce too low. Rei, decidedly dissatisfied with these treaties, feared the worst.

THE NEGOTIATIONS CONTINUE

When the session of the Supreme Soviet had ended, the Soviet leaders were free for the negotiations under way with Finland. Thus it was possible to resume the discussions on November 3, and the first meeting of this round took place at 6:00 P.M. This time Stalin was not present; Molotov and Potemkin participated as Soviet representatives.

The meeting began with Paasikivi's reading of the reply, approved by the President, to the proposals the Russians had made earlier. The following points in the text of this extensive reply should be cited:

The Finnish government maintained its earlier stand on the demands relating to Hanko and Lappohja Bay. It could not permit maintenance on Finnish territory of armed forces or of a naval base of a foreign power. This was not in harmony with Finland's international position or with the unconditional neutrality it had espoused and which the Soviet government itself had approved.

With respect to the outer islands of the Gulf of Finland—Seiskari, Peninsaari, Lavansaari, and the Tytärsaaris—the Finnish government was prepared to conclude an agreement providing for their cession against compensation. Finland was prepared to discuss arrangements concerning Suursaari, taking into account the security requirements of both Leningrad and Finland.

On the Karelian Isthmus the Finnish government had wished to show an understanding spirit with regard to the wishes presented and on this account was prepared, in the interest of reaching agreement, to undertake sacrifices very burdensome to the Finnish people. To this end a new boundary line was proposed which ran from the Gulf of Finland at the mouth of the Vammeljoki River along the line Vammeljoki-Lintulanjoki-Kaukjärvi to the previous line at boundary marker No. 70.

In Petsamo we were disposed to discuss the cession to the Soviet Union of the western part of the Rybachi Peninsula as far southward as Pummanki Fjord, against territorial compensation.

On the computation of territorial compensation, certain observations were made which touched upon the unequal values of the areas to be ceded and of those offered in exchange.

The Finnish government did not consider that it could undertake to destroy the fortified zone created upon the Isthmus, since it had been built up for defense and security reasons.

The communication ended with the assurance that the Finnish government had carefully deliberated upon its proposals and that it had thus in the name of a united country furnished the Soviet Union with positive evidence of its desire to show understanding of the defense considerations which were of importance to that country. The sacrifices which Finland was thus prepared to undergo were very burdensome for the Finnish people, as they involved territory inhabited by Finns for ages. Finally, ratification of an agreement was dependent upon its approval by the Finnish Diet.

When this reading was ended, the exchange of views began. It followed in general the same lines as before. Molotov did most of the talking, Potemkin remaining silent most of the time. As Molotov merely went on repeating what had been said earlier, the discussion got nowhere. It was plainly evident that the intelligence with power to decide was absent from the group and that it was for this reason we were bogged down. Molotov firmly emphasized the importance to Russia of Hanko. We in our turn declared that we could not even speak of the cession of Hanko. Questions affecting the Isthmus were also dealt with to some extent. When we had presented our proposal for a new boundary line, Molotov noticed that Ino remained on the Finnish side.

Finally Molotov declared that the Finnish reply was not satisfactory and that Russia's demands were minimal ones, a statement which we had heard incessantly repeated. We replied that Finland had gone to the maximum limit possible.

Before we left, Molotov said the following dark words: "We civilians can see no further in the matter; now it is the turn of the military to have their say." What he meant by this remained obscure for the time being. Did he intend to ask the views of the military or to deliver the matter to the arbitrament of arms?

This session was comparatively brief. When we parted at 7:00 P.M., neither party said anything about a further meeting or about a continuation of the discussion.

Back at the Legation we turned to our usual analysis of the conversation which had taken place. We decided to let matters rest for the time being and wait to see whether there would be a resumption or whether relations would be broken off. We sent a short cable to Helsinki reporting the way the negotiations had gone.

As the following day, November 4, seemed to be free, we took advantage of it with a program of our own. We visited the famous Tretyakov Art Gallery, where the paintings of the best-known Russian artists are exhibited. Since there were many fine things in the museum, we spent a number of hours there.

In the afternoon from four to five we paid courtesy calls on the ministers of the Scandinavian states, whom we had thus far met only at the railway station. Bolt-Jörgensen (Denmark), Winther (Sweden), and Maaseng (Norway) were naturally much interested in the course of the negotiations. We told them the principal developments.

While we were at the Norwegian Legation, we received from the Finnish Legation a telephone call to the effect that we were wanted for a new discussion at 6:00 P.M.—thus right away. We rushed to the Legation, and were in the Kremlin at the appointed hour. This time it was again Stalin and Molotov who represented the Soviet Union.

At the earlier meetings the conversation had been mostly in the form of general statements, in which the question of a treaty had been touched upon only in broad terms. Now for the first time we came to speak about details. Stalin did most of the talking. He asserted, as Molotov had the day before, that no Russian government save the Soviet government had, as he put it, tolerated the idea of an independent Finland. The Tsar's government had not done so; nor had the interim government and the Kerenski government. But the Soviet government did require guarantees for its own security. In this sense the Finnish Gulf plan was of great importance to them. They could not give it up, and it was for this reason that they required Hanko and Lappohja. So far as they cared, Finland could put the Hanko cession in any juridical form it chose: lease, sale, or exchange.

When we said once more that Hanko could not be discussed, to our great surprise Stalin proposed an alternative—the group of islands to the east of it. He pointed on the map to the islands of Hermansö, Koö,

Hästö, and Busö, around which a red line had been drawn, and asked, "Do you need those islands?"

We remarked that this was a new question regarding which we had no instructions.

On the other demands we got the same old statements. The tone of the discussion was light and friendly.

At length they took up Foreign Minister Erkko's radio speech of a few days before, over which the Russian papers had made a great uproar. We had received a long cabled report on this speech, to judge by which it had been pretty stiff, though indeed not nearly so harsh as Molotov's speech of a few days earlier. At the end of his statement, according to the cable, Erkko had said that now when new commitments were sought of us, we had the right to ask for guarantees that they would be honorably carried out. In our proposals we had shown readiness to accept far-reaching adjustments. But there were values which could not be sacrificed. When fundamental values were at issue, we knew the course we would choose, no matter how difficult.

Both Stalin and Molotov attacked Erkko's speech on the basis of its content. Although the speech had been more forceful than the usual run, even by the report we had received, we expressed our displeasure with the distortions which had appeared in the Moscow press, according to which Erkko was made a true warmonger. Stalin and Molotov claimed that the text as published in Finland had left out the worst parts; they had in their possession both the original and the expurgated text, which made this apparent. We promised to check this report.

On leaving we said we would apply to Helsinki for instructions, especially on the alternative proposal put forward in place of Hanko. They hoped they would see us again in three days' time.

Talking things over in the Legation we were a trifle more optimistic, since the negotiations had not been broken off and the tone maintained in the discussion had been friendly.

We sent in cipher to Helsinki a cabled report of the outcome of the discussion. At the same time we asked the government whether in the next meeting we might offer to the Soviet Union Jussarö in the west and the Ino line in the east.

The next day, November 5, was Sunday, and free so far as we were concerned. We spent most of it at the Legation. I telephoned Erkko in Helsinki to say we would not need instructions till Tuesday. Erkko said the governor of Viipuri province was in Helsinki on account of these negotiations. He was to furnish information to be used in calculating the value of the property in the portion of the Isthmus to be ceded; this the

Soviet Union had promised to pay in cash, above the territorial compensation.

On Monday, November 6, the whole delegation was invited to lunch with Winther at the Swedish Legation. We talked mostly about the current negotiations. Nothing new came to light.

THE ANNIVERSARY OF THE OCTOBER REVOLUTION

In the evening, starting at six o'clock, there was a great ceremony in the Bolshoi Theater, organized by the Soviet government to commemorate the Revolution. The program began with an hour-and-a-half speech by Molotov; in this he went over the accomplishments of the Soviet Union. Afterward there was lighter entertainment: singing, music, and fiery dances. Stalin was present in a box to one side but so much shaded by the curtains that the audience could not see him.

In an intermission the guests were taken to a room at an upper level where many kinds of tasty sandwiches and other refreshments were served. Here Derevyanski, the Soviet Minister in Helsinki, came over to talk to me. Often before I had conversed with him frankly, and I now lamented that the negotiations were going badly and might well come to nothing. He assured me that good would come of them. When I asked on what he based his conviction, he was unable to explain.

The ceremony ended at 12:30 A.M.

The next day, November 7, was the anniversary of the Revolution, a great holiday in Moscow and elsewhere in Russia. We had received an invitation to come to the Red Square and watch the parade. The day was rather raw, and Paasikivi did not want to go to the square and stand for hours, so I went alone. My place was reserved for me among the foreign diplomats, on a low platform to the left of Lenin's mausoleum. It gave a good view of the square. Little by little there gathered upon a platform on the roof of the mausoleum a group of the most prominent leaders of the Soviet Union, including Stalin and Molotov. Many other familiar figures were to be seen as well.

A total of thirty thousand soldiers took part in the parade which crossed the square. They were commanded by Marshal Budenny, whose bristling mustaches readily identified him. Powerful motorized forces drove past. The parade made a strong impression on the spectators— at least on me, no expert in such matters.

The attitude of my neighbor, Laurence Steinhardt, the Ambassador of the United States, was different. At every turn he criticized both the troops and their weapons. Now the tanks were old and clumsy, now the infantry arms were out of date; there was a submachine gun only to about every twenty men, and so forth. Finally, I asked whether he was an expert, whereupon he said he had formerly been an officer. As it was cold, he took a swig of cognac now and then from his pocket flask. He offered me some, but I said thanks, I wasn't cold.

When the military parade was over, a very different sort of procession began. The populace began to flow into the far end of the square in dense ranks. They bore ahead of them an abundance of tremendous pictures of well-known persons, so many pictures that the whole square seemed to be a sea of them. It was said that at least a million persons marched in this fashion past the mausoleum and the leaders standing on the platform built on its roof. When these ranks departed, the spectators left as well. While walking to the Legation I noticed that the whole city was afoot. The streets were full of people. The day was spent as a public holiday.

The celebration of the anniversary of the Revolution went on into the evening, though in another fashion; for at 10:00 P.M. there was Molotov's reception for the diplomatic corps. This took place in the former palace of a wealthy merchant. The Finnish delegation was among those invited. Paasikivi did not care to go, referring to a slight cold, but I gladly accepted the invitation.

At length we took seats in a large hall, where well-known artists performed a musical program. After this we proceeded to other rooms for a late supper.

By reason of the negotiations currently under way with Finland, I had the honor to sit at the hosts' table, with such members of the government as Molotov and Mikoyan. Stalin was not present at the reception. Potemkin and his wife were with us. According to a place card, the famous Beria, head of the GPU, was supposed to sit beside me, but he seemed to have been detained, since his place was taken by his young assistant, Merkulov. Among the foreign representatives at this table were the Ambassador of the Soviet Union's "dear friend and ally," Hitler's Germany, Count von der Schulenburg; Italian Ambassador Rosso and his wife; the ministers of China, Persia, and Estonia, and Mrs. Yrjö-Koskinen. Numerous other guests sat at smaller tables at a distance. There were food and drink in abundance, with half a dozen varieties of liquor alone. Frequent toasts were drunk; I think Molotov proposed at least a score, bravely draining his glass to the bottom each time. He proposed a toast to Finland, wishing success to the negotiations under way with that country. I respectfully rose and returned his toast. Mikoyan, sitting beside Molotov, had evidently decided to ascertain whether "the capitalist woman" could hold her liquor. He toasted Ambassador Rosso's handsome young wife again and again, so that before long her eyes swam.

Conversationally, I was rather badly situated during the course of the long supper. My table mates were not companionable. Merkulov, sitting on my right, was an extremely grave person; when I talked to him I got only brief words in answer. To my left sat the bulky Minister of China, with whom I tried to start a conversation. But no matter what language I tried, he did not understand, nor did I understand Chinese. Consequently, my sole diversion was to follow what went on both at my own table and at the many other tables where the representatives of other nations were placed. At the minor tables things were considerably quieter than at ours.

When the long meal was over and we rose from the table, Count von der Schulenburg introduced himself to me. He said he had flown in that day from Berlin to be present at the festivities. He remarked that in the German Foreign Office they presumed to know that there would be agreement between Finland and the Soviet Union. According to their advices, Finland could offer some island in the neighborhood of Hanko which would satisfy the Soviet Union. I guessed that he meant Jussarö, about the cession of which we had only just inquired of the government, and I was at a loss to imagine how the business could have leaked from Helsinki so quickly. But evidently what was in his mind was Utö, which had been mentioned in the German newspapers.

I said I was by no means sure agreement would be reached, as this depended principally on the Soviet party.

"You surely know best," said Von der Schulenburg.

The conversation then passed on to the difficulty of the negotiations, in which connection I complained that after the German-Soviet treaty the situation had changed to our disadvantage. I remarked that it was not to Germany's interest to let Russia carry its will through in this matter.

Von der Schulenburg answered, "But what can we do? We're bound. At the moment we can't do anything. Now the Russians have the opportunity they've long been waiting for."

After that we talked about conditions in Germany, which he admitted were bad, though not so bad as in Russia. "If the Germans saw the food shortage here, they wouldn't grumble so much."

In general, German-Soviet friendship could not be so very warm, judging from my companion's expressions. He spoke of the Russians in most disdainful terms and at length concentrated his fire on this evening's carouse. "Und mit diesen Menschen müssen wir zusammenarbeiten!" ("And we have to work with these fellows!") he said as we parted.

I managed also to talk to Foreign Trade Commissar Mikoyan, one of Stalin's closest friends. He, too, referred to the negotiations, which he hoped would lead to agreement. I complained to him, too, about the unreasonableness of the Soviet demands, which made it difficult to arrive at an agreement. He was greatly astonished at this, saying the requirements were "minimal," a view which thus seemed to be general within the Soviet government, as it was so constantly repeated. He told me that when they had discussed within their Cabinet the terms to be offered Finland, it was generally thought that Finland should be offered easy conditions. They all had great respect for Finland; there was a saying, "Finnskii narod tvyordyi narod" ("The Finns are a tough people"), and accordingly they had to be treated with circumspection. "Consider," he said, "if there were just Russians in our government, things would be quite different. But Stalin is a Georgian, I'm an Armenian, and many of the rest are minority nationals. We understand the position of a small country very well."

Mikoyan was enthusiastic in praise of Stalin. Lenin was a very gifted man, he thought, but Stalin was a genius—which presumably meant a lot more. Anyway, Mikoyan had had a lot to drink, and the conversation tended to reflect it.

The party was still going on when I began moving homeward, arriving there at 3:00 A.M. As yet the new instructions, which had been promised the day before—Tuesday, November 7—had not arrived from Helsinki.

CHAPTER 5

THE CONFLICT SHARPENS

On the morning of November 8 a coded telegram arrived from Helsinki, and it was deciphered by eleven o'clock. The message set forth new instructions issued by the President, regarding which the Diet group leaders had been informed. According to these instructions Hanko was not to be discussed, whether under the guise of lease, purchase, or exchange. The same attitude was to apply to the Soviet Union's alternative proposal on the islands in the neighborhood of Hanko. Mention of Jussarö was likewise unconditionally forbidden. Even the cession of Ino could not be considered save on condition that Russia abandon its demands for Koivisto and Hanko. Authority was granted to cede in Petsamo only the northern part of the Rybachi Peninsula. Compensation to be required for the cessions on the Isthmus would be given in a second telegram.

We were greatly disappointed by the binding instructions we thus received. We had expected Helsinki to understand that only through additional concessions could agreement be reached. It was in that sense that we had inquired whether we might offer Jussarö in the west and Ino in the east. Since we were now refused this authority, we decided after deliberation to test once more the firmness of Helsinki's negative attitude. As the fruit of our consultation we sent off at midday the following telegram:

"Instructions received. If no agreement on this basis, may we let the negotiations be broken off?"

The answer to our inquiry arrived around midnight:

"You are aware our concessions have gone as far as our security and independence permit. If no agreement on the basis proposed, you are free to break off the negotiations. Erkko."

Thus the new instructions left us no ground for maneuver in the decisive phase of the negotiations. Paasikivi suffered on their account one of his customary rages. He criticized the instructions severely. "Now, if ever, would be the time to fight. But since you of the army (*turning to Paasonen*) can do nothing, it is necessary to avoid war and

back up. None of the army people but Mannerheim understands anything."

Mannerheim had, in fact, said to Paasikivi while they were sitting
together the evening before our departure, "You absolutely must come
to an agreement. The army cannot fight."

The *Svenska Pressen* phoned from Helsinki asking for news. I described the course of events briefly and asked whether the morning papers
had had anything in the way of a government release. I learned that the
Council of State had held a meeting the evening before at eleven o'clock.
Diet Speaker Hakkila and the Diet group chairmen had attended. Those
present had been informed of our report. The afternoon papers would
carry news to the effect that the President had confirmed the general instructions.

Subsequently, I got more detail on the session. The Cabinet and
the group chairmen had recommended approval of the instructions in
the form in which they were sent. Before the Social Democratic group,
its chairman, Mauno Pekkala, had on the same day rendered a report
on the session and on his own stand. After conversing with various members of the group's preparatory committee and of the party board, he
had approved the new instructions as the basis for the negotiations. He
had, however, desired that the negotiators be directed to handle the discussions in such a way that war might be avoided. This was truly a comfortable fashion of conducting business: issue strict instructions from
which there was to be no divergence, but still tell your men to avoid a
conflict!

As for the cable over Erkko's signature, referred to above, it has
remained obscure to me who was responsible for it. President Kallio
declared at the private consultation of the Council of State held on
February 25, when reference was made to this cable, that he had had no
knowledge of its being sent.

NEGOTIATIONS ARE BROKEN OFF

Since the Russians were this day resting up from their celebration,
we concluded it would be well to put off negotiations till the following
day. The day passed in pondering the new instructions and in working
out negotiating tactics. We thought it best to refuse straight off the demand for bases at the mouth of the Gulf of Finland. If that stopped
matters, the negotiations would be at an end. If the Russians abandoned
this demand, we could go on talking about the Isthmus and Suursaari.

On the basis of the compensation figures, received by wire, we drafted
a memorandum concerning the property to be ceded on the Isthmus, to

be used if necessary. The compensatory sum required for the property on the territory we offered came to some 800 million marks.

The next day, November 9, we notified Molotov's secretary that we were ready to go ahead. The time was set for 6:00 P.M.

Stalin and Molotov were present this time too. The discussion lasted just one hour.

To begin with, Paasikivi regretted that his illness had prevented him from attending the ceremonies of two days before. The others asked sympathetically what had been troubling him. I said it had been a gay and pleasant evening. This seemed to please our hosts, who smiled broadly. But the mood soon changed.

Paasikivi began to read our reply, stating briefly that the same consideration which prevented the concession of a military base in Hanko applied also to the cession of the islands suggested. The Finnish government could not assent to this proposal.

The eyes of our opposite numbers opened wide. It was clear that they had expected us to assent gladly to this suggestion.

After this there followed the usual exchanges on the subject.

Stalin pointed out Russarö on the map. "Could you perhaps let go of this one?"

As our instructions prescribed, we replied in the negative.

"Then it doesn't look as if anything will come of it. Nothing will come of it," said Stalin.

At length it appeared that neither party had any more to add concerning a base in the neighborhood of Hanko. All arguments had already been presented.

Next we brought out a chart and said we proposed to offer the southern part of Suursaari.

Stalin replied, "The island will have two masters. It won't do. What do you offer on the Isthmus?"

"There is nothing new to propose," we replied. "We reject your suggested boundary line. We stand on our earlier proposal."

"You don't even offer Ino?"

"We have not asked our government's opinion on that point."

I tried to show, by describing an arc, how well defended Leningrad would be under our proposal. In addition to the Kronstadt and Krasnaya Gorka fortresses, Russia would now have the Gulf islands to be ceded and the whole Terijoki border area.

"The Tsar had them too, but still he needed Ino."

Now the opposing negotiators pointed out the narrows opposite Seivästö. Here there had to be a fortress on both shores. Otherwise the aperture was not closed. The islands to be ceded were merely small "points." Not much could be done with them. "We would just be shooting at each other—you at us, and we at you" (on Seivästö).

Next Stalin and Molotov seized upon the question of Ino again, observing that for its protection twenty kilometers of hinterland would be required.

Stalin remarked, "On that patch of land you offer us we would sit as though on the point of a sharpened pencil"—he indicated the point of his pencil.

I tried to measure the breadth of the area.

Molotov asked, "How much is it?"

"About eight kilometers," I answered.

"There, you see!" said Molotov.

As the conversation went on, I pointed out Suursaari on the map. I asserted earnestly that Finland could not cede any portion of its western half. If the Soviet Union felt it could give up its demands upon Hanko or upon bases elsewhere to the westward, we considered we could satisfy their reasonable aspirations in the eastern parts of the Gulf of Finland, on the Isthmus as well as elsewhere.

But we did not get the sort of answer which would have laid the way for abandonment of the demand for Hanko. Instead, our opponents went on with their demands on the Isthmus. Yet here we could not undertake to offer any concessions, since we had no authority to do so. Moreover, so long as the Hanko request had not been abandoned, the upshot would merely have been that concessions on the Isthmus would be accepted, still leaving the demands in the west unsatisfied. There was no getting ahead that way.

When an hour had been expended in chewing over the suggestions of both sides, the conversation appeared at a halt and its subject exhausted. I then put in the remark that there were apparently such great differences of opinion that at the moment there seemed to be no possibility of hitting upon a solution which would satisfy both parties. Would it not under the circumstances be best to put it on the record that there could be no agreement on this occasion?

Stalin was at once ready to accept the same conclusion. Possibly he expected that we would retract on that account. Negotiations with the Russians had proved on many earlier occasions to be that sort of poker game.

But we had no way of making any new declarations. So we stood up and took our leave.

The parting was friendly on both sides. Stalin even said, "Vsevo khoroshevo!" ("Best of luck") and Molotov said "Do svidania" ("Till we meet again").

On reaching the Legation we sent to Helsinki a long cable in which we reported the conversation. We said we surmised the negotiations were broken off. We urged, however, that this surmise should not be publicized as yet.

This was because we still had a faint hope that not everything was yet at an end. We had, in fact, twice before parted without any mention of a further meeting, and yet there had been a continuation. From all we could see, we had received the impression that Stalin was earnestly for agreement. It was not for nothing that he had devoted so many evenings of his time to the affairs of little Finland. Furthermore, he had sought compromises, he had sounded out the cession of Russarö, which we had been obliged to reject.

I was already in bed when at half an hour after midnight there was a knock at the door and I received a letter which Molotov's secretary had just brought. The secretary had wished to give it to me personally, but when he was told I was asleep he had left it with Nykopp. It referred to the *aide-mémoire* we had delivered during the discussion of the day before. As this had contained the sentence, "Finland cannot grant to a foreign state military bases on its own territory and within its own boundaries," we were accused of misrepresenting here the position of the Soviet Union. The assertion was made that "if the Hanko area or the islands east of Hanko are sold, or exchanged for an area in the Soviet Union, they can no longer be on Finnish territory or within the boundaries of Finland." For this reason our *aide-mémoire* was returned.

I marveled at this remarkable specimen of Russian tactics. Since Paasikivi seemed still to be awake, I entered his room and showed the letter to him. We studied it together. We had a great laugh over this Molotov invention.

"Pettifoggery!" said Paasikivi.

We nevertheless considered that the Russians had clearly again opened the door. Perhaps, therefore, we had a chance to meet them once more and resume the interrupted conversation. But Helsinki would first have to be given a shake. There was no reason to leave this opportunity unexploited. We agreed, however, that we would sleep on the matter first.

I went to bed and had already turned off the light when there was another knock at the door. *Suomen Sosialidemokraatti* was on the telephone, asking for news. The newspaper was given to understand that perhaps on the following day we were to meet again around the council table. I asked the reporter to telephone this in to the Foreign Ministry, so that the people there should not be too nervous about the interruption. The reporter said further that the German news agency, DNB, was spreading the word that negotiations would be resumed in a day or two. After that I got to my night's rest without further interruption.

Having had our sleep, Paasikivi and I began to meditate upon what Molotov had intended through his letter and what was to be done about it. Molotov had evidently not wished to break off the negotiations, and he had hastened to send his letter before we should inform Helsinki. Accordingly, we wired Helsinki that further negotiations seemed possible.

In answer to this we received during the course of the day a wire from Erkko reporting that the government fully approved our stand. They could not really do anything else—we had proceeded precisely as we had been directed.

In the meantime, there was creeping into our minds the suspicion that Molotov might have wished to close the whole affair. But in that case what would be the design back of his returning our *aide-mémoire*? In ordinary practice it would mean that the recipient did not want to accept the expression of views presented therein.

Anyway we came to the conclusion that since Molotov had initiated the correspondence, we ought to continue it. Paasikivi wrote a draft for a letter in reply and I made additions to it. In the letter we reviewed the last phase of the negotiations and asserted that we had represented the proposals of the Soviet Union correctly and factually in all respects. We asserted further that the area at the mouth of the Gulf of Finland whose cession was sought would, contrary to Molotov's contention, continue to be within Finland's boundaries even in the event that Finland should release it to another state. We set forth again the reasons which barred the Finnish government from assenting to this demand, but we declared that Finland was in other respects ready to make great concessions in order to satisfy the aspirations of the Soviet Union. Finally, we represented the hearty desire of the Finnish government for an agreement, aimed at reciprocal understanding, between the two states upon the basis of those concessions which had been suggested by Finland.

When the letter was ready and translated into Russian, we had inquiry made of Molotov's secretary where and when we might deliver it. It was characteristic of the setup there that the secretary could not answer this until he had consulted Molotov. We were already thinking that it would perhaps not be accepted any more than the *démarche* of the Swedish minister had been a few days before. We decided that in this event we would depart at once. But finally word came that the letter might be delivered to the Foreign Minister's secretary at 8:30 P.M.

Thereafter we had to wait and see whether the negotiations would be continued.

But during the whole of the next day, November 11, there was no word from the other party. Time and again we wondered what this might mean. We had not even been clear as to what Molotov's letter meant. If it had been intended as a closing chord, he should have indicated it more clearly instead of accusing us of misrepresenting their intentions. However, if the intent was to keep the door open, it was Molotov's job to answer our letter. We concluded that the letter had in no way weakened our position.

Otherwise the day was spent in social duties. At 1:30 P.M. the Scandinavian ministers and their wives came to lunch at the Finnish Legation. In the evening we were guests of Arne Solanko, secretary of the Legation, for dinner.

We tried to order tickets to *Pique Dame* for the following day but did not get them. We were simply told that the opera was sold out.

Having heard nothing from the other party, we began to plan our return home. We decided to leave on Monday, November 13, if Helsinki was agreeable, and to order the train tickets on the morrow. If that did not suffice to wake the others up, it would be clear how things stood.

The next day, November 12, was Sunday. There was nothing to expect, nor did anything happen. We answered an inquiry of Erkko's regarding the content of Molotov's letter. In a second cable we said we planned to leave Monday evening, if the government approved, unless something happened. Late in the evening the reply informed us that a Cabinet meeting would be held Monday.

I also had a talk with Erkko by telephone, confirming the Cabinet meeting, scheduled for Monday at 10:15 A.M.

The Russian papers were beginning to attack Finland. Both *Izvestia* and *Pravda* that morning carried dispatches from the Tass office in Finland. They also reported an editorial in the paper *Soihtu* opposed to the government's stand; this they said represented public opinion in Finland. The midday *Krasnyi Flot* and *Trud* carried extensive articles hostile to Finland. Some of them threatened that Russia's will would be imposed. As a sample of the editorial style of the papers I reproduce the concluding part of *Krasnyi Flot*'s editorial:

Provocateurs, warmongers, and their henchmen are trying to represent the Soviet proposals as a threat not only to the independence of Finland but also to the security of Scandinavia, particularly Sweden. The Soviet people repudiates with loathing these filthy insults of the international political sharpers. We know that our government's sole motive is and has ever been a concern to restrict the war zone and to underwrite the life and peaceful work of the states which are neighbors of the Soviet peoples. Unshakably faithful to the principles of its pacific policy, the Soviet government will find ways and means to guarantee the security of the extreme northwestern land and sea frontiers of our fatherland.

Most of the day was spent at the Legation, except that we went for a short drive to Sparrow Hill and had a look at the city.

On Monday, while awaiting Helsinki's reply to the inquiry about our trip, we drafted a courteous letter to be sent to Molotov, in which we reported that it seemed logical for us to return to Helsinki, since in our discussions it had not been possible to find a basis for the agreement which had been contemplated. Thanking him for the friendliness with which we had been treated, we expressed the hope that the negotiations might at a future date lead to a result satisfactory to both sides.

The purpose of the letter was to keep the door open for further negotiations.

At three o'clock in the afternoon we had a talk with Erkko. He said that the Cabinet had met at 10:15. The President and the chairmen of the Diet groups had also been present. The government had considered that we ought to come home, and on this point the Diet representatives were of the same mind. We received confirmation of the decision through a cable which arrived at five that afternoon. After receiving this wire we began to busy ourselves about our departure. We sent to Molotov the letter we had composed. We also reported our plans for departure to the protocol division of the Foreign Affairs Commissariat.

Our departure from Moscow took place at 9:50 P.M. At the station to see us off, in addition to the Legation personnel, were the ministers of the Scandinavian countries and Pontikovski, deputy of the chief of protocol, Barkov.

At the station Maaseng, the Minister of Norway, said his government was very uneasy about Petsamo. Norway had already begun to fortify the Varangerfjord.

We reached Leningrad on schedule on the morning of November 14 and stopped again at the Astoria Hotel. We looked around the city during the day and visited the Russian Museum (the former Alexander III Museum), where there are a good number of Repin paintings.

In the evening at 6:22 we left by train from the Finland Station. This time, too, the station platform was completely barred off, and a strong military detachment was guarding it. When the train reached Terijoki and Viipuri, the stations were full of people, who agitatedly sought further information on the negotiations which had taken place.

We arrived at Helsinki on November 15 in the morning. Here also the station platform was full of people. At ten o'clock we called on the

President to report on the negotiations. Prime Minister Cajander and Foreign Minister Erkko were also there. A corresponding report was given to the Council of State on the same day at 3:00 P.M. On this occasion Diet Speaker Hakkila and all the group chairmen were present.

The Diet groups in their entirety also wanted a report. I spoke to the Social Democratic Diet group on November 18, to the Agrarian group on November 21, and to the Coalition (conservative) group on November 23.

I gave a similar exposition of the course of the negotiations to the council of the Social Democratic Party at a meeting on November 26. A lively discussion followed, in which the members almost without exception applauded the way in which the negotiations had been handled. Only K. H. Wiik expressed pessimism, reproaching the party for having become too nationalistic. I was able in my last speech to put on record that "the party council in the course of the discussion associated itself with the stand of the party board, which is that of the government; namely, that Finland should consent to no cession which would endanger the country's independence and security, while at the same time an armed clash must be avoided in so far as possible and an endeavor must be made to loose the knot pacifically."

The party council resolved unanimously to give out a release of this tenor, which was published in the press. The decision was made at about the same time that the subsequently famous "Mainila shooting" occurred.

As Soviet sources later alleged that Finland followed the advice and acceded to the pressure of the great powers in choosing its course, it is interesting to recall the attitudes the great powers assumed during the negotiating stage.

Regarding the attitude of Germany, the Soviet Union's ally at the time, Yrjö-Koskinen related, on the basis of reports current in Moscow diplomatic circles, that Ambassador Count von der Schulenburg had had a talk with Molotov after our second Moscow trip. Molotov had given him a résumé of the Soviet government's demands upon Finland and of the progress of the negotiations thus far. When they met Von der Schulenburg subsequently, the ministers of the Scandinavian countries perceived that he had assumed a very understanding attitude toward the Russian demands. He had believed that Finland would accept the demands, including the Hanko one, this being only a question of a Gibraltar-like arrangement which was not in conflict with Finland's neutrality or a menace to Finland's independence and which was of great importance to the Soviet Union's defenses. An endeavor was made by the Germans to find out from the Swedish Minister whether the Swedish government would be disposed to urge upon Finland an acquiescent attitude toward the Russian demands. Similarly, in the later stage of the negotiations, Count von der Schulenburg had expressed views of this sort. This peculiar attitude of Germany gave rise, even at this early date, to the suspicion that Germany and the Soviet Union had agreed that the Baltic States and Finland were to be included in the Soviet sphere of interest.

It was clear, moreover, that Von der Schulenburg on that occasion had presented, not his own thoughts, but the official view of the German government. From conversations with him I got the impression that he was not a Nazi and that he was much disturbed that Germany could do nothing for Finland. Later it was revealed that he was a member of the opposition to Hitler. He took part in Stauffenberg's conspiracy in 1944, and it was planned that he should become the Foreign Minister of a new government under Gördeler. In this affair he lost his life.

Subsequently, one has been able to read what the famous Swedish explorer, Sven Hedin, relates in his book, "Free-Lancing in Berlin" (*Utan uppdrag i Berlin*), published in 1949 and little noticed in Finland, regarding his conversations of the same period with the German leaders of the day. In the autumn of 1939, when the clouds were beginning to gather over the states on the shores of the Baltic and the Finnish Gulf, he had gone to Berlin to discuss the positions of both Finland and Sweden. As a person in favor with the Germans, he had free access to the highest Nazi leaders. On October 15, 1939, he had a long conversation with Hermann Göring. They went through the whole range of European problems. On that occasion Göring made the following remarks about the consequences of the war:

If the war turns into a trial of strength in which life and liberty are at stake, I fear the neutrals will have cause for grief. As a consequence of the disadvantageous geographical situation of Holland and Belgium, their days will be numbered. The fate of the small Baltic states is already sealed. Finland will be attached to Russia, which will also occupy Rumania. Yugoslavia will be split up. Turkey's position is ticklish, because Stalin, like all Russian statesmen before him, wants the Dardanelles.

When Hedin visited Hitler on October 16, Hitler took another line. The exchanges went like this on that occasion:

Hedin: Herr Reichskanzler, at home in the North we live in mounting uneasiness over the attitude Russia exhibits with regard to Finland.

Hitler: It is my conviction that neither Finland nor Sweden need fear that any major quarrel will break out between Russia and Finland. I believe this because the demands Russia has made upon Finland, so far as we are aware, are reasonable and do not in any case go so far as those presented to the states of the Baltic littoral.

Hedin: But if Finland, contrary to expectations, is attacked from the east, what will your position then be, Herr Reichskanzler?

Hitler: In that event Germany will steadfastly maintain a position of strict neutrality. But I do not believe such a situation will arise.

Hedin: But if Sweden, by reason of its relationships with Finland extending over six hundred years, should either officially or through the medium of volunteers come to the aid of that country in its desperate plight, how would you react to such an intervention?

Hitler: I would still remain neutral. But I do not believe that Swedish aid would mean much in a really serious conflict. I have no great regard for your countries of the North. Ever since I came to power, the papers of Sweden, Norway, and Finland have vied with one another in insulting me personally and my work and in calumniating it. Nothing has been too vile and scandalous to accuse me of. I have truly no reason to feel any friendship toward countries whose press has treated me with such indignity. As for Finland, seeing that Germany in 1918, through Von der Goltz's expedition, helped Finland out of a difficult spot, I should think that we are entitled to expect greater gratitude and consideration than have been accorded.

The attitude of the Western powers toward these negotiations was different. At the time of the meeting in Stockholm of the Northern chiefs of state, in October, 1939, it was asserted that England had expressed to the Soviet government the hope that the demands made upon Finland would be kept within the bounds of reason, so that they might not occasion incidents between the two countries. British quarters were convinced that, despite its threats, the Soviet Union would nevertheless not start a war against Finland.

The United States was even more active in the matter. Finland had a good name in the United States as an honest country which paid its debts and as the home of renowned athletes, on which account the United States gladly gave its support to Finland. On our second Moscow trip the American Ambassador to Moscow, Steinhardt, called on us and told us that President Roosevelt, in a letter delivered on October 10 to Kalinin, then President of the Soviet Union, had expressed his deep concern for Finland. He had declared he would refuse to recognize a relationship between the countries which should be based on force; he also hoped that the relations of friendship and peace between Finland and the Soviet Union would be maintained and reinforced. In Kalinin's reply it was asserted that the negotiations between the Soviet Union and Finland had taken place on the basis of the earlier relationships between the countries and that their purpose was to consolidate these relationships and to foster friendly cooperation in building up the security of both countries. Roosevelt on October 18 sent a cable to the King of Sweden, in which he said he supported the principles of neutrality and lawful order, which the nations represented at the Stockholm meeting also were supporting consistently.

In addition to these great powers, the Scandinavian states took steps on behalf of Finland at the time of the negotiations. Their ministers in Moscow on October 10 each left with the Soviet government a separate declaration of identic content in which they said they expected the Soviet Union not to demand of Finland anything which would prevent Finland from continuing with complete independence in its position of neutrality. These declarations, however, the Soviet government did not accept, since, as the representatives of those countries quoted the Soviet government as replying, "third parties" had no occasion to intervene in matters which did not concern them.

This "influence of third parties," to which Molotov referred in the address he delivered before the Supreme Soviet on October 31, was thus a completely impartial endeavor to bring moral suasion to bear upon the attitude of the Soviet government.

THE WAR OF NERVES

As the negotiations in Moscow had not been expressly broken off but merely interrupted and as our taking leave of the Russian negotiators had been friendly, we in Finland were of the opinion that we had before us Paasikivi's third alternative, that "nothing would happen." We had not reached agreement, it is true, but no ultimatum had been issued, to say nothing of a declaration of war. Here we trusted firmly the Soviet's love of peace, proclaimed constantly for twenty years. Moreover, it was the Soviet Union which had proposed a general elimination of armaments, demonstrating its love for peace in this way as well. From such a government one should not expect measures involving the use of force merely because its small neighbor had held fast to his rights. So we sighed with relief when the disagreeable and nerve-racking negotiations in Moscow ended thus happily.

Life went on in harmony with this optimism. The people who had removed to the country returned to their homes. The schools, which had been closed for weeks, opened their doors anew. The reserves who had been called to the extraordinary refresher exercises began to receive releases. During October and November the show windows of stores had been taped with strips of paper to protect the plate glass against air raids. (The paper protection was wholly ineffective, as was later learned during the bombing attacks.) People began to wash the strips off.

While Finland was thus returning to the tempo of normal life, from behind the border there were ominous signs of anything but peace. The whole Russian propaganda machine was put into motion against Finland.

Lisin, the Helsinki correspondent of the Tass news bureau, daily telephoned in reports falsifying conditions in Finland which the Russian papers assiduously published. In cities of the Soviet Union factory meetings were held at which it was urged that the Russian demands be carried through. Editorials to the same effect appeared in the press. As early as November 3 *Pravda* had already written, "We shall pursue our course, let it lead where it may. We will defend the security of the Soviet Union regardless, breaking down all obstacles of whatever character, in order to reach our goal." The editorials continued in the same tone in the latter half of November. There was no sparing of personalities. Malicious editorials were directed against members of the Finnish government. On November 26 in a columnist's article published in *Pravda*, Prime Minister Cajander was handled with crude irony. He was called "a scarecrow, a fool, a marionette, a clown pirouetting in the circus ring," etc. Nor was Erkko spared, and I too got my share thus early, both in the papers and in the Russian radio programs. Yet these impassioned attacks were not accorded the attention they perhaps deserved. At that time we were not sufficiently acquainted with the political significance of Russian newspaper propaganda. We imagined that by means of a war of nerves they were trying to soften Finland into a state of acquiescence toward making concessions.

But at the end of November the position changed and became more serious. On November 26 the famous seven shots were fired at Mainila, which constituted the overture to the events of the following days. On that same day our Minister in Moscow, Yrjö-Koskinen, received a note from Molotov stating that at 3:45 P.M. the forces located near the village of Mainila had been fired upon by artillery from the Finnish side. Seven shots in all had been fired, which killed three privates and a noncommissioned officer and wounded seven soldiers and two officers. The note went on:

The Soviet government brings this to your attention and considers it necessary to emphasize the fact that during the negotiations recently held with your Messrs. Tanner and Paasikivi the Soviet government remarked upon the danger to which the concentration of numerous forces in the immediate neighborhood of the frontier close to Leningrad gave rise. As a result of the provocatory discharge of artillery, taking place from Finnish territory and directed against Soviet forces, the Soviet government is forced to put on record that the concentration of Finnish forces in the neighborhood of Leningrad does not merely threaten that city but is in itself an act hostile to the Soviet Union and has already led to an attack against Soviet forces and occasioned casualties.

It is not the purpose of the Soviet government to exaggerate the importance of this deplorable act of aggression, which was committed by Finnish army units perhaps badly directed by their leaders, but it desires that such reprehensible deeds shall not occur again in the future. On this account the Soviet government, protesting emphatically against the deed, proposes that the Finnish government withdraw without delay its forces on the Karelian Isthmus further from the border, to a distance of twenty to twenty-five kilometers, thus eliminating the possibility of fresh provocations.

The Finnish government had undertaken an investigation at once upon receiving word of the incident. This established only the fact that at the hour indicated seven cannon shots had been heard from the other side of the line, not from the Finnish side. The Finnish artillery was stationed so far to the rear that their fire would not have reached the border.

However, the incident was regarded by the government as a serious matter. On the very next day, November 27, Yrjö-Koskinen delivered to Molotov the reply of the Finnish government, setting forth what actually occurred:

Investigation reveals that on November 26 between 3:45 and 4:05 P.M., Russian time, firing occurred on the Soviet side of the border in the Mainila region to which you have referred. The place where the shells exploded was visible from the Finnish side—the Mainila village square, which is only some eight hundred meters from the border beyond the common. Judging by the sound produced by the seven shots, it has been possible to conclude that the gun or guns used were situated some one and a half to two kilometers to the southeast of the place where the shells exploded. The shots observed were noted in the logbook of the border guard stationed at the spot immediately upon the occurrence of the incident.

As Molotov in his note had suggested that our forces be moved further from the border, to some twenty to twenty-five kilometers away, the reply stated that on the Finnish side there were situated near the border practically nothing but border guard forces. Furthermore, no artillery was located there which would have been capable of carrying to the other side of the line. Despite this fact, the Finnish government was prepared to discuss the Soviet suggestion with the view that both sides should remove their forces to an agreed distance from the line. The reply noted with satisfaction the statement that it was not the purpose of the Soviet government to exaggerate the significance of this border incident. In order that there might remain no uncertainty about the situation, it was suggested in conclusion that the border agents of both countries be assigned the task of inquiring into the case, as provided in the 1928 agreement relative to border agents.

It might have been supposed that with the dispatch of this factual reply the matter would be settled. This was not the case, however. Foreign Affairs Commissar Molotov on the next day, November 28, showed

Minister Yrjö-Koskinen a new note in which the Finnish government's reply was dealt with in very irritated language. The reply was described as "typifying the deep hostility of the Finnish government toward the Soviet Union and forcing the relations between the two countries to a point of extreme tension."

The note went on as follows:

The fact that the Finnish government denies that Finnish forces fired upon Soviet forces with artillery and inflicted casualties can be explained only as a device to mislead public opinion and as an affront to the victims of the shooting. Only a lack of a sense of responsibility and an attitude of scorn toward public opinion could have motivated this endeavor to depict this detestable deed as Soviet artillery practice at the very frontier, in sight of Finnish forces.

The refusal of the Finnish government to remove its forces, which have perpetrated this shooting directed with hostile intent against Soviet forces, and the government's demand that Finnish and Soviet forces be withdrawn simultaneously, which is presented as based upon the principle of equilibrium, lays bare the hostile desire of the Finnish government to maintain the threat to Leningrad. In reality the positions of the Finnish and the Soviet forces are not comparable in this case. The Soviet forces do not threaten any vital Finnish center, since they are hundreds of kilometers from any of these, whereas the Finnish forces are thirty-two kilometers distant from the USSR's vital center of Leningrad, the population of which is 3,500,000 persons, and thus represent a direct threat. It is idle to point out that the Soviet forces cannot in fact move anywhere, since withdrawal to a point twenty to twenty-five kilometers behind the line would mean their being stationed in the suburbs of Leningrad, which would be irrational from the point of view of Leningrad's security. If the Finnish government rejects this minimal demand, this will mean that it intends to maintain its troops as a direct threat to Leningrad.

The note closed with the remark that the Finnish government, by concentrating in the immediate neighborhood of Leningrad a large force of regular troops, had committed an unfriendly act against the Soviet Union which was not in accord with the nonaggression pact the two states had entered into. The Finnish refusal to withdraw its forces to the stated distance from the frontier after the criminal firing directed against Soviet forces showed that the Finnish government wished to maintain its hostile attitude toward the Soviet Union, that it did not intend to comply with the requirements of the nonaggression pact, and that it had decided to continue the threat to Leningrad. By reason of all these circumstances the Soviet government considered itself obliged to declare that from the date of delivery of the note it regarded itself as free of the obligations which had bound it under the nonaggression pact in question, now systematically violated by the Finnish government.

Thus easily did the Soviet Union free itself of the nonaggression pact, which was not even susceptible of denunciation before 1945.

The Finnish government took the announcement terminating the existence of the nonaggression pact very gravely. On the following day, November 29, Yrjö-Koskinen had the government's answer in his hands. It laid emphasis upon the procedure, prescribed in the fifth article of the nonaggression pact, whereby all disagreements which might arise between the two countries, no matter what their character, were to be settled in a spirit of justice and by pacific means only. Referring to this article the Finnish government proposed that the conciliation commission contemplated in the treaty should, in accordance with the article, be convened, in order to consider the dispute which had arisen. Alternatively Finland was prepared to submit the settlement of the dispute to the arbitration of an impartial third party. In its quest for harmony the Finnish government went even further. The closing portion of its note read as follows:

In order to afford convincing evidence of its sincere wish to come to an understanding with the Soviet government and to refute the assertions of the Soviet government that Finland had adopted a hostile attitude toward the Soviet Union and wishes to threaten the security of Leningrad, the government is prepared to reach an agreement with the Soviet government regarding withdrawal of its defense forces stationed on the Karelian Isthmus, border and customs guards excepted, to such a distance from Leningrad that they cannot be alleged to represent a threat to its security.

Before the Finnish Minister could deliver this note to its destination, he received another. It was brief, but all the more significant:

As is well known, the attacks by units of the Finnish armed forces against Soviet forces continue not only on the Karelian Isthmus but also at other points on the Soviet-Finnish frontier. The Soviet Union can no longer tolerate this situation. By reason of the situation which has arisen, for which the Finnish government alone bears responsibility, the Soviet government can no longer maintain normal relations with Finland, and is obliged to recall from Finland its political and economic representatives.

Through this note the diplomatic relations between the two countries were terminated. From now on further measures were to be expected tending in the same direction.

Despite the breach of relations, Yrjö-Koskinen delivered the Finnish government's note of November 28. No reply was received.

This exchange of notes, occurring over the course of three days, showed that the Soviet Union was acting in conformity with a plan which had been adopted in advance. Despite this fact, in Finland it was still believed impossible that the Soviet Union would have recourse to acts of war.

PART TWO *war*

CHAPTER 6

ATTACK WITHOUT WARNING

The wishful thinking of the Finns came to an end when, unexpectedly and without a declaration of war, the Soviet Union attacked on the morning of November 30 by land, by sea, and by air.

Russian forces crossed the national frontier beginning early in the morning, and aircraft were on their way toward many important communities. The first victims of the war lost their lives under their bombs.

When news of these occurrences was received, the Cabinet was convened under the chairmanship of the President that same morning. The altered situation gave ground for multifarious deliberation, and various decisions were made. The most important decision was the declaration that the country was in a state of war and that Marshal C. G. Mannerheim, who had acted as chairman of the defense council, had been appointed commander-in-chief. Lieutenant General K. L. Oesch and Colonel A. F. Airo became his immediate assistants. In the middle of the session an air raid warning was heard. Defense Minister Niukkanen rose from his seat and called for the suspension of the session and the removal of all present to a shelter. Observing an inclination to smile at this demand, Niukkanen explained brusquely that the Cabinet must surely comply with its own directives. Instructions had in fact been issued as to air raid precautions. The session was broken off.

As there was no bomb shelter in the building, we dispersed each on his own. I retired into my office in the Finance Ministry. Rainer von Fieandt, Minister of Supply at the time, came there with me. Naturally he and I began to discuss our changed position. We were both quite at ease, and we conceived that the attacks which had commenced were merely a continuation of the war of nerves which we had undergone, in ever mounting intensity, for a couple of weeks already. But the situation had indeed become so serious that something clearly must be done. As the Cajander government had failed in its endeavor to bring about a settlement with the Soviet Union, it appeared indispensable to change the government and thereafter to try once more to get the negotiations under way. The conversation was an altogether general and everyday exchange of impressions.

The Cabinet meeting went on after the all-clear. When it was over I remained behind to talk to President Kallio alone. I laid before him the idea which had just occurred to me—that a change of government was called for and that in particular the Prime Minister and the Foreign Minister, who had assumed the most inflexible stand in their speeches and who were the ones most vehemently attacked by the Russian propaganda machine during the preceding weeks, should be brought to withdraw. President Kallio calmly heard the proposal out and studied it from various angles without revealing his own opinion.

A little later I invited the Social Democratic members of the Cabinet to come in and talk things over. At this meeting there was unanimous agreement that urgent steps should be taken which would enable us to avoid war. A change of governments was considered indispensable. In order that it might be brought about rapidly, it was decided that, at the meeting of the Social Democratic members of the Diet which was to be held the same day, the recall of the Social Democratic representatives from the government should be proposed. The principal task of any new government should be to try to put the negotiations with the Soviet Union in motion once more.

When I left the building of the Council of State at about three in the afternoon with one of my colleagues in the Cabinet—I no longer remember who—there was another air raid alert. As we walked across the central market square we saw a number of Russian bombers flying at very low altitude over by the Hietalahti docks, and at once we heard explosions. Yet this warlike spectacle was taken so calmly that the people walking about the streets of the city seemed not to have noticed it. Nor did we take it as a grave matter, but simply continued our walk. Later it was learned that this was in fact the first major bombing of Helsinki, in which the Technical Institute was destroyed. Other bombs had fallen near the Milk Central building, and people had been killed. These last bombs had presumably been intended for the Diet building.

THE CHANGE OF GOVERNMENT

At six in the same evening the Social Democratic Diet group held its meeting in the Diet building. In the darkness of the evening the sensation was different from what it had been in the daytime. Right next to the Diet, the Milk Central building was still burning. It served as a bright guiding beacon to the bombing planes which might again try to bomb the Diet. Since it was not possible to black out the conference rooms in the Diet, the meeting was held in almost complete darkness; there was just one tiny bulb glowing at the chairman's desk. The members of the group sat more grave and quiet than usual during the course of the long meeting.

Mauno Pekkala, the group chairman, led off by saying that the group had been convened by reason of the fact that the Soviet Union had commenced military action against Finland by bombing Helsinki, Viipuri, and Enso, among other places. The chairmen of the various Diet groups had met and agreed that in the Diet session scheduled for this evening, to which the government would present a report on the state of affairs, only one speaker would take the floor on behalf of each group and declare the attitude of his group with regard to the report.

Next it was my turn to present the group with a survey of the situation. This was brief, because the group members were quite well aware of the position from what they had just heard. I said that the Social Democratic members of the Cabinet, after taking counsel among themselves, had come to the conclusion that the only thing to do now was ask for an armistice. The present government could not, however, do this, for which reason the government must be induced to resign this same evening and thus make it possible for a new government to be formed and for the armistice to be sought. Calling for resignation of the government could also be justified on the ground that now was a time for all parties, save the IKL (Nationalist People's Movement), to be taken into the government. We had thought that at least two members of the present Cabinet, Prime Minister Cajander and Foreign Minister Erkko, should be excluded from a new government. I asked the assent of the Diet group to the proposition that the Social Democratic members of the Cabinet be allowed to present their resignation to the President. In conclusion I observed that the line which had been followed hitherto had been, when one took into account the state of public opinion in the country, the only possible one. Making greater concessions had not been possible up to this time. Now things had changed. Now surely everyone would realize that the matter was earnest.

The Diet group decided unanimously to approve the proposal that the Social Democratic members of the Cabinet present their resignation to the President. To appear on behalf of the group in the Diet session which was to follow shortly, the group's chairman, Mauno Pekkala, was chosen.

Next Pekkala presented for the group's approval the statement which he was to make before the Diet and which he had prepared beforehand. It ran as follows in its entirety:

The analysis of the situation made by the members of the Cabinet is in consonance with the information already available in general terms to Diet representatives. The analysis is in its entire accuracy sufficiently clear to all of us, while at the same time it affords startling evidence of the way in which force and violence still strive to rule in our world. The group on whose behalf I have the honor to speak has always been of opinion that differences between states, including also cases where the relationships between a small state and a large one are involved, should be settled by peaceful means, through negotiation. During the existence of the present crisis we have at all times advocated this point of view. Unfortunately, our aspiration has not led to the result sought, for reasons beyond our control. On behalf of the Social Democratic Diet group I ask leave to state that the group has stood behind the government in this matter and that it hopes the crisis will be resolved as promptly as possible.

Chairman Pekkala's draft statement was unanimously approved for delivery on behalf of the group.

When the group meeting came to an end, Speaker Hakkila announced that the Diet session would be at 8:00 P.M. that same evening and that by reason of the danger of bombing attacks it would be held in the building of the Vallila labor center. For those who were not in a position to go there on foot, buses had been reserved.

I walked that long stretch to Vallila with some of my Diet colleagues. In the dark, the walk was somehow terrifying, since in various parts of the city raging fires were reflecting their glow upon the sky. As we walked, we gravely discussed the events of the day.

In the little hall of the Vallila labor center the representatives took their seats in chairs lacking the familiar desks in front of them. All remained quietly in their seats; there was none of the usual running to the coffee room that evening. There was not much chance of service in the coffee room in any case. Reports were presented by Prime Minister Cajander, Foreign Minister Erkko, and Defense Minister Niukkanen.

In his brief statement Prime Minister Cajander said that the Cabinet had been in constant touch with the chairmen of the Diet groups, and through them with the Diet as a whole. Since the situation had reached its present pitch, the Cabinet nevertheless thought it both logical and a matter of obligation to set before the Diet in its entirety, for the purposes and in the manner prescribed in Section 36 of the Diet Act, a complete report on Finland's relations with the USSR, and that the Foreign Minister would present a detailed survey on the subject. From this it would be apparent that the government had at all times done everything it could in order to defend tenaciously the interests and rights of Finland. At the same time it had been prepared to adjust matters insofar as had been possible. "The Soviet Union," he continued,

has tried to cultivate the belief that the Cabinet would not dare to appear before the Diet. The Cabinet for its part would not even hitherto have had the least fear to render account of its proceedings to the Diet as a whole; the government's reserve in this connection has been motivated by altogether different considerations. There was moreover no urgency for such an appearance, since all details of the negotiations have been brought to the knowledge of Diet members through the Diet groups. Their support has, indeed, been a bulwark to the government. Now the Diet is to have an opportunity to speak its mind on the case officially. The other party has undertaken to impose its demands by force. The fashion in which it has acted during the last few days has occasioned astonishment, since Finland never declined to continue negotiating. We continue to be ready to negotiate.

I trust the government will be able to determine that the Diet backs its course of action.

Foreign Minister Erkko spoke at greater length, setting forth in detail the demands of the Soviet Union and the attitude which the Finnish government had assumed with regard to them. As part of his statement the Diet also received a report on the exchange of notes which had occurred most recently and on the breaking off of relations. Erkko concluded his speech with the following words:

By making one positive proposal after another in order to bring about a peaceful solution satisfactory to both parties, the Finnish government has during the past weeks and the last few days shown its sincere desire to reach an understanding with the Soviet government. The Finnish government continues to entertain that desire. It depends entirely upon the other party, our powerful Eastern neighbor, whether that end can be reached. The measures to which the Soviet Union has already had recourse and of which it appears to be availing itself systematically even now will soon show whether its position is final, or whether there may yet be offered a chance for Finland to avoid confiding to the arbitrament of battle the defense of its existence and its independence.

Lastly Erkko informed the Diet that the government of the United States had offered Finland its good offices as mediator. He had informed the representatives of the United States government that Finland welcomed the assistance proffered by the United States and gladly accepted it. Whether the Soviet Union would be in any way disposed to accept the offer was a point on which he had no light as yet.

Defense Minister Niukkanen, wishing that the minutes of this historic session should afford the most complete picture possible, desired to mention briefly the border violations which had been committed by the Soviet Union:

I have found myself forced to marvel at the calm and coolness which the Finnish soldiers on the frontier have displayed during this entire period of tension. Despite the fact that the Soviet Union has earlier endeavored to provoke border incidents here and there, this endeavor has at no point along our long frontier succeeded with the Finnish soldiers. Cool and resolute, they have stood at their posts, and this resolution and coolness have also characterized our forces during the course of today.

After this Niukkanen listed various border violations which had occurred in the course of the preceding days and, more particularly, on that very day. The air raids were singled out for conspicuous attention.

Upon the conclusion of the statements by the ministers, the session had to be adjourned so that the Diet might, in accordance with its rules of procedure, have time to consider them. The interruption was not long this time, because the Diet members had had opportunity to determine their positions in advance. The plenary session ended at 8:57 P.M., and the new session was set to begin at 9:10.

In the new session, held in the same place, each of the Diet group chairmen presented the view of his group with regard to the information furnished by the Cabinet.

Mauno Pekkala, the Social Democratic group chairman, read the statement which had been approved in the group's meeting earlier that evening.

Juho Pilppula, the chairman of the Agrarian Diet group, asserted briefly that "the Agrarian Diet group approves all the acts of the government, the only aim of which has been to protect, by peaceful means alone, the neutrality of Finland and the rights pertaining to our people."

Ragnar Furuhjelm, the chairman of the Swedish People's Party Diet group, declared, in a single sentence, that "the group fully approves the acts of the government, whose aim it has been to order the relations between Finland and the Soviet Union in a peaceful fashion."

Representative K. R. Kares, the chairman of the IKL, spoke a little longer, and in fact gave some play to his feelings. He declared on behalf of his group that

in everything which has to do with the manner in which the government has proceeded in our country's present case the group supports the government's measures. We consider that the government has also acted logically and rightly in not appearing before the Diet earlier, since the Diet groups have always been kept up to date and have been enabled to take part in deliberations of decisive character through their representatives.

In conclusion he read a couple of verses from Gustavus Adolphus' battle hymn, to "hearten the Diet."

Representative Sulo Heiniö, chairman of the Progressive Party Diet group, said that his group had been enabled to follow the course of the negotiations and was in a position to testify that the reports made before this session had been consonant with the earlier statements.

Consequently the group pronounces itself satisfied with the explanation the government has given and supports a return to the order of the day, in the confidence that in its battle for its independence and its neutrality the Finnish people will honorably discharge its task, even though the preponderance of opposing force on this occasion appears to us unprecedentedly great and invincible.

Representative Pekka Pennanen, chairman of the Coalition Party Diet group, also endorsed the government's course of action, and Representative Heikki Niskanen, leader of the Small Farmers' and Countrymen's Party, declared briefly that "we will support a return to the regular order of the day."

As no others asked for the floor, the discussion was declared at an end. Then the Diet unanimously approved the proposal of the Speaker that it return to the regular order of the day.

Before the session closed, Speaker Hakkila announced that the Speaker would issue a special notification of the time and place of the next session of the Diet. The session came to an end at 9:37 P.M.

The representatives at this session proceeded to a train which had been made ready for them and which was to remove the Diet from the capital. Its destination does not appear to have been known to any save the Speaker and his two deputies. It was only later that the representatives learned that they were heading for Kauhajoki in Ostrobothnia.

In deliberating upon where the Diet should be situated from now on, it became clear that only southern Ostrobothnia could be considered. However, there were few towns in that area capable of lodging so large a number of people, and of these some were unsuitable for one reason or another. There was an airfield at Kauhava, military stores at Ilmajoki, and an ammunition factory at Lapua, so that as military objectives they would be dangerous. This circumstance caused the decision to fall upon Kauhajoki.

When the session was over, I remarked to Erkko that his report had contained a point which was not in accordance with the facts. He had said something to the effect that the delegates to the Moscow negotiations had had authority to decide what demands they thought they could approve. This statement was *not* correct, because at the last moment we had been forbidden to make further concessions. Erkko was somewhat embarrassed. He promised to correct the record of his statement in the minutes. In the minutes as printed by the Diet this passage is to be found reading as follows:

At the last meeting it was stated that we would wish to treat of the matter as a whole; and Finland would have been able to consider a settlement going a little further if the Soviet Union for its part had felt that it could give up the Hanko base and Saarenpää. The Finnish representatives were entitled in this respect to go even further than has been indicated above. They were also authorized to discuss the Ino area.

The Council of State had been asked to meet after the session in one of the conference rooms of the Vallila labor center. Before the session began I told Prime Minister Cajander of the decision of the Social Democratic Diet group regarding the composition of the government and asked him to bring the matter up as soon as the session commenced. I also remarked that the most convenient way of handling the matter was for the government to resign as a whole. This was a novel suggestion to him, yet he was ready to fall in with it at once. At the session he brought up the question of the resignation of the government on his own initiative. Basing his proposal on the argument that the situation had changed and that what was needed now was a government which should enjoy broader support, he suggested that the government should present its resignation; this it could do with a good conscience after just having received a vote of confidence. The members of the Council of State unanimously approved the proposal.

As it was necessary to act fast, we decided that word of the government's decision to resign should be brought to the President that same evening. One man from each of the parties represented in the government was chosen to bear the announcement to the President and to discuss matters with him. Thus Prime Minister Cajander, Ministers von Born and Niukkanen, and I set off on this trip. We took our seats in an automobile and were driven by a dark and winding route to a destination which was not known even to me. And although I am aware that I know the geography of the city pretty well, I got over my perplexity as to whither we were actually heading only when I saw that we had come to the Great Kuusisaari island, off Munkkiniemi. The President had moved to a place of safety offered him here in the outskirts of the city, and it was at that place that he resided, in a private detached house, for the whole period of the Winter War.

The President received us in a small, well-furnished room, dimly lit by lamps glowing behind ruddy shades. He listened calmly and without surprise to our report concerning the government's resignation, which was something he was in a position to anticipate by reason of the conversation he had had with me the day before. Since the appointment of a new government was regarded as an urgent matter, he promised that he would promptly see to the change of government. We had some further conversation about the formation of the government and agreed that it had to have a broader basis than the one which was resigning. When the matter was settled, we returned to town.

The next morning (December 1) as soon as the Bank of Finland opened its doors, I went to call on its governor, Risto Ryti. I thought that at this moment he would be the most appropriate person to form a government. He was diligent and conscientious. Having been on several occasions a member of the basic procurement committee of the defense establishment, he was well acquainted with the army's needs. Furthermore he enjoyed a good reputation in all circles, including those of industrialists and businessmen, to whose loyal collaboration we should now have to appeal. These groups had not been so very pleasantly disposed toward the Cajander government.

While I was explaining my idea to Ryti, President Kallio, who as a former director of the Bank of Finland often dropped in for a chat, also entered the room. Without any hesitation he associated himself with the thesis that Ryti was the man who had to form the government. Together, then, we sought to impress upon Ryti that this was his patriotic duty in the hour of the fatherland's peril. Ryti was firmly opposed to the idea, basing his refusal on the contention that he had for many years taken no part in governmental life. We also tried to hit upon a candidate for the post of Foreign Minister, but without finding a suitable man. As the discussion of Ryti's becoming Prime Minister did not seem to be leading anywhere, I made what was probably, from my own point of view, the most imprudent promise of my life by saying that if he, Ryti, would consent to become Prime Minister, I would myself undertake to serve as Foreign Minister in an interim capacity. When we came to discuss the other portfolios we concluded that they could in the main be left in the hands of those who had held them to date. But there was good reason to have with us a man from the Coalition Party, which hitherto had been in opposition. There came to mind first and foremost J. K. Paasikivi, who, since he had participated in the interrupted Moscow negotiations, was thoroughly acquainted with the problems which had given rise to the conflict.

By the time that I was obliged to depart for my office, no decision had been reached, nor had Ryti given his assent. President Kallio and Ryti stayed behind to continue the discussion. A moment or two later the President called me by telephone to say that Ryti had, although reluctantly, at last given his assent and was already busy assembling a government. He was in fact successful in completing his list of ministers on the same day, and it was possible to effect the change of government that very evening. The resignation of the former government was accepted, and the new one was appointed. This was very likely the quickest change of governments in Finland's history. By reason of the state of war it was necessary to carry the matter through without calling the political parties into consultation.

The composition of the new government was as follows:

Prime Minister: Risto Ryti (Agrarian)
Foreign Minister: Väinö Tanner (Social Democrat)
Minister of Justice: J. O. Söderhjelm (Swedish People's Party)
Minister of the Interior: Ernst von Born (Swedish People's Party)
Defense Minister: Juho Niukkanen (Agrarian)
Finance Minister: Mauno Pekkala (Social Democrat)
Minister of Education: Uuno Hannula (Agrarian)
Minister of Agriculture: P. V. Heikkinen (Agrarian)
Associate Minister of Agriculture: Juho Koivisto (Agrarian)
Minister of Communications: Väinö V. Salovaara (Social Democrat)
Minister of Trade and Industry: V. A. Kotilainen (Coalition Party)
Social Affairs Minister: K.-A. Fagerholm (Social Democrat)
Minister of Supply: Rainer von Fieandt (Swedish People's Party)
Minister without Portfolio: Juho K. Paasikivi (Coalition Party)

New men who came into the Cabinet with the change were Ryti, Kotilainen, Pekkala, and Paasikivi. Members of the former Cabinet who had been set aside were Cajander, Erkko, Salmenoja, and Voionmaa. The shift thus went a little further than had at first been contemplated.

In this fashion Risto Ryti began his "comeback" into the field of administrative policy. From his comfortable seat in the Bank of Finland he moved to the palace of the Council of State and at the end of a year into another, that of the President. When six years had passed he moved into still a third official residence, one yet more solitary. To him if to anyone may be applied the words of the song about the men of Bothnia, "From jail to jail drags on my weary way." When he resisted his own induction into the government, he was thus entirely in the right.

Ryti's newly appointed Cabinet held its first meeting on the following day, December 2. This meeting, as well as succeeding ones held during the war, was held in the Bank of Finland. By reason of the danger of air attacks, it was necessary, on this and on later occasions, to hold the sessions in the bank's vault, which could resist even heavy bombing attacks. The Prime Minister set up his office staff in the bank building, so that after a fashion he continued to sit in his own familiar chair during the entire period of the war. Cabinet sessions were ordinarily held in the board room of the bank. The Ministry of the Treasury was lodged in the same building. The other ministries were dispersed about the town in accordance with a plan drawn up by the Minister of the Interior. In fact, one of the ministries—the new Ministry of Supply—was established out of town, in the building of the Labor Academy at Kauniainen. The Foreign Ministry, which had come under my charge, had under the plan been assigned a thoroughly inadequate home in the stadium building. To begin with, the stadium tower, if any object in town, was an easily spotted target for bombers. Moreover, lack of office space made orderly work impossible, and there was no good cellar vault to afford protection. Consequently I was happy when a couple of weeks later the Central Bank for Cooperative Agricultural Credit Societies (OKO), which had moved somewhere out of town, made its comfortable offices available for the use of the Foreign Ministry.

Because of the dispersed locations of the ministries, contact between them was tenuous, in some cases nonexistent. The ministers met each other only in general sessions. It also became a custom to eat together in the Bank of Finland, the kitchen of which, under its accomplished mistress Milma Pake, rendered us good service. There we had a chance to exchange opinions. For the purpose of maintaining contact among the members of the Cabinet there was established a position known by the name of Commandant for the Council of State. The occupant of this position, Martti Hovilainen, was to know at all times where each member of the Cabinet was. In this way, if called upon, he could promptly summon them to a general session.

The other official dependencies of the government were scattered in various parts of the country. Naturally, communications with them were halting throughout the period of the war.

The Soviet radio broadcast throughout the world the news that the Finnish government had "fled to an unknown destination," intending to give the impression that disorder prevailed in Finland and that all organized resistance was at an end. In actual fact the Cabinet never left the capital for a day. The Soviet Union was soon to learn that Finland was capable of unexpectedly stout resistance.

All of this relates to external organization. Internally, the Cabinet organized by selecting for itself, in accordance with its rules of procedure, a foreign affairs committee and a finance committee. To the foreign affairs committee there were named, in addition to the Prime Minister and the Foreign Minister, Ministers Paasikivi, Niukkanen, Hannula, and Söderhjelm. The task of the committee was primarily to be responsible for Finland's foreign relations. There also passed through its hands matters having to do with the conduct of the war insofar as these were dealt with by the Cabinet. In the main, of course, these matters were handled by the headquarters of the Commander-in-Chief. The headquarters liaison officer within the government was General Walden, and he frequently participated in sessions of the Cabinet and of its foreign affairs committee. Among the members of the committee, on the other hand, in fact only the Prime Minister and the Defense Minister were acquainted with matters concerning the military situation and the procurement of arms.

The principal goal of the new government was to ward off the danger of war and to put the interrupted negotiations into motion once more. It was for this reason that the most conspicuous members of the former Cabinet had been left aside. In this sense the Cabinet decided at once in its first session that its principal aim should be the restoration of a state of peace. But the Cabinet adopted no regular program, save naturally that of prosecuting the war with utmost vigor in the event that peace could not be restored at once. Various efforts toward this end were in fact made during the very earliest phase of the war.

On the very day the invasion had taken place—November 30, thus even before the change of government—the United States had tendered its good offices toward the settlement of the conflict through peaceful means. The tender was made to the governments of both Finland and the Soviet Union. The Finnish government answered at once, accepting this friendly offer. The Soviet government on the other hand coldly rejected it.

Yet this was not believed to be the definitive attitude of the Soviet Union. For this reason the Cabinet in its first meeting decided to address the Swedish government with a request for its mediation. At the same time Sweden was asked to assume charge of the interests of Finnish citizens in the Soviet Union for the duration of the war. It was hoped that Sweden as intermediary might suggest to the Soviet Union a resumption of the negotiations. Sweden was likewise to declare that the Finnish government intended to make substantial new proposals. While this proposal was made in Moscow through the intermediary of Sweden, the move was reported to the great powers of Europe, to the other Scandinavian countries, and to the United States.

Winther, the Swedish Minister in Moscow, tried on December 2 to get an appointment with Molotov in order to present the case of the Finnish government. But he had to wait until the evening of December 4. Molotov then rejected the Swedish offer of mediation, saying that the Soviet government had no occasion to take the matter under consideration because it recognized no government in Finland save the "Finnish Democratic Government." He simultaneously rejected the Swedish offer to act as custodian of the interests of Finnish citizens in the Soviet Union because the Soviet government did not recognize the Finnish government which had charged Sweden with this task.

THE TERIJOKI GOVERNMENT

This peculiar answer is to be explained by the fact that between the time the move was made and the time the answer was given there had occurred an event which not only showed what the Soviet Union was really aiming at through the war it had started but which also for a long time constituted an apparently impassable obstacle to any initiative regarding peace negotiations. The Soviet Union had set up for Finland one of those puppet governments, recently become familiar but at that time still unknown even as a concept, and graced it with the style of "the Finnish Democratic Government." The Soviet government had determined to settle the Finnish problem with this government, and to this end it had concluded with it on December 2 a treaty in which there were ceded to the Soviet Union all the areas it had earlier demanded of Finland. In compensation, the "Finnish Democratic Government" received extensive tracts in Soviet Karelia. As this treaty is very little known in Finland, it is well to reproduce it here in its entirety. According to the broadcast of the Moscow radio on December 3 at 10:50 P.M. it ran as follows:

The Presidium of the Supreme Soviet of the Soviet Union on the one hand and the Finnish Democratic Government on the other hand,

Being persuaded that now, when through the heroic struggle of the Finnish people and through the exertions of the Red Army of the Soviet Union there is to be liquidated that true focus of war infection which the former plutocratic government in Finland had created on the frontiers of the Soviet Union for the benefit of the imperialist powers;

And, since the Finnish people have created their own democratic republic, which derives its support entirely from the people, the time has come to establish good relations of friendship between our countries and with united forces to protect the security and inviolability of our nations;

Having regard to the fact that the time has come for the realization of the desire, sustained for centuries, of the Finnish people to have the people of Karelia reunited to the related Finns, incorporating them into a single Finnish people; and also

Desirous of reaching an auspicious solution satisfactory to the interests of both parties with respect to the arrangement of boundary problems, and particularly with respect to the protection of Leningrad and the southern coast of Finland;

With the purpose of reaffirming the spirit and basic principles of the peace treaty of October 23, 1920 (Old Style), a treaty which reposes upon reciprocal recognition of the national independence of the other party and upon nonintervention in the other party's affairs;

Have considered it necessary to conclude between them the following treaty of mutual assistance between the Soviet Union and the Finnish Democratic Republic, and have named as their plenipotentiaries for this purpose,

On behalf of the Presidium of the Supreme Soviet of the Soviet Union: V. Molotov, Chairman of the Soviet of People's Commissars, Chairman of the Council of Foreign Affairs Commissars of the Soviet Union, and People's Commissar for Foreign Affairs of the Soviet Union;

On behalf of the people of Finland: O. W. Kuusinen, Chairman of the Finnish government and Commissar for Foreign Affairs of Finland;

Which representatives, having exhibited their credentials which were found to be in correct order, have agreed upon the following.

[After this there were read over the radio seven separate articles which were incorporated into the treaty referred to.]

The first article relates to the incorporation into the territory of the Finnish Democratic Republic of areas in Soviet Karelia the extent of which comes to 70,000 square kilometers. The boundary will be determined upon by the Soviet Union and the Finnish Democratic Republic in accordance with a map which has already been prepared. On the other hand, Finland declares its readiness to effect certain adjustments of the frontier on the Karelian Isthmus, from Leningrad toward the north, ceding an area of 3,970 square kilometers, in return for which the Soviet Union compensates Finland in the amount of 120 million marks for the value of the railway inventory which is now on the Karelian Isthmus and which is to be removed to the Soviet Union.

[The second article:] Finland declares its readiness

(a) To cede to the Soviet Union for a period of thirty years the Hanko Peninsula and the surrounding waters within a radius of five miles to the south and east and within a radius of three miles to the west and north thereof, and a number of islands lying to the south and east in accordance with a map which has been prepared, for the creation there of a military and naval base such as will be in a position to defend from attack the Gulf of Finland, as a guarantee for the security of Finland and of the Soviet Union, at which time there will be granted to the Soviet Union, to the end of furnishing protection to the naval base, the right to maintain there at its own expense a precisely defined number of land and air forces, the maximum figure of which shall be determined in a separate agreement;

(b) To sell to the Soviet Union the following islands in the Gulf of Finland: Suursaari, Seiskari, Lavansaari, Tytärsaari, and Great and Little Koivisto; also those portions of the Rybachi Peninsula and of the Keskisaari Peninsula on the shore of the Arctic Ocean which belong to Finland; all at an agreed price of 300,000 marks.

[The third article:] The Soviet Union and the Finnish Democratic Republic obligate themselves to furnish each to the other all aid, including military aid, in the event that any European power attacks, or threatens to attack, the Soviet Union through Finnish territory.

[Under the fourth article the parties undertook to refrain from engaging in any alliance or from participating in any combinations aimed against the other party to the treaty.]

[The fifth article:] The parties to the treaty have agreed that they will at an early date conclude a trade agreement and increase the annual exchange of commodities between the two countries considerably above the level of exchange of 1927, when it reached its highest point, namely 800 million marks.

[In the sixth article the Soviet Union undertook to supply the Finnish People's Army on easy terms with arms and other military necessities.]

[The seventh article:] The period of duration of this treaty with respect to those clauses which relate to reciprocal aid obligations between the Soviet Union and the Finnish Democratic Republic—Articles 3–5—shall be twenty-five years, in addition to which, if by one year before the termination of the period specified one or the other of the parties does not regard it as necessary to repudiate the decisions contained in the treaty for that period of time, these decisions shall automatically remain in force for a further period of twenty-five years.

[The last article related to the date upon which the treaty entered into force and to the manner of its ratification.]

This treaty has been prepared in two original texts in the Russian and Finnish languages in the city of Moscow on December 2, 1939.

[Signed:]

V. Molotov
O. W. Kuusinen

At the same time that the treaty with the Kuusinen government, which had its seat at Terijoki, was read over the Moscow radio, it was announced that the intention was to ratify it at the earliest possible moment in Helsinki.

The fact that so extensive a treaty of this character was made ready within a few days after the invasion shows that this step had been carefully prepared in advance. It was at once understood in Finland that the purpose of the war was the conquest of Finland and at the same time the establishment here of Bolshevism. The story went about that the Russians thought it was merely a matter of parading to the national capital, where they believed the Russian forces would find themselves within a week, joyously acclaimed as liberators.

Even during the war we received some information about this first Quisling-type government, which had so suddenly appeared out of nowhere with the assignment of making Finland happy. Certain propaganda leaflets which had been seized contained statements regarding its composition: "On the basis of an agreement entered into between many members of the leftist parties and Finnish soldiers who have risen in revolt, there has been formed a new Finnish government, entitled the People's Government of the Finnish Democratic Republic," on December 1, 1939. Its Prime Minister and Foreign Minister was the revolutionist, O. W. Kuusinen, who had fled from Finland in 1918 and who, at a period when hard times had overtaken many other fugitives from Finland, had managed to save both his life and his position so that he might now be available when required. The Minister of the Interior was Ture Lehen; the Finance Minister, Mauri Rosenberg; the Defense Minister, Aksel Anttila (subsequently a lieutenant general in the army of the Soviet Union); the Minister of Agriculture, Armas Äikiä; the Minister of Education, Inkeri Lehtinen; and the Minister for Literary Matters, Paavo Prokkonen.

This government had indeed its own army, whose strength was supposed to be about 50,000 men but which at best consisted of scarcely more than a thousand men or so. There were a few Finns in it, and in addition Ingrians and Russians. The army was intended to be used for prestige purposes on the march to Helsinki. Its uniform was said to be copied after the uniforms of Charles XII's times, but this report was subsequently characterized as being without foundation.

Later on, after the wars, the formative phase of the Terijoki government became better known.

As early as November 13 (the day the Finnish representatives in Moscow had delivered a written notice of their readiness to continue the negotiations), O. W. Kuusinen, acting upon the instructions of Dimitrov, the secretary general of the Comintern, sent a letter to the secretary general of the Finnish Communist Party, Arvo Tuominen (generally known as Sonny Tuominen), who was then living in Stockholm. In this letter Tuominen was directed to proceed to Moscow with all dispatch. The urgency of this trip rested on the assertion that the negotiations between Finland and the Soviet Union had been broken off, for which reason it was necessary to have resort to more forceful measures with respect to Finland. The character of the measures was not mentioned, but Kuusinen added that they would be of the kind the Finnish Communist Party had long hoped for and that Tuominen would find awaiting him a task which would make him very happy.

Although the letter contained nothing more explicit, Tuominen guessed what that task would be. He had been employed on Moscow's confidential business for many years, but he had been revolted by the fate of many of the Finnish fugitives and his outlook had changed, so that he had no desire to comply with this order. For this reason on November 17, in letters addressed both to Kuusinen and to Dimitrov, he replied that he could not come. He gave no reasons for his refusal. The reply was sent with a special courier who had come from Moscow.

Before the reply had reached its destination, Tuominen received through the Soviet Legation in Stockholm an abrupt verbal demand that he set off at once. As this demand produced no effect, on November 21 there arrived direct from Moscow a special courier who presented a new demand, even stiffer than its predecessors, to the effect that Tuominen must depart on the following day with the Moscow plane. This command was issued by the Politburo of the Russian Communist Party. In addition to handing over this brief written order, the courier said that Russia was about to go to war with Finland. At the same time there would be set up a Finnish popular government composed of Finns living as émigrés in Russia. Tuominen was scheduled to be Prime Minister and Kuusinen the President of Finland. The other members of the government were to be selected as soon as he arrived in Moscow. The emissary further said that some of the highest statesmen of the Soviet Union were back of the invitation. This explanation was thought to be sufficient, since clearly from Dimitrov's and Kuusinen's letters Tuominen had not understood what was really at stake.

Arvo Tuominen's answer was negative this time too.

As has been related above, the Mainila incident took place on November 26, and four days later the invasion began.

When the news of the establishment of Kuusinen's government reached Finland, the Finnish Social Democratic Party and the Finnish Confederation of Trade Unions issued a joint statement in which the desire of the laboring population for peace was once more emphasized. The statement concluded with the following words:

The desire of the Finnish working class for peace is sincere. Yet if the aggressors decline to respect this will toward peace, there is left no other alternative to the working class of Finland than to wage battle, weapon in hand, against aggression and in defense of democracy, peace, and the self-determination of our country.

In the name of these workers' organizations and of many others advices were sent out to brother organizations abroad regarding the attitude of the working class toward the aggression which had begun. The newspapers spoke caustically about Kuusinen's "puppet government." Karl-August Fagerholm wrote in the *Arbetarbladet*, "O. W. Kuusinen's government is a complete failure; its propaganda value is nil."

THE LAST ACT OF THE LEAGUE OF NATIONS

Although there appeared to be very little hope of bringing about a settlement through agreement, we did not yet give up trying to reach one. One possible mediator was the League of Nations, among whose express duties was the prevention of armed conflicts. On December 2 the government charged Finland's representative in the League of Nations, Minister Rudolf Holsti, with the task of addressing the League and sent him instructions necessary to this end. On the following day (December 3), Holsti delivered to Avenol, Secretary General of the League, a letter over his own signature, in which Finland as a member of the League asked the League of Nations to take under consideration the unprovoked aggression directed against Finland. The letter contained the following passage:

Finland has never taken any action against its powerful neighbor. It has spared no effort in the endeavor to live in peace with its neighbor. Despite these facts the Soviet Union, basing its actions upon fabricated border incidents and alleging that Finland has refused to assent to the consolidation of the security of Leningrad, has first denounced the treaty of nonaggression and then rejected a proposal of the Finnish government which urged that the matter be entrusted to the mediation of an impartial power.

Under these circumstances I have the honor, upon instructions of my government, to bring these matters to your attention, requesting that you be so good as to convene the Council and the Assembly on the basis of Articles 11 and 15 of the Covenant, and that you request them to take any steps which may be necessary to terminate the aggression.

The League of Nations went to work with rare alacrity. The secretariat convened the Assembly for December 9. In response to the invitation sent to the Soviet Union the League of Nations received a telegram dated December 4 in which the Soviet government asserted that the Finnish request was without justification. "The Soviet Union," it continued,

is not at war with Finland, nor does it threaten the people of Finland with war. Consequently appeal to Article 11, Paragraph 1, is out of place. The Soviet Union maintains peaceful relations with the Finnish Democratic Republic, whose government on December 2 concluded with the Soviet Union a treaty of friendship and mutual assistance. This treaty settles all the questions with regard to which the Soviet government had negotiated fruitlessly with the representatives of the former government of Finland, now ejected from office.

On these grounds the Soviet Union refused to send its representatives to the meeting of the League of Nations.

The telegram went on to say that the government of the Finnish Democratic Republic had on December 1 approached the Soviet government to request its assistance by force of arms in suppressing, through joint endeavor and as promptly as possible, the extremely perilous threat of war with which it was confronted at the hands of the former rulers of Finland.

Despite the negative position of the Soviet Union the Assembly of the League of Nations, in which Finland was represented by Ministers Rudolf Holsti and Harri Holma and by Colonel Aladár Paasonen, took the matter under consideration. In its name another cable was sent to Moscow on December 11, in which the governments of the Soviet Union and Finland were urged to end hostilities at once and, availing themselves of the mediation of the Assembly, promptly to initiate negotiations for the reestablishment of peace. At the same time it was stated that Finland had accepted this recommendation and that the Soviet Union was invited to declare before the evening of the following day whether it was disposed to accept the appeal and to cease hostilities without delay.

The Soviet Union, expressing its thanks for the invitation, declined to accept it and in justification referred to the telegram which it had sent earlier.

The Assembly nevertheless continued its consideration of the case. It rendered an opinion in which it assumed an attitude in all respects most understanding toward the position of Finland and which was completely in Finland's favor. The fact was noted that at no stage of the controversy had Finland rejected any peaceful measures. It had assented to direct negotiations with the Soviet Union. It had consented to consider cessions of territory even though it would have been entitled to appeal to its treaty with the Soviet Union in order to thwart any proposition directed against the inviolability of Finnish territory. Further, it had made counterproposals which in its opinion went as far as it was possible to go. With respect to the Mainila incident, Finland had proposed that the border agents of both states should carry out a joint investigation. When the Soviet Union repudiated the nonaggression pact, the Finnish government had requested that the mediation procedure specified in the pact should be applied. Finland had accepted the offer of mediation made by the United States. On the other hand, the Soviet government was shown to have acted on six separate issues in a manner which was not in harmony with the obligations which that country had undertaken.

On the basis of all the foregoing, the Assembly "formally condemned the action of the Soviet Union against the Finnish state." It furthermore appealed to all members of the League "to furnish to Finland in the measure of their ability material and humanitarian aid, and to refrain from any action which would be calculated to reduce Finland's ability to resist."

Upon the Soviet Union's refusal to accede to the summons to attend the session of the Assembly, that body further found that the Soviet Union had not merely been guilty of violating an obligation based upon the Covenant of the League but that through its action it had placed itself outside the Covenant, for which reason the Council of the League of Nations was entitled to make such decisions as the situation called for.

The Council did in fact make these decisions on December 14, when it declared that by reason of its actions the Soviet Union had placed itself outside the pale of the League of Nations. Consequently it was no longer a member.

The upshot of our having had recourse to the League of Nations was that the behavior of the Soviet Union was unanimously condemned and that on this account, again unanimously, that country was expelled from the membership of the League of Nations. This was the last act of the League.

The various states of the world had in addition been urged to furnish Finland with aid both material and humanitarian. This decision made it possible for Finland to secure access both to arms and to financial credits. In many countries, moreover, there were founded national societies for the collection of aid to Finland. Particularly in the Scandinavian countries, in Switzerland, and in the United States the organizations which sprang up were very active. With respect to the League's decision, the further fact may be mentioned that it subsequently gave rise to negotiations of many sorts both with emissaries of the League of Nations and with numerous other persons who came to Finland.

The reasons the Soviet Union gave the League of Nations for its refusal to attend the session differed considerably from the stand the Soviet Union had maintained in earlier sessions of the League.

At a meeting of the Assembly of the League in 1937 the Soviet Union's Commissar for Foreign Affairs, Litvinov, had spoken as follows:

It is quite clear that under international law no assistance is to be given those who are in revolt against a lawful government; any assistance given to rebels in the form of war materials and particularly in the form of men would be a gross violation of international law; the recognition of the ringleader of the revolt as chief of state in the government does not improve the position, since in this way it would be possible to legitimize any revolt or revolution whatsoever through a simple declaration that the rebels constitute the government; recognition of the rebels as the lawful government in itself constitutes intervention.

On the same occasion Litvinov further said: "Aggression is always aggression, no matter under what mask it tries to hide. There is no international principle which would make lawful an attack, or an unauthorized march into another country, and the violation of international treaties."

At the time when these truths were spoken, the Soviet Union was worried about the aspirations of the Ukraine toward independence. It had occasion to suspect that the formation of a Ukrainian revolutionary government under the leadership of Hetman Skoropadski was being plotted in Germany.

INDEPENDENCE DAY, 1939

As we were trying our best to fit ourselves into the impossible premises of the Foreign Ministry in the stadium, to keep the wild interchange of cables under control, and to receive visitors, including foreign ones, there suddenly came to mind the thought that we must try to commemorate our Independence Day in some manner. It was wartime, to be sure, and everything was looking very gloomy. But on the other hand it was precisely to assure our independence that we were fighting, so that it would be well to do conspicuous honors to this remembrance. There was in addition a propaganda consideration which had influence in leading us to wish that despite all difficulties the day should not be seen to pass without a commemoration. Had not the Russian news bureaus disseminated throughout the world the report that the Finnish government "had fled to an unknown destination"? It was important to show that the government was at Helsinki in its entirety and that its demeanor was confident. For this reason, too, it would be worth while to get up at least a makeshift reception on Independence Day. And we would invite the foreign journalists and photographers to the reception, too, so that they could say the watchers were still upon the ramparts.

I no longer recall who was the first to think, amid the general turmoil, of the commemoration of the day, nor on what day it came to mind. I believe this happened only the day before, because we in the Foreign Ministry were in a fine rush getting our reception organized. There was indeed some trouble. Quite plainly, it was not so easy to arrange as under normal conditions.

As the Presidential Palace, where Independence Day receptions were ordinarily held, was not available, we had to think of other quarters. I gave the Foreign Ministry official Päivö Tarjanne, who is now Finnish Minister in Denmark, the job of going to the salon of the Council of State (generally known as the Smolna) to arrange for the reception there. A few moments later he called in from downtown to say that there was no way of getting into any part of the building and that the janitor was nowhere to be found. After he had hunted up the keys in some other building he called again to say that the building was quite unheated and that on this account we would be unable to use it. That difficulty might perhaps be overcome by stoking the place thoroughly, so I urged him to have the heating fired up. I assured him that by the next day we would have it warm enough to be bearable. But before that obstacle could be tackled there came from the building another of Job's messengers, and this one crushed us. The windows of the building could not be blacked out, because there was not enough blackout curtaining. Under the bombing threat of those days, however, it would have been madness to give a party with brightly illuminated windows. Then, too, we had issued strict blackout orders.

There was nothing for it but we must hunt up some other hall. Mr. Tarjanne got the job of asking the various public rooms whether they could take on the reception to be offered. He asked all the hotels and restaurants, but at first we got only negative responses from all quarters. At last we were told that the Hotel Kämp could indeed make available its principal reception room with its accessory rooms, but that the hotel had nothing to serve us nor the personnel to serve it. Well, something could be done about that. I telephoned Severi Koskinen, the superintendent of the Elanto restaurant chain, to ask whether he could manage on short notice to arrange coffee and refreshments if the place and the service utensils were made available. In his usual hearty fashion he promised, despite the short time at his disposal, to take care of that side of it, and so we had our business settled.

Under the direction of Rafael Hakkarainen, the Chief of Protocol, the invitations were promptly sent out. It was possible to invite many by telephone. The list of guests of course did not even approach the number the President was accustomed to invite to the Palace on Independence Day. But it was not indispensable that it should, nor were there so very many people in Helsinki at the time. In any event we sent off invitations to the representatives of foreign powers who were in Helsinki, to the representatives of the foreign and domestic press, and also to as many others as we thought the room would hold. As it was our intention to arrange the party in the simple, frugal fashion called for by the war, it was indicated on the cards that street dress might be worn on this occasion. Now, so far as the Ministry was concerned, the thing was done. The reception could be given, and at the same time the new government would be able to present itself.

When on December 6 at 6:00 P.M. we entered the Hotel Kämp under a moist fall of snow, I was a little uneasy how everything would go off. Had the hotel heated the hall sufficiently, and above all, had Elanto been able to handle the service side of it in respectable fashion? Everything seemed to be in satisfactory order. The guests paid their compliments to Elanto's coffee and its good cakes and biscuits. For of course in a way it had been a question of honor with Elanto to be charged with the service on such an occasion as this in the town's best hotel.

The guests had settled the question of dress in the fashion suggested by the cards. No one wore tails or a dinner jacket, as had been customary at receptions of this sort. The ladies appeared to have had a few problems to solve in choosing their dress. The most difficult dilemma seems to have been the uncertainty as to whether on such an occasion they should appear with hats or without. One uniquely clad guest drew my attention through his attire. Uuno Hannula, the Minister of Education, had come to the reception wearing a gray woolen shirt and red-heeled boots. When I eyed his clothing a shade critically, he explained without being asked, "This *is* my street dress." And it was, too. Hannula went about during the whole Winter War in this sort of garb, and what was more, he had tied around his arm the white ribbon of the reporters. He said that with this on he got in anywhere he wanted much more easily.

Although the thoughts of all were naturally revolving about the critical problems of the war, the atmosphere did not seem to be depressed. The President passed the time of day gaily with the guests, and the guests tried to appear as easy in mind as they could. The newspapermen hovered about suitable victims the whole evening long, and the flash bulbs of the photographers flared frequently as they snapped the evidence, which they would send to papers at home and abroad, that the President and the Cabinet were present at the reception in the flesh.

During the course of the evening one Swedish journalist, more curious that most, asked Paasikivi why the Moscow radio daily reviled Tanner and left him, Paasikivi, in peace. Paasikivi explained that it was perhaps because since Tanner knew less Russian than he did, the times Tanner took the floor the statements had generally been very brief and on most occasions had consisted of the single word *nyet*, while he himself had had to make longer explanatory statements. On the substance of the matter, to be sure, we had been quite of the same mind while negotiating at Moscow. On a later occasion, when Paasikivi was in Moscow as Minister, he gave the same explanation to Foreign Affairs Commissar Molotov, who at that time was much given to attacking me. Perhaps it is indeed one explanation of how I happen to have got into Moscow's black books, while Paasikivi nevertheless enjoyed—at least for a long time—the rays of the Moscow sun.

In other respects the evening passed without any awkward incidents, and those present seemed to be pleased that the day had not been forgotten but had been celebrated despite the war. I recall particularly a long conversation I had with Schoenfeld, the American Minister. At once upon the outbreak of the war the United States had exhibited a great sympathy for the cause of Finland, offering its mediation in the interest of peace, even though this had not proved successful. The Minister explained the position of the United States to me at length and was eager to hear our views on the situation.

When we left this unique reception late in the evening, we had it brought home to us the moment we got outside the hotel doors that we were living in wartime. The darkness was if possible even more impenetrable than before. A complete blackout was in effect, and the overcast sky did not permit the feeblest glow to light the march of the homeward bound. But the evening had in any case served its purpose. That one could tell from the world press, which never again carried the legend about the government which had "fled to an unknown destination."

TWO RADIO SPEECHES

In the initial phase of the war we tried several ways of getting in contact with the Soviet government. These efforts, however, were failures. Among the endeavors to make contact may be listed the radio speech which I delivered on December 15 in Russian, Finnish, and Swedish. It was addressed to Mr. Molotov in Moscow. In the speech reference was made first to the negotiations in which we had engaged in Moscow. In these negotiations we had been prepared on Finland's behalf to assent to far-reaching concessions even though the Soviet government had no legal right to present such demands as it did. Upon departing we had expressed our hopes that the negotiations were to continue. But this had not happened; the fault was entirely the Soviet Union's, which by breaking off diplomatic relations had made them impossible and which had then attacked our country. Even thereafter we had in many fashions shown our desire to solve the dispute in a pacific manner, having recourse now to the intermediary of the United States, now to that of Sweden, now to that of the League of Nations. Yet all had been in vain. The Soviet Union had shown that it did not wish to hear our proposals.

"And still the air is free. On the air, then, by radio I address you to ask a few questions."

Then I inquired whether the defense of Leningrad had been the true concern of the Soviet Union upon its presenting the demands. How did the establishment of the Terijoki "democratic" government fit in with that? This clearly showed a desire to subject all Finland to the power of the Soviet Union.

I further referred to that catch phrase of Mr. Stalin's which I had read on the wall of one of the buildings of the great agricultural exhibition in Moscow: "We do not want an inch of foreign territory, but neither do we want to cede an inch of our own territory to anyone." How did that fit in with the Soviet Union's attack upon peaceful little Finland?

"Why this shedding of blood before all alternatives have been exhausted?"

"Are you prepared to resume negotiations and thus to show through deeds that your principles are something more than advertising slogans?" These were my closing questions.

I asked for an answer through the same medium which I had used for my questions.

There was no answer. The only indication that the questions had been heard was a release distributed by the Tass news bureau to the effect that an answer would hardly be given.

Prime Minister Ryti also delivered an important speech on the radio on December 8, solemnly declaring that Finland's will to peace was powerful but that it would oppose the aggression with all the forces at its disposal. In the event that the country were to be occupied, the people would go on demonstrating that they did not accept the fact.

CHAPTER 7

SEEKING A WAY TO PEACE

At once upon assuming the reins of administration we of the foreign affairs committee of the Council of State began to ponder in what way it would be possible to get out of the war. This question came up as early as the meeting of December 4. On this occasion the committee was informed that word had been received through the Swedish Minister in Moscow, Winther, to the effect that at the moment there was no way of entering into discussion with the Soviet Union. The Soviet Union had not even accepted Sweden as a mediator because it had reached agreement upon Finnish problems with the Kuusinen government. I said my own impression was that the change of government had clearly come too late, since the Soviet Union had already managed to set up the Terijoki puppet government. There was no way out for us just now save battle, to which end weapons must be procured for the army. Paasikivi was of the same mind—that there was no way of getting discussions started for the moment. Therefore we should approach the United States and England and appeal to them at once for arms. We could proceed to negotiations only after the Soviet Union had suffered defeats.

So for the time being we worked along that line. We started to gather arms and ammunition and everything needed in warfare from various parts of the world. A special office, with V. A. Kotilainen, the Minister of Trade, at its head, was set up to conduct this activity and to engage in commercial discussions. This office had available an abundance of volunteer forces. Well-known businessmen placed themselves at the disposal of the government without compensation both in planning domestic orders and in conducting negotiations regarding their counterparts abroad. In the difficult months to come these so-called "mark-a-year-men" (for that was their salary) were of great assistance.

Along with this activity, everything possible was done to awaken the world's conscience in defense of Finland's just cause. Nor were there any difficulties here. The press of almost the whole world treated Finnish affairs in an exclusively favorable spirit, and Finland was constantly the beneficiary of demonstrations of sympathy. It was a great help here that at the same time there was no fighting in any other part of the world. The World War fronts were quiet, and the world's attention was thus concentrated undividedly upon the unequal struggle in Finland, where a small country had to fight against the unprovoked attack of a state fifty times its size.

In order to arouse the sympathies of the world, President Kallio even considered sending to all chiefs of state a letter over his own signature in which he would explain Finland's position and ask them to take steps to mediate for peace. This idea of the President's was discussed at a meeting of the foreign affairs committee on December 9, but the device was held impracticable and it was not considered likely to lead to concrete results.

The Diet also cast its weight into the scales by approving, on December 10, an appeal addressed to all peoples. This set forth the fact that our eastern neighbor had directed a brazen attack against Finland, which for its part had not offered the slightest provocation. Consequently we had been forced into a conflict without being in a position to exercise the least choice in the matter. As our struggle was in defense of the cause of all humanity, the appeal expressed the hope that the civilized world would not leave us to fight alone against the numerically overwhelming enemy. The appeal was brought to the attention of foreign governments through official channels.

These appeals had at least the advantage that our country began to receive arms from various quarters, principally Sweden, France, England, and the United States. Financial credits were also available. So we could continue the fight, although the Commander-in-Chief had pessimistically reported ammunition would last for only two weeks.

When the first attacks had been successfully repulsed and the situation on the front had thus to some degree become stabilized, it was time to return again to the question of getting peace negotiations under way. It was upon this point that the discussions in the foreign affairs committee were concentrated from the beginning of January, and thereafter the question did not disappear from its agenda. The tendency was encouraged by the circumstance that generous suggestions with a view toward peace and direct offers to undertake mediation began to come in from all sides. Paavo Pajula, our Minister in Copenhagen, asked on behalf of the Danish government whether we would like Denmark to try to get Germany to take a stand in Moscow in favor of peace. Sweden gave us to understand that it would be prepared, to the same end, to offer its services once more. Yet the moment was not considered opportune. Foreign Minister Halvdan Koht of Norway wrote me a friendly personal letter from Oslo in which he, too, dealt with the possibility of peace. He felt it would be well to offer the Soviet Union the cession of Hanko in exchange for the neutralization of the Finnish Gulf. If this idea were to receive support, he would be glad to advocate it in Moscow. As the idea had already been studied in the negotiations we had had with the Soviet Union, it seemed useless to bring it up again.

From Estonia there came a report, vague at first, that the Soviet Union had realized it had plunged into a mistaken venture and that it would now be willing to engage in further discussions with Finland. Later we received a more precise confirmation of this in a telegram from P. J. Hynninen, our Minister in Estonia. He said the Estonian Foreign Minister, Ants Piip, had got word through the Estonian Minister in Moscow, August Rei, that Finland could have peace by making further concessions. Among these, Hanko was in first place. There was furthermore the demand that the Finnish Foreign Minister should resign. It was decided to answer this announcement by saying that Hanko could not be ceded under any circumstances and that it did not behoove the Soviet Union to dictate how the Finnish government was to be composed.

There were also discussions of our chances for peace with the former Swedish Foreign Minister Rickard Sandler, who was visiting in Finland. He had been acquainting himself with northern Finland and at my request had scheduled his return trip via Helsinki. Ryti and I had a long conversation with him in which we explained our position and the encouragements to peace we had received, as well as the inquiries which were on foot. He agreed with our view that peace was necessary, without however being able to propose any sure way of attaining it. He regarded continuation of the war as dangerous, above all because it might force Finland and possibly the other Northern nations to abandon their neutral stand and to drift into the World War on the side of the Allies. He warned us in particular to see to it that the Western powers should not penetrate into Petsamo or into Murmansk.

These various possibilities were earnestly debated in the foreign affairs committee without clear decision as to which course it would be best to try. It was considered safest to address Germany, at that time the Soviet Union's ally. In case this should lead to no result, it was believed the effort of mediation would meet with best success if a number of countries were to take joint measures in Moscow, offering to mediate. We felt it would be most appropriate if this were to be done on the initiative of the United States. Prime Minister Ryti had had some casual discussions of the matter with Schoenfeld, the American Minister at Helsinki. When I in turn came to continue this discussion with Schoenfeld, he doubted the moment was suitable, yet believed that the United

States was ready to offer its services at any time we might request it. "In any event, Finland must hold out until political conditions change," was his concluding observation.

On January 9 the foreign affairs committee finally decided to ask the United States, through a request to its government via Minister Schoenfeld, to address the governments of the Soviet Union and Finland jointly with the other major neutral power, Italy, offering such mediation as would be necessary to bring about between them both an armistice and the initiation of a peace conference. It was further proposed that the United States should suggest to Italy that for its part that country should simultaneously try to press both Germany and Sweden to approach the Soviet Union and Finland with the same purpose.

The intention was to bring about a joint representation on behalf of Finland. Minister Schoenfeld promised to act in the fashion suggested. But the enterprise petered out and led to no result.

FAILURE OF THE GERMAN MEDIATION MISSION

As has been said above, in the foreign affairs committee of the Council of State we thought Germany had the best chance of succeeding in a mission of mediation, since it had made a treaty with the Soviet Union and was, in a way, its ally. On this account Professor T. M. Kivimäki, on departing on December 15 for Germany, was assigned the task of making soundings there. These, however, came to nothing. Clearly the time was too early.

At the beginning of January, Finland had had considerable successes on various fronts. This gave ground for the optimistic view that one might begin little by little to try to bring about peace negotiations. The aim was first to determine whether anything could be accomplished in this sense through German mediation.

In order to secure an idea of the German attitude, on January 4, 1940, I invited the German Minister in Helsinki, Wipert von Blücher, to come in and discuss the situation. Von Blücher was a skillful diplomat and a widely informed man. He was ordinarily glad to talk and on such occasions revealed his knowledge. Thus we had had frequent earlier conversations about Social Democracy, and particularly its history, during which I had been astonished at his familiarity with this field rather alien to him. Actually he did not seem to be a convinced Nazi, though he faithfully served his masters.

This time, too, his visit led to a comprehensive discussion which bore at first on relations between Germany and Finland and in which both sides took an aggressive part. When I expressed surprise at Germany's current attitude toward Finland, Blücher began to attack Finland's stand, reproaching us for ingratitude despite the help we had received in 1918. He would have it that of late years Finland had borne itself in downright unfriendly fashion toward Germany. I tried to lead the conversation toward the possibilities of ending the Finnish war which might at the moment exist. I strove to show that the flaring up of a new front in the north was not to Germany's advantage. There was always that danger if the war went on for long. For its part Finland wanted to remain neutral and not to be swept into the train of either of the combatting groups of powers.

My criticism of Germany's attitude was occasioned by the fact that Germany had tried in many ways to keep Finland from acquiring arms. It had not permitted German factories to deliver to us arms orders placed even before the war had broken out. Nor had it permitted transit through Germany of arms ordered from other countries. For example, a shipment of Italian planes had got all the way to Stettin, when Germany—surely upon Soviet demand—refused to permit them to go on. Thereupon they had to be returned to Italy. To me, all this showed that Germany wanted to be on our enemy's side.

Without undertaking to explain Germany's past refusal of transit permission for arms, Blücher said that, for all Germany cared, other countries might freely help Finland and furnish arms and even volunteers. Germany would also permit munitions en route to us to pass through its territory. But Germany could not permit the Western powers to secure bases in the North. If such a concession were made to them, it would be a *casus belli* for Germany. As for Germany's attitude toward the Finnish war in other respects, he phrased his thought in these terms: "An dem finnischen Kriege ist Deutschland unbeteiligt." ("Germany has no part in the Finnish war.")

But my real business was to discover whether Germany could come forward as a mediator between Finland and the Soviet Union, and little by little I moved toward this main purpose. I did not, however, at this stage believe that there was occasion to ask straight out that Germany act as intermediary. Declaring that Finland would gladly seek peace, I limited myself to saying that I should like to learn through him whether the German government could give Finland counsel as to how one might reach the desired goal of peace. This question perceptibly enlivened Blücher, and he began to ask questions in order to learn more. Above all he wanted to know what Finland would propose to suggest in the event it should prove possible to discuss peace. But I did not think it possible to enlarge upon my inquiry.

Blücher remarked, as his own impression, that the present moment was bad for beginning negotiations because thus far in its war with

Finland the Soviet Union had met with nothing but reverses. He nevertheless promised to inquire of his government regarding its attitude and to return to the subject later.

Now that we had dealt with this principal matter I took up the further subject of trade between Germany and Finland, which was not moving even though it had been decided, in the very last days of the preceding year, to extend the trade and payments convention between the two countries. I urged that the German vessels which lay idle in Germany's Baltic ports should be sent to Finland with cargoes, and should similarly carry back return shipments. He explained that Germany's unwillingness to send its ships here arose from the fact that the Soviet blockade of Finland prevented their free passage. He suggested the vessels should be cleared for Stockholm. Finland should carry its own export shipments thither, and receive its imports there. He asked that the Finnish government should seriously consider this proposal. It was clear that Germany did want Finland's export goods, but that as an associate of the Soviet Union Germany did not want to injure this fellowship by infractions against the blockade.

Here the conversation ended. It was necessary to wait and see what chance Germany, as the Soviet Union's ally, would have of making its voice heard in Moscow.

It was intended that this step be kept most confidential, because at the beginning of a war neither party gladly sees its ideas made public and talked about. But it soon became plain that we were to have no luck in this. The news leaked out. The first word came from our Minister in Copenhagen, Paavo Pajula, who was able to report that the German Ambassador in Moscow, Count von der Schulenburg, had told the Danish Minister there that Germany hoped there would be a peace between Finland and the Soviet Union. After this there began to appear in the world press items reporting the German purpose to mediate. It was said, indeed, that Germany had already made a peace proposal at Moscow. Perhaps it was on this account that Snow, the British Minister in Helsinki, visited me to inquire what foundation there was to these German mediation rumors. Naturally I could not tell him what part we had in the matter; I merely said that no peace proposals had been made to us. I further related what we had heard via Denmark regarding what had been said in Moscow.

With regard to the same rumors our Minister in Paris, Harri Holma, reported his opinion that these rumors had been started by Moscow itself so that the aid plans of the Western powers with respect to Finland should get a dose of cold water. According to his report the Paris papers had warned Finland against believing these stories.

In actuality the stories were perhaps well-founded, insofar as Germany, on Blücher's recommendation, had begun to explore the terrain in Moscow. Thus in a sense the affair was under way. But it went forward slowly. The halting progress began to make even the German Legation in Helsinki nervous. Its counselor, Reiner Kreuzwald, had dropped in for a chat with Tapio Voionmaa, the permanent undersecretary, on January 17 and had complained that thus far Blücher had not received any sort of reply to his inquiry. Von Blücher was much distressed on this account. Moreover I learned from the secret police that Blücher had lamented the same circumstance in a conversation with Berlin and had said at the same time that he could not make so bold as even to show his face at the Foreign Ministry. The information we gathered gave us reason to assume that Germany and the Soviet Union were seriously pondering the matter.

We had had no great hopes that the approach through Germany would lead to any results, although we did wish to try out this channel first. Even these minimal hopes were dissipated when on January 19, 1940, Blücher put in another appearance. This time he came on his own initiative, but it was high time, two weeks having passed since our earlier conversation. Blücher began by talking about various minor matters. He set forth *in extenso* his ideas on how the German war and the Japanese-Chinese war would end, and to be sure he was optimistic as to both. For my part I brought up facts intended to show that our war was exceptionally difficult for a small country to bear up under. As for the German war, I remarked that it had not really begun yet. This remark of mine somewhat astonished him, but when I added that the war would surely spread further and take on new aspects, he was prepared to admit that this might well be so.

Next Blücher came to his real business, namely, to present a reply to the question I had posed two weeks earlier. He said that on the preceding evening he had received a telegram from Berlin which stated that "the German government is of the opinion that for the moment there are no prospects of settling the conflict."

On the basis of his announcement a further discussion developed, in which Von Blücher, as though to alleviate the impression produced by the answer, wondered whether the Finnish people, after its great victories, would even be disposed to make peace. I assured him that at least the Finnish government was ready. He asked further whether we had really expected that Berlin would move to mediate for peace. Clearly he wanted to leave me with the impression that no representations on Germany's part had been made in the matter, but that the German government, after thinking the matter over, had come to a negative con-

,clusion. I then told him confidentially what we had learned via Denmark regarding the attitude of the German Embassy in Moscow and also that the German Ambassador, Count von der Schulenburg, had on various occasions declared that his preoccupation was to bring about a peace. Herr von Blücher spent some time in astonishment over Von der Schulenburg's statements, and perhaps also over how small the world is, after all, and how in it everything becomes known.

Neither of us had anything more to say this time on mediation toward peace. I understood that along this path, at any rate, there was no chance of arriving at a peace. Perhaps it was the Soviet Union, concerning whose desire for peace we had received word through other channels, that did not wish to remain under a debt of gratitude to Germany.

Still, I took up some other questions which were open at the time, primarily the renewed obstacles to trade between the two countries. I belabored Blücher with the fact that trade between our two countries was not moving, and that no agreement regarding the principles which should govern it had even been reached. I expounded to him the new proposal made by Finland in Berlin, with which he did not seem to be acquainted. In his view the obstacle was that the German exporters had not received what was due them because, by reason of the war, Finland had been unable to export anything to Germany. I said that despite the war our exports were holding up pretty well, but that we did not *want* to ship goods to Germany until there was a clear agreement. Above all, we did not care to send copper, which as a belligerent nation Germany was most eager to obtain. This was for him an entirely new way of looking at the matter. In further explanation of his government's negative stand, he said that the Germans had shipping difficulties and that everything depended on whether German ships would be able to reach Finnish ports. According to him, negotiations on this subject were under way in Moscow even now. In order to give a picture of the German shipping difficulties, he said that in the Baltic the Russians had sunk three ships and that three others had been fired upon but not sunk. When I expressed surprise at this manifestation of German-Russian friendship, which led to the sinking of German vessels only, he mentioned as a consolation that at least one Swedish vessel had been sunk too. In his opinion it was not worth while for Professor Kivimäki's currently planned trade mission to go to Germany before unobstructed passage of German shipping to Finland was assured. He consistently advocated the use of Stockholm as an entrepôt.

I had yet another talk with Blücher about the chances of making peace. Counselor Kreutzwald of the German Legation had inquired

through Permanent Undersecretary Voionmaa whether I would care to
see Von Blücher before his trip to Germany, which was scheduled for a
few days ahead. Although this was a slightly odd fashion of sending
a message and the aim was clearly to tempt me into taking the initiative
in resuming our interrupted business, I invited Blücher to come in for a
chat. He did come, on January 24, the day before he planned to depart.
Before his arrival I had seen from the secret police report of telephone
conversations that he had talked with Von Grundherr in Berlin, who
held the Finnish desk in the German Foreign Ministry. Von Blücher
had pressed hard for action on some matter relating to Finland, and presumably this matter related precisely to the peace mediation. Von Grundherr had shown very little interest and was opposed to the business. But
the next day, when the telephone conversation was resumed, the tone was
different. Von Grundherr had said that the matter might be considered.
Armed with this foreknowledge, I was prepared to receive Blücher.

When he came in, I again touched on the subject of trade relations,
which were important to Finland at that time. A long discussion again
ensued. It became clear that the key to the whole matter was, as before,
free access to Finnish ports for German shipping. When I said that
Germany had no need to heed the Soviet blockade, which others were
disregarding, he emphasized once more the fact that several of their
ships had been sunk. He said that Von Ritter had just traveled to Moscow
on Germany's behalf to negotiate a trade treaty with the Soviet Union,
and he hoped that the matter of sea trade with Finland would be cleared
up in this connection. He also reverted to his earlier assertion that German exporters feared they might lose what was due them from Finland.
When I said that at the moment Finland owed Germany only about a
million Finnish marks and that Finland could easily pay this amount
with its exports as soon as trade should open up, it became apparent that
he had not been informed of this. He promised that in any case he would
talk about the trade matter when he got to Berlin.

But his real concern was to return to the subject of mediation, as I
had in fact divined. He began by lamenting that we had let Germany's
mediation plans leak out. I denied this sharply and read to him, to sup-
plement the information I had given him before, the report we had received through the Estonian Foreign Minister, Piip. This information
made it plain that Von der Schulenburg had talked to someone in Moscow
about the possibility of peace, and it was from this source that the reports had leaked to the world press. In order to get on, Von Blücher
asked whether I had any information on this matter to send with him to
Berlin. Clearly, he would have wished to try to get the peace plan under
way once more. I replied that, since only a few days earlier we had got

SEEKING A WAY TO PEACE 123

a completely negative answer from Germany, I did not consider it possible to make fresh proposals. "It is unpleasant to knock at the same door twice," I said. Von Blücher looked a little taken aback; apparently he had expected I would gladly accept the offer. The discussion continued in very frank fashion from here on. I described the chances we had in the war and expatiated upon Germany's doublefaced attitude toward Finland. He regarded himself as a victim. "All my work in Finland to date is smashed to bits," he said.

Such was the end of our attempt to make use of German mediation in order to bring about peace. The ally was unable to open the door in Moscow.

PEACE FEELERS THROUGH STOCKHOLM

When I had given Blücher a flat refusal upon his almost offering to attempt a mediation once more, I had not done so out of pure caprice. Among ourselves we had come to take an attitude of doubt toward the German mediation, and we had in a fashion laid the groundwork for inquiries through other channels.

On New Year's Day Mrs. Hella Wuolijoki* had written to me from her farm at Marlebäck, Kausala, a letter suggesting that she might be assigned the task of going to Stockholm to meet her old acquaintance the Soviet Minister, Mme. Aleksandra Kollontai. I regarded this proposal most skeptically. I well knew Mrs. Wuolijoki's imaginative temperament as well as her difficulty in keeping her feet on the ground, but in such a situation it would not do to be too delicate in selecting one's instruments. After taking counsel with Ryti and Paasikivi I asked Mrs. Wuolijoki to come to Helsinki. She reached town on January 8 and was given the job of trying to find out through Mme. Kollontai what the war aim of the Soviet Union was and what course Mme. Kollontai would suggest in order for us to bring about peace. Mrs. Wuolijoki left on her journey on January 10. The first word from her came by phone, and she reported in guarded language that she had met Mme. Kollontai, who had received her as an old friend and had been prepared to initiate inquiries in Moscow. Mme. Kollontai had also judged that the moment would be appropriate, whereas a couple of weeks earlier the attempt would have been impossible. A few days later I received another telephone report to the effect that a pair of experts were coming from Moscow to Stockholm to discuss the matter further. Mrs. Wuolijoki seemed to be optimistic about the outcome. I was able to gladden her with the news that

---

* Hella Murrik Wuolijoki, Finnish playwright, born in Estonia in 1886. She married Sulo Wuolijoki, a Finnish Social Democratic leader, and later moved into the Communist camp and held a left-wing salon. An old friend of Mme. Kollontai, she played a prominent role in postwar Finland. She died in 1954.

she had meanwhile become a grandmother. It chanced that I took this call at the residence of the American Minister, Mr. Schoenfeld, at Kauniainen. I was there for dinner; a unique occasion, as during the whole Winter War the Foreign Minister attended no other social gatherings. But to be sure, there was no time or opportunity for them during the war.

Then written reports began to come in from Stockholm, both from Mrs. Wuolijoki and from the Finnish representative in Stockholm, Eljas Erkko, with whom Mrs. Wuolijoki had been instructed to keep in touch; for Erkko had been named Finnish Chargé d'Affaires in Stockholm upon the outbreak of the war. According to these reports the Soviet representatives had arrived. The first contact with them had taken place on January 21. In subsequent letters it was reported that these representatives —Yartsev (our old acquaintance from Helsinki) and a person named Grauer—had merely asked about conditions in Finland and had in other respects been very reserved, for which reason the business had remained at a standstill for several days. Even on January 26, when I asked Erkko by telephone where the negotiations stood, he said the affair was indeed alive, but that they had not come down to details yet. The Russians apparently wanted to assure themselves that we were in earnest and not just negotiating to gain time.

In the meanwhile a discussion of the need for peace had taken place at headquarters, in connection with Prime Minister Ryti's visit there. Reporting on this discussion, Ryti declared that Mannerheim had said that in war one never really knows how it is going to turn out in the end, but that at this moment the situation was good and gave no grounds for a spirit of panic. In his view we might at this moment amplify our territorial proposal by offering the area southwest of the line Lipola-Seivästö. On the other hand, it was difficult to concede a base at the mouth of the Gulf of Finland. During the discussion it had further become clear that if his matériel requirements were at least partly fulfilled, the Commander-in-Chief would not be at all pessimistic. Above all he needed heavy artillery and at least twenty-five to thirty thousand additional men. If the guns were procured, he believed he could get by, since our air force would be adequate once the four hundred promised planes had arrived. He had just completed his requirements schedule and had cabled it to Ironside and Gamelin, the British and French Commanders-in-Chief. Mannerheim had asked Ryti whether he might give this list of our needs also to Sir Walter Citrine, Secretary General of the British Trade Union Congress, who was visiting headquarters at the moment. Ryti had urged him to do so, as Citrine was a man of influence and might for his part consider it a demonstration of mistrust if we did not show him the list. Citrine had, by the way, remarked at headquarters that the British Prime Minister, Chamberlain, had at first been emphatically opposed to granting arms to Finland, considering Finland's case hopeless, so that the arms furnished would simply fall to the Russians. Halifax and Churchill, on the other hand, had advocated sending the arms.

At last, on January 29, there was a change in the Stockholm conversations. We in Helsinki got word of it through the press attaché of the Stockholm Legation, Otto L. Hjelt, whom Erkko had sent to bring the news to Helsinki. He had flown by special plane to Turku and driven by night from there to Helsinki carrying a letter regarding the imminent arrival of which Erkko had informed me the day before. In his letter Erkko reported that when he had visited Foreign Minister Günther on January 29, Günther had told him that just a short while earlier Mme. Kollontai had called to read to him a telegram in French which she had received from Foreign Affairs Commissar Molotov. The cable's text was designed to be brought to the attention of the Finnish government in the following terms:

The USSR has no objection in principle to concluding an agreement with the Ryti-Tanner government.

As regards the initiation of negotiations, it will be necessary to know beforehand what concessions the Ryti-Tanner government will be prepared to make.

If the USSR does not have definite assurance that a basis for the initiation of negotiations exists, it will be vain to talk of any agreement. It is also indispensable to note that the requirements of the USSR are not limited to those which were presented in Moscow at the time of the negotiations with Messrs. Tanner and Paasikivi, because since those negotiations blood has been shed on both sides, and that blood, which has been shed contrary to our hopes and through no fault of ours, calls for augmented guarantees to the security of the frontiers of the USSR.

It must also be noted that the promises the government of the USSR made to the Kuusinen government are not applicable to the Ryti-Tanner government, nor can the government of the USSR consent to make such promises to the Ryti-Tanner government.

Günther, Erkko wrote, had remarked to Mme. Kollontai upon the danger the Russian proposals were exposed to with regard to Hanko Cape, whose status was precisely what the present fighting was about. He had observed that it was impossible for Finland to yield Hanko and that, furthermore, Sweden did not in any way desire to influence Finland in this matter. Günther's impression regarding Molotov's telegram was that the Soviet Union now wanted to get in touch with Finland directly. He had also drawn attention to the fact that there was in the telegram no mention of further territorial cessions, only of additional guarantees. Günther had taken a pessimistic view in talking to Mme. Kollontai, telling her that he did not believe Finland could accept the Russian proposal. To this Mme. Kollontai had replied that the most important thing was that Finland should say plainly and frankly what it would assent to.

The most important news in this telegram was the declaration that the Soviet Union was prepared in principle to make peace with "the Ryti-Tanner government," the lawful government of the country, and that it had thus thrown overboard the government of its adopted son, Otto Wille Kuusinen. The hints at peace conditions, on the other hand, were disturbing. Even acceptance of the demands made upon us in the fall would no longer be a sufficient precondition to the making of a peace! The justification for this—"the blood which has been shed contrary to our hopes and through no fault of ours"—was badly out of place in a communication from those who had started the war.

Erkko asked for an answer to this telegram as promptly as possible so that he might leave it with Günther for forwarding. The matter was to be kept strictly confidential. In the Finnish Legation only Erkko knew of it, and in the Swedish Foreign Ministry only Günther, who had not let the telegram out of his hands even to be typed in a clean copy. The importance of this secrecy had been further emphasized by Mrs. Wuolijoki when she came in from Mme. Kollontai to see Erkko just before his letter was sent off.

Nor did the news from Stockholm stop at this point. In a letter he sent on the following day, Erkko told us that when he had sent to Mme. Kollontai, via Mrs. Wuolijoki, an assurance that the matter would be kept strictly confidential, he had through the same channel received from Mme. Kollontai the following advice and greetings:

1. The negotiations were to be held with the knowledge of the Swedish government, because it was impossible to keep them secret from it and because Sweden had earlier offered itself as a mediator.

2. It was the purpose of the Soviet government in this way to link Sweden to the peace negotiations, thus making it bear its share of the responsibility and leading it to bring pressure to bear upon Finland. (Günther had realized this and had at once rejected the idea.)

3. In this way there would arise the advantage that, in the Russian view, Sweden would be split off from England. (At this point Erkko had added in his letter, "How far this is to Sweden's and Finland's interest is another matter. The result of it would in any case be that all prospects of aid from that quarter would disappear and we would be in the clutches of Germany and the Soviet Union for good. England, indeed, is the country which has helped us most effectively to date.")

In addition to all this, Mrs. Wuolijoki had further told Erkko, as coming from herself but as having (according to her assertion) Mme. Kollontai's approval:

1. That although concessions might be made, they might be retrieved on the quiet;

2. That compensations might be obtained within the framework of a trade treaty;

3. That industries which had existed in Finland in Tsarist times might be rebuilt for the purpose of supplying manufactured products the Soviet Union needed.

In a letter she sent to me Mrs. Wuolijoki added that in Mme. Kollontai's view the main thing was that negotiations be got under way with the Finnish government, even though they were to be on the basis of the Kuusinen program (meaning the treaty between the Soviet Union and the Kuusinen government). Thus during the negotiations we would be in a position to speak of saving Koivisto for Finland. For Hanko Cape or the Hanko islands the Soviet Union could give us all eastern Karelia. As negotiators Mrs. Wuolijoki suggested Paasikivi and Kivimäki, the latter being in Stockholm at the time.

This was great news after all our groping in the dark. Moreover, at least as glossed by Mme. Kollontai's and Mrs. Wuolijoki's comments, it was in part so good that it was difficult to take it seriously. Later events showed that it was necessary to deal cautiously with reports from both ladies.

We had to think this news over in Helsinki. But first we had to take care of the delegation from the British Labour Party which was visiting Finland under the leadership of Sir Walter Citrine and with which we were discussing the procurement of arms from England, among other matters. It was only on the afternoon of January 30 that we came to consider the reply to be sent to Stockholm. Ryti, Paasikivi, and I deliberated on the matter for an hour and a half. Paasikivi was pessimistic and believed the whole thing would go on the rocks if a base at the mouth of the Gulf of Finland were not surrendered at once. Ryti and I believed it would be best at first to give only a general answer as Mme. Kollontai herself had recommended, since the Soviet Union had not made any detailed proposals either. It was in this sense that I drafted a reply which Ryti and Paasikivi went over in the morning.

In the reply we pointed out first that it was not Finland that had broken off the earlier negotiations, nor had it wanted the war or begun it. Moreover, during the period of hostilities the Finnish government had on several occasions declared its eagerness to find an acceptable solution to the conflict. Since common ground could be found only through compromise, one might take as a point of departure the position at which the Moscow negotiations had ended. Over and above that, the Finnish government was disposed to make additional concessions such as might be deemed necessary for the security of Leningrad. One might further consider the neutralization of the Gulf of Finland through international agreement. Cession of territory could, in the government's opinion, be undertaken only in the form of exchange. Finally, the government considered it self-evident that compensation must be paid for the property of private citizens in areas which were to be ceded.

The reply was taken to Stockholm by Prime Minister Ryti, who was going there to discuss the procurement of heavy artillery and of auxiliary forces. He discussed these matters both with the Swedish Defense Minister, Sköld, and with Generals Thörnell and Rappe. The gentlemen in question were favorable to the proposals, but Prime Minister Hansson, who was present at one stage of the conversations, was cautious in what he had to say.

The first word of the reception accorded our reply came to us in a letter from Erkko dated February 2. He said he had delivered the reply to Günther, and that the two of them had gone over it together. On Günther's recommendation and after consultation with Helsinki, a few phrases in the reply were made a little softer. Günther said on this occasion that Mme. Kollontai had paid him a special visit to say that she had received word, confirmed by Moscow, to the effect that the Soviet Union could not give over its demand for Hanko Cape. This was surprising news, as the government's reply had been based upon the telegram received from Molotov, in which Hanko Cape had not been mentioned. Erkko had, in fact, asked whether after this it would be worth while transmitting the reply at all. Günther, however, had felt that it should be delivered, since it was of a positive character throughout. Günther went on to ask what the attitude was of the Finnish government at the moment regarding the cession of Hanko Cape, to which Erkko had replied that he had no information but that he assumed no change had occurred with respect to that point. Günther said he had told Mme. Kollontai the same thing and that he had lamented her reply. Mme. Kollontai had also spoken of peace with Finland to certain other persons, including Prime Minister Hansson and an attorney, Georg Branting. About an hour after Erkko's visit Mme. Kollontai called on Günther and received the Finnish reply.

At the same time that this exchange of views with the Soviet Union was taking place through the intermediary of Sweden, plans affecting

Finland were being incubated in England and France. Our Paris Minister, Harri Holma, had frequently referred to them in his letters. The same day that our reply was delivered in Stockholm, a letter came from him which asserted that France was planning a military expedition to Murmansk, in which Finland also might participate. If this were to be carried out, we would find ourselves taking part in the World War. Finland's position was thus becoming a little complicated. On the one hand, we were defending ourselves, and to this end we were calling upon the Western powers for arms, which they gave us in the belief that we were fighting on their side too. On the other hand, however, we were negotiating for peace with the Soviet Union. This position of ours between two fires continued during the following weeks, making it difficult to reach decisions.

The Diet, which at once upon the outbreak of the war had been transferred from turbulent Helsinki to the quieter surroundings of Kauhajoki, held its concluding session for the 1939 term on January 31, 1940. It would normally have been my duty to be present, but this was impossible as I was drafting the reply to be presented in Stockholm. I decided to set out on the evening of that day, so that I reached my destination only in time for the first session of the succeeding Diet term, on February 1. I now had an opportunity to see the conditions under which the Diet had been working for two months in that distant rural center of Bothnia. The committees met in the classrooms of a school, and most of the representatives lived in the local commercial school, where they also ate. The activity as a whole was more halting than in the comfortable rooms of the Diet building at Helsinki, but the work seemed to be progressing in an atmosphere of good will. Yet contact with Helsinki, and particularly with the Cabinet, was exceedingly defective. For this reason it was readily comprehensible that the Diet representatives demanded a review of the situation from the Foreign Minister who had come to attend their opening session. At an unofficial meeting of the Diet I reviewed the course of the war to date, yet without being able to tell them anything about the peace feelers we had sent out. The Diet members appeared to be altogether too sanguine regarding the final outcome of the war.

I return once more to the reply we sent to Stockholm, and to its fate. Erkko reported in a letter of February 3 that Mme. Kollontai had on the day before received our reply from Günther and had read it carefully. She had had no comment to make with regard to it. Günther had orally informed her that the reply offered the opportunity to discuss all questions which were pending. Mme. Kollontai then said that she would have to transmit our reply to Moscow. But the following day she again called on Günther in a very nervous state, which was unusual with her. She wanted to put it on record that the fact she had accepted a copy of the Finnish reply did not by any means signify that she approved its content, but merely that she would transmit it to Moscow for information. She then returned once more to the Hanko Cape question, making use of the familiar Gibraltar analogy of which Stalin and Molotov had frequently availed themselves during the Moscow negotiations. Günther gave as his own opinion the view that cession of Hanko Cape would be unthinkable for Finland, for reasons of internal politics if for no other, and all the more so if considerations of foreign policy were to be taken into account. He added, however, that he believed the Finns would perhaps be prepared to discuss other questions of similar character if only the necessary groundwork and trust were to be created.

These conversations had shown that Mme. Kollontai had said and promised more than the Soviet government was prepared to approve, that the feeble contact with Moscow which had been established was threatening to break down, and that on this account the enterprise might founder. For this reason Erkko thought it necessary for me to come to Stockholm, where it would be possible to arrange a meeting between me and Mme. Kollontai. This would afford opportunity to discuss our affairs in greater detail and more freely than we could through the services of the Swedish Foreign Minister as intermediary.

In his letter Erkko went on to say that Günther had told him that the Prince of Wied, the German Minister in Stockholm, had been fishing for information about a Finnish group which had come to Stockholm in order to appeal for Sweden's entrance into the war on Finland's side. The information the Minister had secured had, however, been so faulty that it had been easy for Günther to characterize it as quite without foundation. At the same time the German military representative, Gutmann, had declared that if Western forces came to help Finland, Germany would not tolerate it and would proceed to confront its enemies wherever they might be. On the basis of these assertions people in Sweden had begun to believe that Germany was planning to intervene in the Finnish war, which would be most disturbing to Finland's own plans. This intervention, it was supposed, would take place by Germany's taking over southwest Finland, leaving the remainder of Finland as a Soviet sphere of interest. These rumors reminded one greatly of the reports which had earlier been current regarding the content of the Treaty of August 1939 between the Soviet Union and Germany, insofar as it affected Finland.

Erkko's idea with respect to my going to Stockholm was supported on the same day also by Mrs. Wuolijoki, who, referring to the reply we had sent on February 3, telephoned us in the following guarded terms:

"The play has been under scrutiny, and the examiner concerned has refused to pass it. The first point of the play would have to be according to specifications. In that event old hopes might be realized."

I understood this in the sense that Mme. Kollontai had not forwarded our reply but was pressing us to yield Hanko in addition to our other concessions. If we fell in with this, Finland might receive in compensation parts of Soviet Karelia.

Nevertheless I asked for certainty's sake whether the reply had been forwarded.

Mrs. Wuolijoki said that "it has been examined and certain changes have been suggested." She then asked: "Are you quite tied down? Couldn't you come to the dress rehearsal here? My colleague [Erkko] hopes you can."

Tanner: It is not impossible. I'll try to think it over.

Mrs. Wuolijoki: I am going to meet the examiner [Mme. Kollontai], and I shall ask her opinion and phone again during the evening.

At 9:00 P.M. I received another call from Mrs. Wuolijoki. This time she said that Mme. Kollontai sent me cordial greetings and considered my coming important.

To make sure, I asked once more whether the play had been forwarded. She replied vaguely, "The business has been reported and kept in hand." Apparently only a report had been sent to Moscow, but the text had failed to be transmitted.

As it appeared that a face-to-face conversation with the representative of the Soviet Union in Stockholm might be of service to our case and as Mme. Kollontai was looking forward to one, we decided, after consulting with Ryti, that I should make the trip. At the same time we agreed on the basis of what I was to say. In the event that purely formal alterations in the reply we had sent were desired, I was authorized to assent to them. On the other hand, no authority was granted for making changes of substance. An opportunity to meet Mme. Kollontai and, it might be hoped, to obtain a direct explanation from her was regarded as important.

PROCUREMENT OF MATÉRIEL AND MANPOWER

The wartime activity of the Foreign Ministry deviated in many respects from the norm. To say nothing of external characteristics, such as the fact that neither the Minister nor the officers were troubled with official lunches or dinners—I attended only one such—the internal activities, too, had changed. No new legations were opened, no trade or other conventions were drafted, nor was there deliberation about the bestowal of decorations upon meritorious foreigners. All activity was concentrated exclusively on matters which in one fashion or another were related to the war. If one leaves aside the endeavors to bring about a peace, regarding which the officers of the Ministry had no knowledge, it was the satisfaction of the army requirements which perhaps occasioned most labor. Matters of this sort were, of course, worked out in other quarters as well—at headquarters, in the general staff, etc.—but the Foreign Ministry came to be entrusted with the conduct of the intermediary duties which they involved. It was not possible to do much about this by correspondence, as the mails were slow. As a result, the quantity of telegraphic communications swelled enormously. Matters relating to munitions, volunteers, aid, foreign loans, and other such subjects were dealt with by telegraph. It was particularly the messages relating to the procurement of munitions which were responsible for the growth of the telegraphic traffic. I made no endeavor to delve into this branch of our activities, since it was a field entirely alien to me. I sent all the exchanges of telegrams on this subject directly to Prime Minister Ryti, who seemed to be acquainted in detail with both our supplies and our needs.

I have not the remotest idea how large an amount of arms was eventually brought to Finland. As this matter may, however, be of interest to the reader, I may remark on the quantities which the most important sources—France, England, and Sweden—subsequently declared that they had sent us.

In his reply to an interpellation Premier Daladier of France asserted in a session of the Chamber of Deputies on March 12 that France was foremost among those countries which had shipped arms to Finland. From the beginning of December to the day on which he spoke, France had sent, according to his statement, 145 airplanes, 496 cannon, 5,000 machine guns, 400,000 rifles, and 20,000,000 rounds of small arms ammunition.

Prime Minister Chamberlain of Great Britain informed Parliament on March 19 concerning the British shipments: Airplanes of various descriptions promised, 152; sent, 101. Cannon of various sorts promised, 223; sent, 114. Shells promised, 297,200; sent, 185,000. Vickers guns promised and sent, 100. Gas shells promised and sent, 50,000. Aerial bombs promised, 20,700; sent, 15,700. Antitank guns promised and sent, 200. In addition, an abundance of clothing and other supplies, such as knapsacks, tents, etc., had been sent.

Sweden was especially important to us as a source of munitions, since as our closest neighbor it was capable and desirous of assisting us quickly. An official announcement on March 19 indicated that Sweden had sent us 90,000 rifles, 2,000,000 rounds of ammunition, 80 antitank guns, and 250 other cannon, among these 100 antiaircraft guns, of which at the beginning of the war Finland itself had had only four.

These are official reports furnished by the countries concerned. To what extent these shipments reached their destination is a matter of which I am uninformed. In any event, these figures show that many a country had a marked desire to furnish assistance to our country in the hour of its emergency. Without this aid the war could by no means have been fought. It is true that these shipments later had to be paid for.

But war is not fought with arms alone; there must also be men to use them. As a small country, Finland was not able even at the start to arm a force sufficient to face the inexhaustible hordes of the aggressor. And the longer the war went on, the more sensible this lack became. For this reason it was readily understandable that we were eager to accept volunteers from other countries. They were offered in abundance, too, from various quarters, but their arrival here was difficult to arrange. There was a good deal of groping and fumbling in this business. At the end of December there were sent to all the missions of our country abroad the instructions of headquarters regarding the registry of volunteers. They were advised that we could accept only Scandinavians, Britishers, Frenchmen, Italians, Hungarians, Spaniards, Poles, and Americans. These were required to be trained men and to come in organized groups under their own officers and with their own supplies and arms. Exceptions to these rules were to be at the discretion of the Commander-in-Chief, who would also decide upon the acceptance of specialists. Russians and Germans were not to be registered.

As it proved impossible to secure any volunteers at all on the basis of these instructions, it was subsequently necessary to alter them. Around the middle of January the earlier instructions were rescinded and we announced that we would accept individual and untrained volunteers. By then, however, time had already become short.

The question of volunteers gave us work to do during the entire period of the war. Recruitment offices for volunteers were set up in many countries. Sweden was one of the first which undertook to try helping Finland in this respect as in others. During the initial phase of the war there was set up in that country the office for the organization of aid to Finland, which went by the name of Finlands Kommittén. Its chairman was Professor Andreas Lindbom. The office took over, among its other duties, the volunteer question, and Major Helge Malmberg stood at the head of this activity. The chief of the military division was Lieutenant Colonel Viking Tamm; of the administrative division, the bank director E. von Stedingk, with Nils Palme as his principal assistant. This Finlands Kommittén in the last days of December, 1939, announced its dispositions with respect to volunteers. Volunteers were promised that they would be furnished with all supplies and arms free of charge. All questions having to do with pay, insurance, and the like were also settled; for this purpose funds collected in Sweden were used. The Swedish volunteers were to be under the command of the Swedish Lieutenant General Ernst Linder. Despite these sound plans the recruitment of volunteers, for which a number of offices had been established, got under way slowly. As a result, Finland approached the Swedish government on several occasions, expressing its hopes that ready-trained volunteer formations might be sent here.

In other places, too, work was done toward sending volunteers to Finland. At a comparatively early stage the British government gave special permission for the departure of volunteers to Finland. In Hungary a group of volunteers numbering in the hundreds was gathered, but its arrival was delayed because Germany prohibited their transit across its territory. There were also abundant offers from Poland, Austria, and Italy; the Finnish-Americans went to work vigorously, and many of them did succeed in reaching the front in the course of the last phase of the war. Of those who set out from other places, not many arrived at their destination before the war was over. The final result was thus comparatively meager when compared to the great planning activity and exchange of cables which it had occasioned.

While we are on the subject of personnel, it will be advisable to touch upon certain domestic questions which relate to the attitude of labor toward the Civic Guard. Around New Year's Day there were discussions about the conclusion of some sort of agreement on reciprocal relationships between labor and the Civic Guard. On the Social Democratic side the attitude toward the Civic Guard had since the civil war of 1918 been one of aversion; from time to time the dispersal of the organization had even been demanded in the Diet. But during the period of the war which was now under way both those who were associated with the Civic Guard and those who were outside of it had fought at the fronts shoulder to shoulder as good comrades, and this had given rise to the idea of burying the old disagreement. I had heard that discussions of this character were under way, but I had no precise idea of what was afoot until one day in February there came to my office a group of people, among whom I recall the commander of the Civic

Guard, General Lauri Malmberg; Mr. J. W. Keto; and the secretary general of the Social Democratic Party, Aleksi Aaltonen. They came as a result of the discussions to date in order to suggest that an agreement should be made in which the Social Democratic Party would declare that workers were free to join the Civic Guard; the Guard's leadership would in turn make it plain to its members that members of the Social Democratic Party were to be accepted upon their making application and that they were to be treated as equal partners in the organization.

It was Keto in particular who spoke on behalf of the proposal; he had been eager for the project and appears to have been its real father. My attitude toward the suggestion was fairly cool; but since I was assured that substantial opinion was back of it, I did not feel I could oppose it. The agreement was in fact drawn up, and it was officially signed on February 15. It lasted, however, only over the war period, and even during that time it does not seem to have met with particular favor on either side. Subsequently it was bitterly criticized by the more extreme wing of the Social Democratic Party and was consigned to oblivion.

Not only major matters occupied the day-to-day activities of the Foreign Ministry. There also were many other sorts of business which set their stamp upon its wartime activity.

A great number of suggestions were made to us from abroad with the intent to help us carry out properly our difficult task. Peace hints came in from various quarters, but when they had been studied with care they proved to be for the most part more inspired by good will than founded in actuality. Some of the IKL people insistently demanded that they be sent to discuss Finland's case with Hitler, "since what the government says carries no weight in that quarter." The government was not of the opinion that this would be productive of any advantage, as the trip later made by P. E. Svinhufvud to Berlin was in fact to demonstrate. Interests abroad which were opposed to Communism would have been glad to see Finland let itself be harnessed in the service of propaganda directed against the Soviet system and financed by foreigners. To this group of proposals belonged, among others, the imaginative suggestion that we should invite Trotsky to Finland and furnish him with a small strip of territory in the neighborhood of Repola, for instance, to serve as a domicile for a provisional government of Russia. Trotsky and Kerensky were to have been the heads of this government. The plan was presumably intended as a sort of riposte to the Kuusinen government at Terijoki. Back of these ideas there were usually White

Russians who had been forced to flee their country and who expected that the Finnish War would be the beginning of the end of Soviet rule. Coudenhove-Kalergi, the father of the well-known Pan-Europe idea, proposed that Finland, invoking the anti-Communist treaty between Japan, Italy, and Spain, should ask those countries to supply it with military aid. A stroke of genius was the device someone hit upon whereby Finland was to secure sorely needed replenishment for its fund of cash. Captured enemy guns were to be struck into commemorative medals which were then to be sold abroad at high prices. One could go on listing without end the well-meaning suggestions of this sort which we received.

While we are on the subject of replenishment of our cash funds, it is well to mention the fact that our Minister in Washington, Hjalmar J. Procopé, was, even before the war began, assigned the task of requesting from the United States a loan of sixty million dollars. The subject was studied with the thoroughness characteristic of the United States, with the result that it was only in the last days of February that the Congress reached a decision on the basis of which Finland got a credit of thirty million dollars.

A great number of permissions to go abroad were sought. Many businessmen offered to busy themselves in forwarding the matter of shipments to be procured from abroad, as has been mentioned above. A few solicited permission to travel in order to make their way to other countries where conditions were more peaceful. Certain persons were sent out to make Finland's cause known in foreign lands, primarily in our neighbor countries. Many Finns went to Sweden to deliver speeches, and similarly to Norway and Denmark. As a matter of special interest one may record the fact that Santeri Jakobsson, mayor of the borough of Lauritsala, offered to go to Sweden to arouse the sympathy of the Jewish world on behalf of Finland. This he was able to accomplish through the assistance of the world-famous Chief Rabbi Marcus Ehrenpreis. The trip cost Jakobsson his official position in Lauritsala. August Kuusisto, a member of the Diet, went all the way to the United States to arouse the Finnish colony on behalf of Finland. He traveled for months about the Finnish centers there, delivering hundreds of speeches, and succeeded in getting the Finns in that country to take a very favorable attitude toward activity on behalf of their old homeland. This mission bore much fruit in time.

FOREIGN GUESTS

Being the center of the world's attention during these months of war, we came to receive an abundance of visitors from abroad. Part of these came to acquaint themselves with the situation in order that upon returning to their own countries they might bring their influence to bear in favor of Finland. Others seemed to have come out of curiosity, and these were of course less welcome. We were warned in advance against a number of applicants, the observation being made that they were simply coming for espionage purposes.

The swarm of journalists was overwhelming. The principal news bureaus of the world kept their representatives in Finland during the whole war, and in addition many large papers had their resident correspondents here. Most of them made their headquarters in the Hotel Kämp, and thus it came about that this most familiar of Helsinki hotels constantly resembled a beehive, where news was exchanged and also manufactured. The foreign journalists were not entirely satisfied with the way they were treated here. Liaison men were provided for them by the Foreign Ministry and by the State News Center, which had been established early in December; it was the task of the liaison men to keep the journalists up to date. This was done principally through the aid of the front communiqués from headquarters supplemented by additional news. The news office was for the most part under the charge of Urho Toivola, chief of the press division, but of course he had a number of assistants. Still the journalists and photographers wanted to get to the front, but in this respect headquarters was adamant. Reaching it meant surmounting many hurdles, and very few indeed were favored with an opportunity to leave for the front. "This is no movie, this is a war," the Commander-in-Chief remarked dryly when he was pressed on this matter. It was indeed a pity that it was impossible to arrange more frequent trips to the front for journalists and photographers. There they would have secured a great amount of worth-while news material which would have had an effect abroad. During the final phase of the war, when the foreign press was already printing news on the coming peace, and even on its terms, dissatisfaction among the journalists was general, since it was not considered possible to give them information on the progress of the peace negotiations.

Many private persons from abroad visited us, sometimes forming whole delegations. I had no particular contact with them, save with those who had been sent by the labor parties of other countries. The first such group arrived as early as the second week of the war—I think around December 10. The Swedish Landsorganisation (the central trade union confederation) had sent a couple of its agents here to make observations on conditions in our country. They traveled about a little and returned to their own land to report on what they had seen.

Welcome guests were the labor delegations of Sweden and Norway,

six persons in all, who arrived here on January 11. The group consisted
of the chairman of the Swedish trade union confederation, August Lindberg; the secretary of the same organization, Fritiof Thunborg; and the
manager of the information service of the Social Democratic Party,
Gunnar Lundberg. For Norway there were the well-known editor-in-
chief of *Arbeiderbladet,* Martin Tranmael; the vice-chairman of the
Labor Party, Einar Gerhardsen (later Prime Minister); and the treas-
urer of the trade union confederation, J. B. Aase. After making a
general survey of the situation in the capital they toured the front for
several days.

When the delegation had returned to Helsinki on January 16, the
Social Democratic Party board invited its members to a coffee party;
also present on that occasion were the representatives in the capital of
the Scandinavian Labor press, the Socialist ministers of the government,
and the members of the party board. When I welcomed the guests to
Finland, I remarked that we hoped that they, who had seen how matters
stood in our country at the moment, would have good advice to give us.
Lindberg and Tranmael spoke in reply. The former said that their
advice would clearly be superfluous, since without it we seemed to be
doing very well. They had received only favorable impressions on their
trip, and they were amazed at the calm resolution of the Finnish people.
Tranmael's talk breathed a mighty hope for the future of our country.
Finally, Eero Vuori thanked the guests and hoped that they would be
able to exert their influence in their homelands for the benefit of our
country.

Of more significance was the visit of British Labour representatives
a little later, a matter to which passing reference has already been made
once or twice. Aleksi Aaltonen, secretary general of the party, and
Eero Vuori, chairman of the Central Confederation of Trade Unions,
had at the beginning of January sent to Clement Attlee a cable in which
they expressed the hope that persons would be sent from Great Britain
to Finland in order to study the situation on the spot. At the headquarters of the Labour Party it was at once decided that the invitation should
be accepted, with the result that a four-man Labour delegation arrived
in Finland. They were Sir Walter Citrine, secretary general of the Trade
Union Congress, as representative of the trade union movement; Philip
Noel-Baker, M.P. (later a minister in Attlee's Cabinet), as representative
of the Labour Party; John Downie of Scotland, representing the cooperative movement; and Ernest A. Bell, as their secretary. Of these I had
known Downie for many years back, having frequently met him at international meetings of the cooperative movement.

This delegation came to Finland via Sweden, where they were subjected to advance interviews and were particularly questioned as to whether England intended to help Finland. In Turku and Tammisaari the members had opportunity to see the damage the Russian bombers had inflicted upon the working-class residential districts and upon civilian housing in general. The guests reached Helsinki on January 25, remaining there a couple of days and then continuing to the front.

While they were in Helsinki the guests met the members of the Cabinet on several occasions. They were persons of position, and they had come to our country at an important moment. We had both a lunch and a dinner with them. On the latter occasion a considerable company was present, including the Prime Minister and other members of the government. At this gathering I addressed the guests, describing how Finland came to be in the war and our need for assistance. Sir Walter spoke in answer, remarking that little Finland had shown that it intended to defend its rights. The task of the British labor movement was to try to find means to back this struggle. Although he could not speak officially in England's name, he assured us that official England felt the same sympathy toward Finland as the labor organizations of the country did and that England would do everything within its power under present conditions to help Finland. Noel-Baker also spoke, expressing admiration for Finnish equanimity and coolness.

It chanced that just at this time there was in Helsinki the Swiss Colonel Henri Valloton, who had earlier been the Speaker of the Swiss Parliament. He had also been invited to the dinner, and he brought us the greetings of Switzerland's former President Motta and of the Swiss army. He referred in his speech to the similarity of the destinies of Finland and Switzerland, emphasizing the will of his country to defend its independence.

Citrine appeared to be an intense jotter down of memoranda. He filled his notebook every evening before going to bed. But in this way as soon as he got home he had a travel book all ready. It was published as early as February, under the title *My Finnish Diary,* and in it he conscientiously recorded day by day his experiences and observations, including workers' living conditions and wages. I cannot resist transcribing from it one story which involves me.

While we were having lunch at a hotel, according to his book, somebody had teased me by saying the Russians called me a White Guardist. From there the story went on with some other Finn saying to Noel-Baker, "Now you are 'Comrade' Tanner's guest, but this evening [at the official dinner] you will be the guest of the 'White' Foreign Minister Tanner." This jest had made the guests laugh, wherefore I replied by saying, "Not white, but blue-and-white!" I do not remember this exchange myself, but evidently I had hit on the right reply for the occasion; since at that time "blue-and-white" (the colors of our flag) was certainly what we all were.

Our British guests and Colonel Valloton continued on to the front with Eero Vuori and Aleksi Aaltonen as their guides. They had an opportunity to see the game of war close at hand. Marshal Mannerheim also received them.

While on the subject of books I should remark that Colonel Valloton also published a book on his trip under the title *Finlande 1940: Ce que j'ai vu et entendu*. Many journalists published books on the Finnish war and on their observations here. A number of these were well illustrated. Some of the authors sent copies of their books to me. The outstanding Danish journalist Peter de Hemmer Gudme even published two books, the first in December, 1939, *Finland, Eastern Rampart of the North*, and the second in 1940, *Finland's People in Battle*. All the books I have mentioned were written in a spirit exceptionally sympathetic toward us.

But there were also books of another sort. In January, 1940, D. N. Pritt, a member of the British Parliament at that time, published a book most unfriendly to us, under the title *Must the War Spread?* In this book he fully accepted the Russian thesis and opposed England's intervening in our war. Pritt later became a member of the Communist Party. Another book on the Finnish War, maliciously false, saw the light of day in 1942, also in England. It was concocted by W. P. and Zelda Coates, evidently a man-and-wife team. The book's title was *The Soviet-Finnish Campaign*. In every respect it took the Soviet side, alleging that during the whole war the Finnish headquarters gave out false news. In the view of the writers these releases were taken at face value only because correspondents were not allowed to go to the front. Does one suppose foreign correspondents were allowed at the front on the Russian side?

As evidence of the way in which the last-named book looked upon Finnish matters, I shall quote a small sample which deals with the Terijoki government:

As a matter of fact the relations of the Soviet Government with the Terijoki Government illustrated strikingly the Soviet respect for the independence of Finland. No doubt when the Terijoki Government was formed it was thought or hoped that it might receive sufficiently wide popular support among the Finnish people to overthrow the bourgeois Government of that time and the military and Fascist cliques which to a large extent were the real rulers of Finland. This did not eventuate—whether because the Schutz Corps (protective guards) and

Fascists were too strong or because the masses of the Finnish people were not yet prepared for a wholehearted Socialist Government is immaterial to the argument—but the fact was that the Terijoki Government did not gain power over the whole of Finland.

Any Imperialist Power faced with this position and having Finland at her mercy as the Soviets then had, would undoubtedly have simply ridden roughshod over the bourgeois Central Finnish Government and forced upon the country the Government which she had recognised a few months previously. . . .

The Soviet Government acted otherwise, it declared that the form of Government in Finland was the affair of the Finns themselves and after consultation between the Soviet and Terijoki Governments the latter agreed to dissolve itself.

CHAPTER 8

THE STOCKHOLM ROAD

From the foregoing excursions I return to my proposed journey to Stockholm.

As we had agreed, I set out on February 4 at 1:00 P.M. for Stockholm. I departed from Helsinki by car, accompanied by two policemen; in the car were snowsuits and a machine gun for air attacks. At Salo there was an air raid warning, and a couple of houses were afire. We did not stop, even though the wardens ordered us to, but drove straight on for Turku. All day Turku had been under alert for air raids. About thirty bombers had flown over the city and dropped bombs; fresh fires were still to be seen in various parts of the city. As we drove, we saw the damage and destruction caused to city and harbor by earlier raids. The bombings had left considerable traces, but not so much as was related in Helsinki. We went to the Turku airport about 4:00 P.M. and were told that the plane would leave Stockholm at 5:00 P.M., so that its return from Turku to Stockholm could take place only about 7:00. As we waited, the Turku people told us that this had been their thirty-fifth air raid.

When we took off, the field was lighted up for only a minute or two, in order that the plane might stay on the runway.

The flight to Stockholm took place in complete darkness, as all the plane's lights were extinguished. In a way it was a unique experience, since we could not see even the people inside the plane, let alone any view. The flight was without incident, and we reached Stockholm on schedule. The lights of Stockholm greeted us from afar, and the descent was as though one were coming into an altogether different world.

Erkko was at the airport to meet me. He had reserved a room for me at the quiet Plaza Hotel, where I established myself incognito. That very evening I had a talk with Erkko and Mrs. Wuolijoki in my hotel room, going over our business. Mrs. Wuolijoki told us at length about her conversations with Mme. Kollontai, who was of the opinion that our reply had not been drawn up in satisfactory form and so had been impossible to use as a basis for discussions. Our proposal had not included the base at the mouth of the Gulf of Finland. Consequently,

Mme. Kollontai had sent it to Moscow merely as a matter of information. Since the business was thus stalled, Mme. Kollontai had considered it important that I should come to Stockholm to deal with her. This was what had given rise to Mrs. Wuolijoki's telephone call to Helsinki. On receiving my favorable answer, she had arranged with Mme. Kollontai for the meeting and informed me of it. On Sunday it had become apparent from what Mme. Kollontai said that she had received Moscow's permission to meet me, although originally she had made arrangements for the meeting on her own initiative.

Mrs. Wuolijoki spoke warmly in advocacy of peace and recommended concessions on the base question. She deemed that Stalin would be prepared to make great sacrifices in order to have his way there.

We finally agreed that the next morning at ten I should meet Minister Günther, and only thereafter at eleven Mme. Kollontai at Mrs. Wuolijoki's room in the Grand Hotel. Accordingly, on the morning of February 5, I went to the old Crown Prince Palace. Günther, whom I had not met before, was friendly and received me with good cheer. I said that I had wanted to meet my Swedish opposite number, and at the same time I thought it only correct to inform him that I was meeting the Soviet representative on the soil of his country. He had no objection to this.

We spoke of the possibilities for peace. He realized that Hanko Cape was a difficult problem for both sides.

I asked him a few questions:

Tanner: Does Sweden hope we will make peace?

Günther: Sweden warmly hopes so. Why, we are almost parties to the business.

Tanner: If conversations regarding peace do occur and if the question of a base at the mouth of the Finnish Gulf proves important, will Sweden then have any misgivings if a base should be handed over?

Günther: We do not think so.

Tanner: If negotiations take place, is it your hope that this could be with Sweden as mediator?

Günther: We are prepared to help in any fashion. If Sweden's mediation is desired, that is agreeable to us.

Tanner: I should think it would be easier for Sweden to stay out of it and thus have no responsibility for the consequences.

Günther: That would suit Sweden very well too.

I told Günther about the Murmansk campaign France was planning and about its design to send an auxiliary force to Finland, and I remarked that presumably this very day, February 5, the Supreme Council of the Western powers would decide the matter. Finland would then come to a difficult crossroads, as it would have three courses before it, in this order of preference:

1. To make peace;

2. In the event of continued war, to receive aid from our neighbors in the North, thus keeping the war a northern one;

3. In case of insufficient aid from the Scandinavian countries, to secure aid from the Western powers—a dangerous course which would draw us into the major war.

Günther had not heard of the French Premier's plan and was to a degree surprised at the news. He considered the offer of the Western powers dangerous not only to Finland but to Sweden and all Scandinavia. For this reason he agreed with my order of listing the possibilities. He inquired as to my ideas on the amount of the aid required from Sweden and as to how soon it would be needed.

I said the military command calculated it would need some thirty thousand fresh regular troops, which should be made up of volunteers already organized into units, as the enrollment of volunteers to date seemed to be taking a long time. A decision on this should be reached in the next few days and the force must be at its destination within four to six weeks.

Günther promised to take up the matter in the Cabinet at once.

He further went on to speak of the statements of the German Ambassador (the Prince of Wied) and the German military attaché, Gutmann, in the same terms as Erkko had reported in his letter, to the effect that Germany would regard it as a *casus belli* if Sweden were to help Finland on a major scale. For this reason Sweden feared it would be crushed between the warring great powers. He asked me to give him further information on the progress of Premier Daladier's plans and on the decisions of the Supreme Council after I had received more precise data regarding them.

We also discussed Sweden's taking part in the fortification of the Aaland Islands. Günther felt that the matter should be allowed to rest for the time being, at least until the Finnish war was settled. Fortifying the Aaland Islands might well make the Soviet Union nervous and cause it to intervene.

Finally Günther asked whether I was acquainted in detail with the content of the treaty concluded in August, 1939, between the Soviet Union and Germany, insofar as it affected Finland. When I replied that I was not, he said he knew something about it. The Swedish Consul General in Paris, Nordling, who was an old friend of Daladier's, had had a chance to read a copy of the treaty while visiting him. Through the treaty Germany had granted the Soviet Union the right to proceed in the Baltic countries just as it later had done. As for Finland, Germany had given the Soviet Union a free hand with respect to land areas as far west as Viipuri and also the right to acquire a part of Petsamo. If the Soviet Union could not obtain possession of these areas through peaceful arrangements, it was entitled under the treaty to resort to force. If in this way the Soviet Union should come to take from Finland areas greater than had been contemplated, Germany, in order to preserve the equilibrium in the Baltic area, would be entitled to take some part of southwest Finland (the Aaland Islands?). Nevertheless, Günther was not in a position to certify that the paper in Daladier's possession had been accurate.

After an hour's conversation I thanked him and left.

The copy of the treaty in Premier Daladier's possession cannot have been accurate. As may be seen in the collection of German documents published in the United States after the war, Germany and the Soviet Union seem to have made, in connection with their nonaggression treaty of August 23, 1939, a secret agreement regarding which a "confidential protocol" was made. Therein appears the following:

The plenipotentiaries signing the nonaggression treaty between Germany and the Soviet Union considered in a strictly confidential conversation the question of the boundary between the spheres of interest of both parties in Eastern Europe. This conversation led to the following conclusions:

1. In the event that territorial and political reorganization takes place in areas pertaining to the Baltic states (Finland, Estonia, Latvia, and Lithuania), the northern boundary of Lithuania shall constitute the line of demarcation between the spheres of interest of Germany and the Soviet Union. . . .

MADAME KOLLONTAI

At eleven o'clock I went to Mrs. Wuolijoki's room in the Grand Hotel. As I might have been recognized coming in by the main entrance to the hotel, I entered by a back way, without meeting anyone on the stairs or in the corridors. Present in the room already were Mrs. Wuolijoki, who left at once, and Mme. Kollontai. Mme. Kollontai, earlier a celebrated beauty whom I had seen for the first time at an international Socialist congress held in 1910 and later during the revolutionary disturbances of 1917 in Finland, was now a woman of sixty-eight. She had suffered a slight stroke, for which reason she moved with a little difficulty. Her demeanor as we met was very courteous, almost cordial. Born in Finland, she had a special interest in Finnish affairs, and she said she grieved for Finland. She said that for the Soviet Union the war had not yet really begun, and that as spring progressed the attacks and the destruction would increase, as bombs would be used of as much as a ton.

She said that Foreign Minister Günther had inquired previously whether Sweden could mediate between Finland and the Soviet Union, but at that time she had not believed it would be possible, so the matter had been dropped. On January 25 Günther had again offered mediation. Prior to that date the initial conversations in Stockholm had already taken place, and Yartsev had returned to Moscow. On the basis of Günther's offer, Mme. Kollontai had sent a telegram to Moscow, to which she had received a reply on January 29, the same day the information had also been sent to the Finnish government. Finland's answer had been sent to Moscow, but merely as a matter of information. Mme. Kollontai had added as her own comment the remark that the reply would seem to be unsatisfactory as a basis for conversations. Shortly thereafter an answer had come from Moscow, the sense of which was that the Finnish response did not afford grounds for discussion. For this reason she had wished to meet me.

Mme. Kollontai said she understood very well what Hanko Cape meant; she judged it to be the crux of the whole discussion. I told her what we could concede to the Soviet Union without misgivings. I was inclined to think we could reach agreement regarding the line to be drawn on the Isthmus and suggested the area southeast of the Lipola-Seivästö line. With regard to Hanko Cape, however, opinion in Finland was so firm that I did not believe it could be surrendered.

Mme. Kollontai said the Moscow government well understood that Paasikivi and I had sought peace in the negotiations during the autumn, but that the Finnish government and public opinion in the country had been unable to go so far as the Soviet Union required. Now that the war had started, all means must be used to end it. It might in fact go on for years. The difficulty on both sides was the question of face. Could not Finland find some solution, some compromise, with respect to Hanko Cape? I presented the idea of neutralizing the Gulf of Finland, earlier the subject of discussion, which we had planned to offer in place of Hanko Cape. This plan Mme. Kollontai did not seem to grasp, nor did she think it would carry the matter forward.

I proposed we should be frank and speak our own thoughts rather than merely the official attitudes of our governments. I was prepared to suggest the cession of one island at the mouth of the Gulf of Finland, and I was ready to work in favor of the recommendation. In that event it would be necessary to receive a major land area as compensation in order to satisfy the Finnish people. The cession of the Repola and Porajärvi areas to Finland might be a satisfactory compensation.

proposed she wire Stalin about this as being my personal suggestion.

Mme. Kollontai seized upon this idea with alacrity. For safety's sake I repeated the suggestion twice and wrote down for her the names Repola and Porajärvi. She asked me whether we could cede the island in such a location as would correspond to the original need. I said I had in mind an island which would fill the requirements laid down, since it was opposite Paldiski on the Estonian shore.

Mme. Kollontai promised she would cable my suggestion to Moscow.

We went on to talk about the technical side of the negotiations to be initiated. I said we were prepared to go to Moscow, but that we had assumed the Soviet Union wanted to keep the negotiations secret. Tallinn was too small a spot for negotiations of such a character. Perhaps Stockholm would be more suitable. In that case I thought it would be best to negotiate directly, without Swedish mediation.

This caused Mme. Kollontai to ask whether I could tell her if we had any agreement with the Swedish government. Had Sweden registered a protest against the cession of Hanko Cape?

I assured her that Finland had acted alone. Neither Sweden nor the Western powers had advised us, and no ties of state bound us. We were free to decide the matter for ourselves. This seemed to be a surprise to her.

I urged her to deliver her reply through Mrs. Wuolijoki, who would communicate it to me through Erkko. This suited her, though she had thought to pass the information on through Günther. She asked whether Günther would be aware of this meeting. I told her I had visited him just before I came to see her, since it would have been discourteous to meet the representative of a foreign country without his knowledge. Mme. Kollontai was satisfied that this should be so. When I asked whether Moscow knew of this meeting, she replied that without Moscow's consent she could not have come to meet me. However, the other members of the Legation staff did not know of our contact. The code clerk also knew of the meeting, but he could be relied on to keep it secret.

I thanked her for her friendly offer of assistance and said good-bye. The meeting had lasted an hour.

As I left, Mrs. Wuolijoki, who had stepped out by agreement for an hour, was coming down the corridor toward me. We agreed that she should talk to Mme. Kollontai a little longer, trying to form impressions, and that she should then come to see me.

Mrs. Wuolijoki came to my hotel at 12:30 and said that Mme. Kollontai had left at once to telegraph the outcome of the discussion. Mme. Kollontai had hoped that I would remain the following day in Stockholm in order to await the reply from Moscow. It might even come that same day.

I promised to stay if Prime Minister Ryti had no urgent news. I telephoned from the Legation to Helsinki and reported to him the conversations I had had. We agreed that I should stay in Stockholm another day.

The next day, February 6, Mrs. Wuolijoki arranged a further meeting with Mme. Kollontai at the same place at 12:30. Mme. Kollontai's look was tragic, and she announced that she did not have good news. That morning she had received a telegram which read briefly (her own words, in Swedish): "Sorry; the proposal does not afford sufficient basis for negotiations." She deplored the result but was unable to do anything about it. She felt, however, that the tone of the cable was friendly, and she urged that this slender thread not be broken. She asked what island I had had in mind in my offer. Perhaps with that as a point of departure we could continue. I told her that at this stage I could not reveal the name of the island, since it was necessary first to ascertain in principle whether negotiations could start. I asked whether she knew what Moscow required. She replied that she did not, but she presumed that Hanko Cape was, as before, the most important demand. In the reply there had been nothing about the possible cession of Repola and Porajärvi as compensation.

Finally, I had to say that I could make no other proposal and that even what I had told her had been on my own responsibility. I then dictated to her a reply which I asked her to telegraph to Moscow, and for precision's sake I wrote it down for her in the following words in Swedish: "Regret reply. Cannot make new proposals. Should appreciate learning Moscow's proposal."

Now that we had reached the conclusion that this time we could do no more, I took my leave.

At 3:00 P.M. Mrs. Wuolijoki and Erkko came to see me in my hotel. We agreed that Mrs. Wuolijoki should stay on in Stockholm to see whether any further information on the matter would come up. If a new phase did not open up, she might depart. Thereafter the exchange of information might take place through the intermediary of Foreign Minister Günther.

I urged Erkko to call on Günther the following day and tell him that the business did not seem to be prospering in Moscow. At the same time, making reference to the plans of France, he was to accelerate the sending of Swedish auxiliary forces.

At 4:00 P.M. I left Stockholm by plane. From Turku I came to Helsinki by automobile.

COMPETING PLANS

Upon my return home there were on my office desk a great number of cables, from which it became plain that in other quarters things had been developing fast. The most important was one from Minister Holma in Paris, which reported that the Supreme Council of the Western powers had held, on February 5, the meeting with regard to which we were already informed. There it had decided unanimously to send troops to Finland. The Western powers had also decided to make representations in Stockholm and Oslo in order to assure the right of transit for them. On the same occasion there had been further discussion of the Petsamo expedition. But there was a lack of further details regarding these plans, above all regarding the forces which the Western powers proposed to utilize in the expedition.

With this information in hand, the situation had become decidedly more complicated. All three alternatives—the initiation of peace negotiations, the military assistance requested from Sweden, and the aid offered by the Western powers—were being considered, and we had to choose among them now. It was a critical situation, even though it might also be an advantage to be in a position to weigh all three alternatives at the same time. But personally I was not happy over the news. I had done what I could to clear the path for peace, and for this reason I feared that this new offer by the Western powers would influence opinion toward throwing our support in that direction. I was furthermore astonished at Holma's actions in Paris. Without special authority or instructions from Helsinki, he and Colonel Paasonen had zealously tried to secure the assistance of the Western powers, and the fact that matters had reached this stage was clearly, in part, the result of their actions. Helsinki was also to blame, since, although even in earlier reports Holma had indicated that something of this character was afoot, I had deliberately left him without instructions, so that I might not prematurely bind the Cabinet to any plans with which we were unacquainted.

On the same day, February 7, General Walden brought to my attention a letter from Marshal Mannerheim reporting on the visit to headquarters of General Ling of Great Britain and of other military representatives of the Western powers, and on their proposals for the organization of military aid to Finland. The Marshal was not kindly disposed toward the plans of the Western powers for a Petsamo expedition, since in his opinion this would not help us and would be certain to bring Germany in on Russia's side. Walden was highly exasperated by this plan and also by the decision of the Supreme Council, which he now learned of for the first time. He insisted that a cable be sent to Holma at once, calling upon him to report details of the plans of the

Western powers. But I postponed the dispatch of the cable until we should ourselves be clear as to what steps we ought to take.

I had left Stockholm under the impression that the conversations there had come to an end. Yet a couple of days later, on February 8, a cable came in from Erkko in which he said that Molotov had inquired through third parties what island Finland had thought of offering to the Soviet Union. Evidently the Russians were still desirous of continuing the conversations, but only on the condition that their demand for a base at the mouth of the Gulf of Finland be acceded to. Erkko also reported that he was continuing to press in Stockholm for the urgent dispatch to Finland of trained forces, and that on the same day the Swedish Cabinet was to meet and consider the matter.

Paasikivi, who as Minister without portfolio remained at home for the most part and had only rare contact with the other members of the Cabinet, now received a report on the events of recent days. Although up to this point he had firmly advocated working toward an early peace and in this sense had been associated with the preparation of the talks in Stockholm, he now began to vacillate between the several alternatives. He was almost delighted with the possibilities which the aid offered by the Western powers might open up. If with this assistance we could weaken the Soviet Union, it would be a great deed in history. Could such a mighty matter fall to the lot of little Finland? In that case a new frontier against Russia might perhaps run from Lake Ladoga through Lake Onega to the White Sea. But could such a line be lasting? Could Russia ever give up scheming for a road to the Atlantic? Such were the possibilities that occurred to him in the first moments of enthusiasm.

Among the events of the day was a visit by Ryti and Walden to my office in order to discuss our attitude toward this new problem. The result of our consultation was that we should not yet reply to Stockholm on what island to offer. Paris and London were to be asked for further information on the expedition planned by the Western powers, yet without in any way committing ourselves. At the same time we would continue pressing Sweden for military aid. In order to consult on these questions with the military command, Ryti and I would leave on the following day for a visit to headquarters. During our discussion Ryti was decidedly optimistic: if we could only play our cards right and use the offer of assistance from the Western powers in order to bring pressure on both the Soviet Union and Sweden!

I at once sent off to Paris and London the requests for information. Replies were promptly received to the effect that the aid contemplated by the Western powers would be unlimited. They no longer had any thought of approaching Stockholm and Oslo beforehand to ask for permission to march through. This would be done only when everything was ready and it would be possible to present Sweden and Norway with a *fait accompli*.

Thus far the conversations in Stockholm had taken place in great secrecy. I had not dared to say anything about them within the Cabinet. I knew the attitudes of most Cabinet members and I also knew that within the Cabinet it would have been impossible to come to a favorable conclusion on undertaking peace negotiations. Here at home these conversations were known only to Ryti and Paasikivi in addition to myself and, from this stage on, to Walden—in other words, only to persons who aspired to bring about a peace. My Swedish trip had been carried out completely incognito. At this time, however, I thought it appropriate to report the matter to President Kallio as well. On February 8 I visited him in the afternoon at his official residence and reported on the situation at the moment as well as on the conversations which had taken place in Sweden. Kallio was by no means pleased with this news.

In the evening Mrs. Wuolijoki inquired from Stockholm when I could inform Mme. Kollontai of the island to be offered. She said that the Soviet Union required in advance my personal assurance that if the proposal was made it would also be approved. Otherwise nothing could be done. During further discussions it must also be possible to speak of more extensive areas. I promised to give her a reply on February 12 and, in the meantime, to determine whether there was support for my proposal. Mrs. Wuolijoki also said that she was going that evening to see Mme. Kollontai, who continued to foster the further progress of the matter.

The next morning I telephoned Erkko in Stockholm to inform him that I could give an answer to the Soviet inquiry regarding the island by February 12. I also advised him that the decisions made by the Supreme Council in Paris had seriously complicated our plans with respect to the conversations which were to be undertaken in Stockholm. Nothing, however, was yet to be said about these decisions to Günther. Erkko told me that the Swedish Cabinet was then earnestly debating the dispatch of auxiliary forces to Finland. He also had learned through Mme. Kollontai that the Soviet Union continued to insist on the cession of Hanko Cape.

A VISIT TO HEADQUARTERS

On February 10 Prime Minister Ryti and I reached headquarters at Mikkeli, traveling overnight by special train. The Commander-in-Chief with his closest assistants resided at the People's Institute near Otava station. Consequently, we got off there.

Marshal Mannerheim was at the station with his staff to receive us. The whole day, from 9:00 A.M. until 11:00 P.M., was devoted to explanations of the present military position. The chiefs of the various branches reported on the quantity of arms, equipment, ammunition, the number of casualties, etc. Thereafter we discussed our position. The generals were perhaps a little overoptimistic, but they nevertheless called for more men and guns. I set forth my own program for the arrangement of our business, according to which the pursuit of peace should be first in order of preference; the limitation of the war to the Scandinavian area should be second, and, if both of these proved fruitless, only in the last extremity should we place our reliance upon the aid of the Western powers, which would inevitably draw us into the major war. I also reported on the most important recent events in the field of our country's foreign policy.

The subject gave rise to an extensive discussion in which the majority took position in support of this program. It was encouraging to observe that the military command in general favored peace even at a sacrifice.

I then presented for consideration the question of what to offer the Soviet Union in the way of a base at the mouth of the Finnish Gulf, since without the cession of such a base we would clearly make no progress. I suggested, starting from the west, Utö, the Örö islands, or Jussarö. At the same time there was the question of how far back on the Isthmus we might propose that a new line be drawn. Within the Cabinet there had been talk of one approximately through the points Suvanto-Seivästö.

After an intermission the defense council met to consider these questions. By statute this body included, in addition to the chairman, the chief of the armed forces, the chief of the general staff, and the commander-in-chief of the Civic Guard, and, besides these, three generals appointed for one-year terms by the Minister of Defense. During the Winter War period the council was made up as follows: Marshal Mannerheim, chairman; Lieutenant General Hugo Österman, chief of the armed forces; Lieutenant General Lennart Oesch, chief of the general staff; Lieutenant General Lauri Malmberg, commander-in-chief of the Civic Guard; and Major Generals Rudolf Walden and Väinö Valve and Lieutenant General Harald Öhqvist, appointed by the Minister of Defense.

Marshal Mannerheim's résumé of the deliberations was somewhat as follows:

The Finnish army has held out well to date. It has, however, great needs. Above all it needs artillery and a sufficient number of men.

Regarding the choice to be made among the alternatives proposed, the defense council considers that the attainment of peace should have first place, and

Swedish aid second place, though this should be sought with great urgency. Sweden should be asked to supply trained units, as the recruiting of volunteers goes too slowly. In the opinion of the defense council, the inadequately prepared aid of the Western powers should be assigned last place. If an appeal to this alternative is contemplated, there should be discussion between the military commands of Finland and the Western powers regarding its amount and the manner and time of its being carried into actuality; it must furthermore be made ready with great care.

With respect to the peace conditions to be proposed on behalf of Finland, the defense council believes it possible to augment earlier offers, including those with reference to a base at the mouth of the Gulf of Finland. It considers Jussarö as least important to Finland, since maritime traffic would be interrupted with Hanko by the cession of the Örö islands and with Turku by the cession of Utö. On the Isthmus an additional strip of coast between Ino and Seivästö extending ten kilometers inland might be ceded. Suursaari might be ceded in its entirety.

If Finland is to make such considerable additional offers, the Soviet Union for its part must give up its demands upon the Rybachi Peninsula and in compensation for these concessions must give Finland Repola and Porajärvi.

The defense council further hopes that upon the conclusion of the war the government will consolidate the country's defense system. Among other matters, Finnish "Maginot Lines" should be put in good order.

This declaration of the defense council coincided in almost every point with the program I had proposed.

During the course of the discussion it came to light that headquarters had more exact information on the details of the expedition planned by the Western powers than we had in Helsinki. Colonel Paasonen had sent from Paris several letters reporting on these operations. I asked for copies and was promised that they would at once be sent.

Generally speaking, headquarters lived extremely modestly. Lodging and food were very simple. For breakfast, for example, no hot food at all was served.

At. 11:00 P.M. on that same day we returned home by special train.

Back in Helsinki, Ryti and I reported the discussions to the President. The conversation lasted two hours in all. At first, President Kallio was most averse to additional concessions or territorial cessions, but at length we were able to establish that we were of one mind at least with respect to the cession of Jussarö. In other respects as well we ended up at the line proposed by headquarters.

As the foreign press was beginning to spread rumors concerning peace negotiations in progress, I suggested to the President that a statement be issued to refute them. This publication was considered necessary, because rumors of this sort were calculated to subject our conduct of the war to difficulties. The statement was given out in my name and was published in the papers of February 12. It declared that the Cabinet had no knowledge of the peace mediation plans which, according to the information spread abroad by the foreign press, were expected to be advanced on the part of a certain great power. It was pointed out that our army, solely through its own forces and almost exclusively through its own armaments, had for ten weeks successfully waged a defensive struggle against opposing forces many times superior. The statement added the gratuitous boast that, now that aid was on the way in the form both of equipment and of auxiliary forces and was to be delivered from various sources in accordance with the decision of the League of Nations, Finland would continue to be able to ward off all attacks. Consequently, peace terms could not be dictated to it. In conclusion the statement held it possible that the peace rumors had been put out only with the intention of crippling future aid activity abroad.

DIVIDED OPINIONS

Thus far during the war period the foreign affairs committee had dealt for the most part with the possibilities of securing armaments and auxiliary forces, and from time to time with the question of whether we should endeavor, through the intermediary of some foreign state, to get in touch with the Soviet Union with a view to peace. The most recent development of our affairs had not been reported to the committee, since I feared it would reject additional concessions. Now, however, discussions had gone so far in various quarters that it was impossible to keep the foreign affairs committee in the dark any longer. I convened it on February 12. Present were all the members of the committee: Prime Minister Ryti and Ministers Hannula, Niukkanen, Paasikivi, and Söderhjelm, as well as myself. The President of the Republic had also desired to be with us in order to follow the discussion.

Without going into detail as to what had already been done toward peace, I described various theoretical possibilities. As a background for the discussion I reported on the course of events at the front and on the extent of aid received from abroad. Since it seemed impossible to get through the war on our own resources, I said that we must try either to bring it to an end or to have more effective foreign aid. I set forth to the committee the alternatives of (1) making peace, (2) getting assistance from Sweden, and (3) getting the assistance of the Western powers. If we wanted peace, it was up to us to take the initiative. In that connection there would first come up the question of the terms on which we could make peace. It was clear that peace was no longer to be had on the terms formerly offered by Finland. So we should have to think of making further concessions. It had been proposed that the boundary on the Isthmus be shifted further westward. In the north, too, we should have to offer more. Everything had gone to show that a base at the mouth of the Gulf of Finland was also a demand the Soviet Union had no thought of renouncing. Thus far we had firmly resisted this demand, and it was on this account that the war had actually started and that we were now fighting. Possibly the cession of an island, such as Jussarö, in the neighborhood of Hanko, would not harm Finland's own interests. Örö and Utö were other possibilities. Suursaari should also be included in the offer. If against these concessions we could get Repola and Porajärvi from the Soviet Union, Finland would have made an honorable peace and one which would also find support among our people. I asked the committee to answer two questions: Which course should be chosen? And, if peace, what terms could be proposed to the Soviet Union?

The discussion proved extensive. The matter was considered from many points of view, and the consequences of each step were debated. Unfortunately the conclusions of the members of the committee were strikingly divergent.

In Niukkanen's opinion there was no chance of making peace. At the front the expected new major attack of the Soviet Union was under way. If the Finnish forces had more guns, it would be possible to bring the attack to a halt. Our efforts should therefore be concentrated solely upon securing ammunition and guns. Talk of peace and peace terms was quite futile; battle was the thing now. During the spring thaws our situation would improve considerably, since the Russians would no longer be able to cross the lakes and marshes. Niukkanen took into consideration only two alternatives—Swedish aid and Western aid, in that order.

Paasikivi, who had at all times promoted the conclusion of peace and who was also acquainted with the previous discussions, now again set peace first among the alternatives. What chances of getting it were open to us we knew not. For ten weeks we had talked of securing aid, but what had in reality arrived? Under the best conditions, aid from abroad would be considerably delayed. The Western powers were interested only in their own major war. The expedition they planned was so vague that no one knew what might come of it. This possibility, however, must be held open. It would be impossible for the Soviet Union to make peace without appreciable gains. He judged that Sweden would be very glad to see peace made. If Sweden could open the road to peace, then we ought to take that route.

Hannula did not believe in the possibility of peace. On the conditions proposed, the Diet would not consider it. Peace on such disadvantageous terms as I had described was impossible after the hard fight we had waged. He was not afraid of becoming involved in the major war, for which reason he proposed we place our reliance on Western aid. My proposal had been a great surprise to him.

Söderhjelm, too, thought it too early to talk of peace terms, since battle was now the main thing. But as opinions on the peace terms had been sought, his view was that the cession of a base at the mouth of the Gulf of Finland was impossible. The Finnish people believed they were fighting over just that point. It would be decidedly dangerous if there were even talk of a base. Nevertheless, he was prepared for concessions on the Isthmus, and similarly for the conclusion of a special agreement on the Gulf of Finland. The cession of Jussarö was not a mere question of prestige. It was near the coast, and ceding it might prove to be dangerous.

Ryti held that, if at all possible, peace should be made on the terms I had set forth. If peace negotiations could not be started, aid should be accepted wherever available, either from Sweden or from the Western powers. However, the poor shape of our artillery was an argument for peace. Sweden should be brought to declare publicly that it would send auxiliaries to Finland's aid. In conclusion, he suggested that the Foreign Minister be sent to press the Swedish government for both artillery and auxiliary forces.

President Kallio expressed his opinion last, setting the aims of the government in the order I had proposed and supporting the peace endeavor. Thus far he had rigidly opposed the cession of a base at the mouth of the Gulf; but, if we could get by with the cession of Jussarö, that was merely a question of prestige. He supported Ryti's proposal that first of all I should be sent to Sweden, since that could be done with the greatest speed.

During the concluding phase of the conversation I remarked that the spirit in the committee seemed to be high, because we had been successful for the time being on various fronts. With the first defeats, morale among the people would drop, and after that it would be difficult to prevent the emergence of pessimism. I considered it certain that the Diet would approve a peace on the terms I had set forth. I also remarked on the dangers which involvement in the major war would bring with it. In that event Germany would clearly intervene by attacking either Sweden or Finland or both. Finland would become involved in the major war, possibly until it ended, unable to make an independent decision regarding peace.

The results of this discussion were exactly as I had feared earlier. Three members of the committee (Niukkanen, Hannula, and Söderhjelm) were firmly opposed to making peace. Three members, those familiar

with the progress of the peace discussions before this point (Ryti, Paasikivi, and I), were in favor of making peace. Moreover, the President
of the Republic had joined us in support of peace. The sole positive conclusion of the debate was the resolve that I should go to Sweden to ask
the Cabinet for aid.

After the meeting of the committee, President Kallio, Ryti, Paasikivi,
and I met separately and decided that, despite the negative outcome of
this discussion, we would continue in the course upon which we had set
out. The first job was to inform Foreign Minister Günther that Finland
was prepared to offer the island of Jussarö as a base. The committee
had agreed unanimously that I must go to Sweden, so I set off on my trip
the very same day, by the same route as before, to Turku by car and
from there by plane to Stockholm.

A SECOND TRIP TO STOCKHOLM

At Turku I received a letter from Erkko reporting that Mme. Kollontai had informed Günther of the Soviet Union's peace terms. The demands embodied therein were far-reaching indeed. Finland must give
up Hanko Cape, the Isthmus, and the eastern shore of Lake Ladoga.
Thus the positions of the two nations were very far apart. Instead of
further discussing the cession of a small island, the Soviet Union was
demanding the inclusion of whole provinces on its side of the line. The
letter made me very pessimistic; the conclusion of peace was still a long
way off if the Russian demands did not lessen.

I arrived in Stockholm on February 13. Erkko had arranged ap-
pointments both with Foreign Minister Günther and with Prime Minister
Hansson, at ten o'clock and at twelve o'clock.

The conversation with Günther dealt with the question of peace and
with the procurement of auxiliary forces.

He had not yet delivered to Mme. Kollontai my statement that we
were prepared to offer Jussarö. He had only received this statement the
evening before. Mme. Kollontai was coming in to see him that morning,
and he would tell her of it then. He went on to say that she had brought
him an answer to the question I had asked, on my earlier trip, regarding
what the Soviet peace terms would be. These were the same sweeping
demands Erkko had reported in the letter I had received in Turku.
Günther said he had told Mme. Kollontai that the demands were impossible and that he could not present them to Finland.

He smiled at the sly tactics of the Russians. The Soviet Union wished
to make special proposals regarding the use of the Aaland Islands to
appease Sweden, and to pass over Petsamo without mention to appease
Norway.

A more extensive discussion developed with regard to the chances of securing auxiliary forces. The Swedish government was not disposed to send trained units but had planned to send volunteers in considerable groups. I remarked that this would take a long time. It was now a month and a half since recruiting had begun, and not one Swede was yet at the front.

But Günther feared that if trained units were sent to Finland, the Western powers would break off relations with the Soviet Union. Then they would join in the war, and Germany would go into action. Germany had let this be plainly understood.

I said that, according to information in our hands, Germany would consider as a *casus belli* only the establishment by the Western powers of bases in Scandinavia. This information was new to Günther. I went on to say that Finland was fighting the war for Sweden as much as for itself. Sweden was even now in it and could not get out.

Günther felt that the Swedish people would hardly understand it if Sweden, by sending trained units, were to find itself involved in the war. They had to look out for their own domestic politics as well. If, however, the Western powers should come to Finland's aid, Sweden would perhaps have to withdraw its forces from Finland. In his view the best course was to make peace.

I said I thought so too. But the desire of the Soviet Union for peace would mount considerably if Sweden declared it was with us in the war.

Günther, on the contrary, feared that Soviet prestige would in that event even more urgently require that Russia win the war.

At noon I went to the Chancellory to meet Prime Minister Hansson. At my request he had with him Defense Minister Sköld and Foreign Minister Günther.

I set forth my case in this fashion: Finland sought peace. But the steps in that direction had not led to anything. For this reason we must go on with the war for the time being. Finland could not fight on its own resources and therefore it must procure aid. We would prefer to limit ourselves to aid from Scandinavia. Yet the recruiting of volunteers was too slow a course. Consequently, the matter should be taken over by the government. Sweden ought to send volunteers as trained units, in the same fashion as the German Kondor forces had functioned in the Spanish Civil War. If Sweden should do this, it would certainly help negotiations toward peace. If Finland were not to secure assistance of this character, it would have to rely on Western aid. This, however, could have weighty consequences. Finland would become a participant in the major war, and possibly Sweden and Norway as well.

With all this in mind, the Finnish government wanted to know the attitude of the Swedish government toward the procurement of increased aid.

Prime Minister Hansson spoke first, echoing Günther's remarks that the Swedish people would not understand it if the government should adopt this course. He did not even see how it would be technically possible. They were not in a position to insist that anyone in the armed forces transfer to such a unit. Moreover, it was not a matter the Cabinet could decide but an affair for the Riksdag. If it were undertaken, it would entail grave consequences abroad. The Western powers would break off relations with the Soviet Union, and Germany would invade the Scandinavian countries. Germany knew very well what the Kondor forces had really meant in the Spanish Civil War, and it would regard the employment of similar forces as a serious matter. The situation would become still more grave if the Western powers were to come to Finland's assistance.

In reply to these counterassertions, I declared that the Swedish government clearly had wrong information. The information in our hands ran in a different direction. Germany would hardly start an attack on the Scandinavian countries if Sweden were to take a firmer hand in the Finnish war—hardly even if the Western powers were to send auxiliary forces to Finland, provided they made no effort to take over bases for themselves. I reviewed in general terms the plans of the Western powers and the decision of the Supreme Council and told them that a military commission from these countries was coming to Finland for discussions. In case Finland had to rely upon Western aid, the Western powers would inevitably request the right of transit through Norway and Sweden. Then those countries would find themselves in a difficult situation. It would not be easy to reply to that request. But, of course, Norway and Sweden would answer in the negative.

Hansson agreed with this.

The conversation ended by my saying that I had received the Swedish government's answer. We must select our own course in accordance with it.

During the discussion Prime Minister Hansson had done most of the talking. Sköld spoke briefly and with a degree of coolness; Günther remained silent.

Since the Swedish spokesmen were constantly referring to the possibility that Germany might attack Sweden if that country were officially to assist Finland, it will be well to point out that in Finland we had at all times exactly the contrary impression. I refer here to an extract from a conversation which took place as early as December 6, 1939, between Count Rosen of Sweden and Hermann Göring. Before relating this conversation, I should point out that on the preceding day Rosen had asked Göring several questions and that Göring had talked with Hitler about them. Armed with the information thus received, Göring gave the answers set forth below:

Rosen: If Sweden bceomes involved in an armed conflict with Russia, may Sweden be assured that Germany will not through armed force or otherwise help Russia against Sweden?

Göring: Sweden may be entirely at ease in this respect, as I continue to be Sweden's friend.

Rosen: May I consider this reply as meaning that it is quite sure that Germany, in the event of a possible armed conflict between Sweden and Russia, will not assist Russia against Sweden?

Göring: Yes. It is absolutely certain, provided that Sweden in other respects maintains a position of neutrality with regard to the struggle between Germany and the Western powers. I cannot even understand how there can have cropped up in Sweden the notion that Germany might attack Sweden if Sweden were to become involved in a dispute with Russia.

During the evening of the same day I returned by plane to Turku, whence I continued by car to Helsinki. I had hardly reached home when Ryti telephoned me at midnight. He did indeed have important news to communicate, making any sleep that night impossible. At Summa on the Isthmus the Russians had broken through our defense lines. True, the breach was not large, but it was dangerous. An attempt was being made to close it.

This thirteenth day of February was in every sense a day of adversities. First Erkko's letter in the morning, setting forth for the first time the augmented demands of the Russians; then the negative reply of the Swedish Cabinet to our request for auxiliary forces; and now this news that the front had been broken through at Summa. The last phase of the war was in sight, but a month was still to pass before the final action.

On the following day I reported to the President and to the Prime Minister the negative outcome of my trip.

AN INCIDENT IN SWEDEN

As a postlude to my Stockholm visit, there was played out there an unpleasant scene which for some days clouded relations between Finland and Sweden. On February 16 the Stockholm afternoon paper,

Folkets Dagblad Politiken, published a news item which had the impact of a bombshell. Under large headlines the paper proclaimed my secret visit to Stockholm and the negative answer Hansson had given me. This was a decidedly unfortunate occurrence for Finland. The misfortune became still greater when Prime Minister Hansson, on behalf of the Cabinet, issued a statement in which he confirmed the report in unfortunate terms:

. . . The Finnish Foreign Minister discussed this matter last Tuesday, February 13, with the Prime Minister and the Foreign and Defense Ministers of Sweden. The hope was expressed that Swedish military units might be moved into Finland. The Swedish parties made reference to the general guiding principles applicable to aid furnished Finland by Sweden, which were set forth in the statement made before the Riksdag by the Prime Minister on January 17 of this year, a statement which has been generally supported. No change in the attitude then expressed has occurred since that time.

When this statement became available in Finland, it occasioned great disappointment. Almost without exception the papers commented upon it. Karl-August Fagerholm wrote an editorial in the *Arbetarbladet* under the title "A Chilly Statement," part of which read as follows:

Prime Minister P. A. Hansson's statement declaring that the Swedish Cabinet has rejected Foreign Minister Tanner's request to the Swedish government for military assistance was not in itself by any means a surprise to those who have had opportunity to follow the development of the matter. The fact that even these persons were taken aback on reading the statement is to be attributed solely to its exceptionally chilling language. There is not a ray of warmth in it, nothing which might be calculated to encourage a brother nation fighting for its existence. For this reason the statement has occasioned anxiety and concern in Finland. On this account P. A. Hansson's words have been received in Moscow with applause. It would not have been difficult to draft the statement in such terms as would have created quite the opposite impression. If P. A. Hansson had said to the young men of Sweden: "There are reasons why Sweden finds it impossible to send military units to Finland, gladly as we would do so; but every young man who goes to Finland as a volunteer will have Sweden's blessing, because Finland's war is Sweden's war"—if P. A. Hansson had said something like that, the volunteer movement would have gained impetus and the question of regular units need not have come up at all.

When Hansson's statement was published, the Swedish papers generally devoted their attention to it. Numerous journalists asked me for more detailed information regarding the authenticity of this news.

There was still a further post-mortem over the business. A number of members of the Swedish Cabinet were much annoyed over the tactless publication by *Folkets Dagblad Politiken;* they blamed the Finnish

Cabinet, and me in particular, for the leak of information. For this reason I felt it necessary to inform Günther via Erkko that there had been no leak on the Finnish side, which would be improbable in any case since the information which had come out was most disadvantageous to Finland. Consequently, I added, the publication of the news had been a great surprise to us too.

A couple of days later Ryti telephoned to lament the army's lack of antitank artillery. The Russian tanks were coming through the line, and we had no weapons to oppose them. Our own guns, very few to begin with, were worn out or smashed. We needed at least one hundred new cannon, and our military authorities had asked Sweden for them. He then urged me to support this request, so I telephoned both Prime Minister Hansson and Defense Minister Sköld and assured them that on our side nothing had been revealed regarding my latest visit there. Hansson at once accepted my assurance in full, but Sköld claimed that Flyg, editor of *Folkets Dagblad Politiken*, had told him differently. As for getting the guns, neither of them thought they could offer us much hope, but they did promise to discuss the matter with their Cabinet. Thus, for the time being, our army had to fight almost unarmed against the Russian tanks. True, we had learned to use gasoline-filled bottles in antitank defense, but these were of little value save as a close-range weapon.

The source of the *Folkets Dagblad Politiken* story was never definitely established. On one of my later visits I went into this question with members of the Swedish Cabinet and tried to ascertain how the story had come out. They told me that a member of the Finnish Cabinet had stayed with the Swedish rightist political leader, Domö, during a visit to Stockholm and had told him that I had come to Stockholm, all ignorant himself of my business and of the answer I had received. As this rightist leader was acquainted with his government's decision, he was able to put two and two together. Then through the imprudence of one or the other of them, the story came to the knowledge of the editor of the *Politiken*.

This merely confirmed my earlier experience to the effect that nothing could happen in Sweden without news of it leaking out. We have had the same experience. No matter how cautiously you handle important matters of state, there are always involved in them persons who, in order to enhance the impression of their own importance, whisper the facts to some good friend, who in the same fashion shows off before the next man. By this time the matter is ordinarily so widely known that it finds its way into the columns of the press. This is perhaps the reason why all countries establish a severe press censorship during times of war.

This press story did not stop with the incident described above. Newspapers all over the world took a hand in it. All the Swedish papers wrote about it, and most of them berated their government for its stand. In the opinion of certain papers, Sweden itself would be endangered if Finland was forced to ask aid of of the Western powers. The British papers harshly criticized the Swedish reply and foretold that there might come a day when Sweden would have occasion to regret bitterly that it had not furnished the aid when it was sought.

In Moscow the news of the Swedish position was greeted with great satisfaction and was interpreted to mean that Finland's fate was now definitely decided. Aid from the West could no longer save Finland.

As the press barrage still continued, even the King was brought in to defend the position of the Swedish Cabinet. On February 19 a statement was published by the King which did something to alleviate the awkwardness of Hansson's statement but which nevertheless joined in support of the Cabinet's attitude. This royal statement definitely ended hope of aid from Sweden.

CHAPTER 9

THE TORTUOUS ROAD TO PEACE

On February 14 there arrived a cable from Holma, the Finnish Minister in Paris, saying that authorities there had sensed Finland's hesitancy about accepting the Western aid offer, since Finland had made no request that forces be sent. He also reported that Sweden was working against this offer in Paris. He further informed us that Colonel Ganeval was to come to Finland from France in order to discuss arrangements for the dispatch of aid. We replied to Holma that we doubted the aid offered would turn out to be sufficiently effective.

The League of Nations, which in December had urged that humanitarian and economic aid be extended to Finland, now showed some activity. On its behalf there came to Helsinki Mr. Bertil Renborg, under whose direction had been placed the organization which, within the framework of the League, was to provide aid to Finland. He described to us the new plans of the League's Secretary General, Avenol, for carrying out this activity. We got the impression that the direct activity of the League of Nations seemed to have withered into insignificance.

But through other channels "humanitarian aid" came in abundantly. Our closest neighbor, Sweden, went to work on this with speed. At the very start of the war the prominent industrialist Torsten Hérnod had put into motion the collection of funds among industrial establishments and businesses. This collection bore unexpectedly abundant fruit. By February some 60 million kronor had been gathered. The plan was to use 50 million of this to equip the volunteers who should come to Finland, and the rest was to be placed freely at Finland's disposal. The fund drive was initiated among the rural population, too, and yielded about the same amount. Generous help came from Sweden through other channels also: thus the sugar trust gave us a million kilograms of sugar. Our own countrymen in the United States and in Canada worked energetically with their limited means, with considerable results.

CONVERSATIONS WITH FOREIGN POWERS

Thomas Snow, Great Britain's Minister in Helsinki, who had fallen into disfavor and been transferred elsewhere perhaps primarily because he had lost his nerve when the first bombs fell, paid a farewell visit to the President. I was present on this occasion by reason of my office. Naturally we talked about the war for the most part. We suggested to him that he take it upon himself to present to his government our hope that England would declare to the Soviet government that it was interested in Finland's case. England was also to declare that, if peace were not to be made on decent terms, England would take a hand in the Finnish war. Snow was decidedly enthusiastic over this mission. I have no knowledge whether any representations were made to the Soviet Union as a result.

The German Minister, Von Blücher, had been trying to see me for several days, but by reason of other concerns I had been unable to reserve an hour for him. On February 17 he came in, and a fairly prolonged discussion took place between us.

To begin with, he seized upon the statement I had given out the Sunday before, twisting it every way and interpreting it as aimed against Germany. I explained the matter, but the exchange threatened to prove interminable. Finally I had to ask him to go on to something else. He was a little taken aback by my request, but he dropped the subject.

Next he sought to refute all rumors to the effect that Germany had helped the Soviet Union against Finland. He asserted that Germany had furnished to the Soviet Union neither officers, nor pilots, nor arms, nor any other aid. There followed a pessimistic survey of our chances in the war. In his view not much reliance was to be placed upon Western aid. It would merely create another front in the major war. It was only after this that he came to his principal business: the chances of peace. He said Germany continued to find it impossible to mediate since the moment was not yet suitable "for the adjustment of the conflict." At length he put forward a proposal which he described as his personal idea. It might be a path toward peace, a slender link which might either grow stronger or be broken. If Finland so desired, he was prepared to suggest that Foreign Minister von Ribbentrop advance in Moscow the idea of sending representatives from each side to Berlin, where they could ascertain each other's aims. As a suitable candidate on Finland's side he brought up the name of J. K. Paasikivi, who should, in order to avoid attracting attention, come to Berlin by an indirect route—by way of Italy, for example. Von Blücher was prepared to send a telegram to Von Ribbentrop about this. There were, however, two unknown factors in the scheme: would the German Foreign Ministry consent to handle the matter, and would Moscow assent to the proposal?

I thanked him for his concern. We agreed that I should ask him in if we were to take him up on his proposal. Yet I felt it was clear in advance that there was no reason for us to grasp at it, despite the fact that it obviously came from the German government. For, of course, we knew the Russian requirements already, through our Stockholm conversations.

When I discussed this subject with several members of the Cabinet, those present were interested in Blücher's proposition. They wanted further clarification as to whether there was anything more behind it than what his words indicated. I was asked to get in touch with him again and inquire further about details. I promised to do so, and on February 20 I invited him to visit me again.

Von Blücher had said that Germany did not regard the moment as suitable for making a mediation offer. Since, despite this fact, he had put forward his own idea, I said that there seemed to be a certain contradiction. His suggestion would in any case go to the German Foreign Minister, who would decide on behalf of his government whether the matter should be carried further. I inquired how his idea was actually to be understood.

Von Blücher replied that there was no contradiction in what he had suggested. He had said that the German government did not consider that it could *mediate*. For that reason he had thought up a device through which there might be established a sort of *contact*. As to whether it would lead to anything, he could not say; nor could he give any assurances. He again observed that there were two unknowns: Von Ribbentrop's attitude and Moscow's attitude.

Tanner: So you cannot give any assurance as to how the suggestion would prosper. It would be extremely important for us to establish this point. We do not want to plunge ourselves into any uncertain venture.

Blücher: I am unable to give any guarantee.

Tanner: Being acquainted with diplomatic procedure, one might presume that your proposal had been discussed with government officials and that this course had been chosen as a result of that discussion. Might I so judge?

Blücher: I can make no reply to that question.

Tanner: Then there is nothing known as to what conditions Moscow might propose either?

Blücher: Nobody knows.

Tanner: Thanks for the information. [Then I had in fact understood him; but I had wished to make quite sure.]

Blücher: Then that's all.

Tanner: It is.

Blücher: May I in turn ask a question? There are rumors that Finland has asked for assistance from powers that are at war with Germany. Is there any foundation to these rumors?

Tanner: I can make no reply to that question.

Blücher: Am I to take it that you do not wish to answer?

Tanner: Exactly.

There ensued a long pause. Von Blücher was trying to force more out of me by silence. But I began to ask him about his housing troubles. He caught the point, and left.

The conversation had been brief and a little on the cool side.

When I communicated the result of my conversation with Von Blücher to Ryti and Walden, we considered that his suggestions had offered nothing noteworthy. Accordingly we decided, without securing authority from the Cabinet, to ask Sweden on our own initiative to put peace mediation measures into operation. In event of need we could promise cession of Hanko Cape.

Walden left the same evening for headquarters in order to ascertain its opinion regarding this new turn.

Other foreign powers also began to show interest in the latest phases of Finland's case. Prime Minister Ryti received the visits of Count Bech, who had come to Finland from Italy as Foreign Minister Ciano's special envoy in order to inquire into our situation. Ryti gave him the information he needed, suggesting finally that the great powers not at war, Italy and the United States, should together undertake to mediate for a conclusion to the war. Ryti assured him that on Finland's part such a mediation offer would be accepted gladly. Bech had judged that Italy would be able to urge Germany to make a mediation offer. But nothing was subsequently heard of this matter.

The Norwegian Minister, Michelet, also came to see me. To begin with, he complained about the *Altmark* incident (the seizure of a German vessel by the British in one of the Norwegian fjords, resulting in the liberation of a number of British prisoners of war). In his view, England had through this act grossly violated Norwegian neutrality. His principal purpose was, however, to learn what Von Blücher had said during his visit to the Ministry. (So that visit had become known, too.) Had Blücher brought a German offer of mediation? I denied this, and assured him that there had been no offer from any quarter.

In Paris, meanwhile, the dispatch of auxiliary forces to Finland was still being planned. Our Minister, Holma, was making inquiries even about such details as what airfields were suitable for planes equipped with landing gear and what was the composition of our soldiers' winter rations. He further said that Premier Daladier of France had issued an order to the effect that the auxiliary forces must be ready ten days earlier than had previously been scheduled. A couple of days later Holma reported that the expeditionary force of the Western powers would be ready to leave at the end of February or the beginning of March.

TOWARD A SOLUTION

As affairs had developed toward a decisive stage in many fields— uncertainty at the front, the Soviet demands, Sweden's negative attitude, the aid offered by the Western powers, etc.—it was necessary to communicate with the Foreign Relations Committee of the Diet, so that we might get a clear idea of opinions prevailing in Diet circles. This was in fact now less difficult, as the Diet had considered it requisite to come closer to the center of operations and had moved to Helsinki around the middle of February. I asked the chairman of the Foreign Relations Committee, Voionmaa, to convene the Committee on February 21. By reason of air raid alerts the committee was assembled at the early hour of 8:30 A.M. But before we even started, there was an alert, and twice during the session we had to go into the Diet building's bomb shelter.

I began by recalling that three weeks earlier I had furnished the Diet, at an unofficial session held at Kauhajoki, with a survey of events up to that date. At that time there had been reason to be satisfied with the development of the situation, since till then we had enjoyed considerable success in the war. But subsequently the position had changed, and in particular after the middle of February it had, by reason of the Russian breakthrough, taken a decided turn for the worse. We had come to perceive that we would be unable to last out the war on our own resources. For this reason auxiliary forces as well as arms and money would be needed. I told them what had been done to secure aid both from Scandinavia and from the Western powers. I also reported the offer of assistance from the Western powers and remarked that the difficulties and dangers involved had been noted.

After this I advised them that in the Cabinet the view was held that the endeavor to conclude a peace should be put in first place. In this sense soundings had been taken in various quarters. Several states had offered their services as mediators. Further, it was known that the Soviet Union was desirous of peace and that the so-called Kuusinen government was no longer an obstacle. At this point the question of making peace involved a matter of prestige for the Soviet Union: its great losses in the war called for some sort of indemnification. Making peace therefore depended upon the terms offered. The cession of Hanko Cape was clearly a condition for attaining it. In other respects, too, the terms would prove more severe than in the fall when we negotiated on the subject in Moscow. I now wished to learn the committee's attitude: were they prepared to make peace even if we had to cede Hanko Cape and accept other conditions more burdensome than those required in November? Deeper into details than this I did not feel I could go, nor could I report more fully on the conversations which had taken place.

The committee members spoke substantially as follows:

Ikola: Peace negotiations were not even to be thought of if cession of Hanko Cape was a prerequisite.

Reinikainen: Peace should be sought with all zeal, since aid did not appear to be available in sufficient quantity.

Salmenoja was of the same mind as Reinikainen. He hoped, nevertheless, that it would not be necessary to cede Hanko Cape. Thus far we had held our end up brilliantly in the war, but we could not continue to do so. When the future of our people was involved, sacrifices must be made.

Kukkonen: Now that Sweden had rejected our request for more abundant aid, the people had come to look toward the Western powers. If discussions with them should lead to positive results, we should be prepared to take part even in the major war. If Finland were forced to make a peace without honor, a difficult crisis would result. Once the talks at headquarters with the representatives of the Western powers were finished, the committee might be convened again. Then the committee would be in a better position to deliberate on the question.

Chairman Voionmaa said that we had come to a turning point. The question was whether Finland should be tied to the leading strings of the Western powers, to become a mere instrument in their hands. It would be difficult to get sufficient aid from that quarter. There could be no confidence that such aid would be of a decisive character. Peace should be sought, and no illusions should be entertained. We should proceed to initiate negotiations.

Ikola: Is there any hope of aid from Germany?

This question led me to describe the discussions with the German representative here. In January the first soundings had been made in that quarter, and the last a few days before. Both times the response had been negative.

Vesterinen: Now Sweden's negative attitude had become plain, it was time to deliberate on the matter from other points of view. The war would prove too much for us if no aid was to be had. The assistance offered by France and England was extremely vague. Troops could not be brought through the Scandinavian countries. What was the significance of such aid in that case? If the Western powers could guarantee that our country would not be despoiled by the Russians, one could attach some importance to the offer. The course of peace should be of first importance.

Kekkonen: When the war broke out, we had had no word of aid coming from abroad. Nevertheless we had stood firm on Finland's vital interests. Now the situation was different. If Hanko Cape were to be sacrificed, this would be merely proof that we had squandered men and money in vain. There could not even be any talk of peace on the present terms. We must get a clearer definition of the other party's desire for peace. This was no time to be talking of peace, even among ourselves.

As no one else had asked for the floor, the chairman finally determined that each of the committee members had presented his personal views during the discussion. In the chairman's opinion there was no reason to go further into the matter at this stage or to determine the attitude of the committee as such.

Only two of the committee members had taken a stand decidedly opposed to the prerequisites known to govern peace negotiations. This was a sufficient directive for the members of the Cabinet.

Thus, on various sides there had matured the idea that the work of making peace should be energetically taken in hand. In talking and fumbling we had lost three weeks, which might cost us dear, since the battles at the front were at the same time taking an unfavorable turn. But now we could continue resolutely along the road we had started on. That same evening I telephoned Erkko in Stockholm to urge that he approach Günther with the suggestion that Sweden, in its own interest and to prevent Finland from turning to the Western powers, undertake to mediate toward the conclusion of a peace. As a practical measure I suggested that a representative from each side go to Stockholm to discuss the principles of a peace. As a further justification Günther might be told that Finland was now at a crossroad. If Finland turned to the Western powers with a request for aid, the war would spread to the whole Nordic area. It was to Sweden's interest to prevent this. As both parties were prepared for peace in principle, a course toward its realization ought to be found.

According to Erkko's report, Günther was ready to undertake the measures I suggested. He had deemed that the moment was now opportune. He promised to advise Moscow through the Swedish Minister, Assarsson, and at the same time to inform Mme. Kollontai in Stockholm regarding the proposal. Günther was happy that we had wished to make use of Sweden's services.

THE WEST AND RUSSIA CLARIFY THEIR STANDS

Walden returned from headquarters on February 23 and at once sought to communicate his news to a restricted circle. At a talk in the Bank of Finland, with Ryti, Niukkanen, and myself present, Walden reported on the discussions at headquarters with General Ling of Great Britain and Colonel Ganeval of France. He presented a memorandum on the course of the discussion, from which it was apparent that the Western aim in the North was to block the sale of Swedish iron ore to Germany and in the South to keep Germany from getting Baku oil. As gaining possession of Baku was difficult, the Western powers would have to bomb it, but in the North they were prepared to send a military expedition to Finland. The expeditionary force would amount to three and a half divisions. These forces would arrive in Finland via Norway and Sweden. Finland was to make all possible representations in Sweden to further the matter. First of all, we were to ask Sweden for military aid, pointing out that if our request came to nothing we should be obliged to ask England and France for help. In the same connection we were to request transit rights for the Western forces. On a second approach we were to advise Sweden that we had already turned to the Western powers and again ask for permission for their auxiliary forces to pass through. At that time the Western forces would already be off the coast of Norway, ready to land. The Western powers judged that under such circumstances Norway and Sweden would consent to grant transit rights. The Western powers were doubtful only regarding the limited carrying capacity of the Norwegian and Swedish railways, which would make it difficult to transport the forces and in particular to assure a supply route.

On the basis of the information thus received, we assumed a pretty doubtful attitude toward the assistance offered by the Western powers. It was too limited to meet our needs, and there were many obstacles in the way of its reaching its destination. At the same time we went over the position at the front, on the basis of the information Walden had secured. We learned that the enemy was already near Viipuri. The line to be defended was weak, and losing it was only a question of days.

Niukkanen having inquired what were the plans of the Foreign Minister and the Prime Minister, I described the need for peace. The offer of aid from the Western powers was a very feeble instrument of defense. The aid would clearly come to a halt at the coast of Norway. If it did get through Norway and Sweden, it would carry us into the major war without securing for Finland any advantage.

Ryti spoke cautiously, without assuming any definite stand. We must go on trying to get help from Sweden and from the Western powers, but at the same time we must act in the interest of peace.

Niukkanen called attention to the aid offered by the West. We must get busy about this at once. Was there even a chance of getting peace negotiations under way?

I replied that we had at our disposal channels for getting conversations started, if only we secured authority to use them. Thus far, however, it had been impossible to muster support in the Cabinet foreign affairs committee for the initiation of peace negotiations. I made reference to the conversations with the Western powers. They had always been late to act. Before their aid reached us, all southern Finland might be occupied. In such circumstances, the aid would cost us very dear— at least Hanko Cape, and perhaps more.

Niukkanen denied that he had earlier opposed our proceeding to peace negotiations, although in the meeting of the Cabinet foreign affairs committee on February 12 he had sharply rejected the peace line.

When Niukkanen left the meeting, the three of us who stayed on decided to act zealously in pursuing the peace endeavor, even though it should entail various losses. I was directed to ascertain at once whether Foreign Minister Günther had received an answer from Moscow.

On the same day, February 23, in the afternoon, Erkko telephoned from Stockholm and said that at about midday he had received information concerning the precise Soviet demands. Molotov had communicated them to Assarsson, the Swedish Minister in Moscow, through whom they had reached the Swedish Foreign Ministry.

As minimal military requirements for the initiation of negotiations, the Russians demanded (1) the cession of Hanko; (2) the cession of the Karelian Isthmus, including Viipuri; (3) the cession of the northeastern shore of Lake Ladoga, including Sortavala—approximately the line of Peter the Great in 1721. On the other hand, the Soviet Union was prepared to evacuate the other areas, including Petsamo. A defense treaty concerning the Gulf of Finland was to be concluded between the Soviet Union, Estonia, and Finland.

Further, the Soviet Union indicated that it attached no significance to the aid offered by the Western powers. If the demands presented were not accepted now, there would be fresh ones later. In this connection Moscow had once more hinted at the possibility of making an arrangement on the Aaland Island question in concert with Sweden—which Günther had disregarded, however.

By reason of these new demands, this time precise, it was necessary to convene the Cabinet foreign affairs committee and to acquaint it with the detailed terms. The meeting was held at 6:00 P.M. and was attended by all members of the committee and by President Kallio.

To begin with, I presented a fundamental review of the situation and especially of the various alternatives at our disposal. The review gave rise to an extensive discussion, in which the advantages and drawbacks of the various alternatives were weighed. The members of the committee thought the Soviet terms formidable and difficult to accept, because they would break up Finland's geographical area.

Walden reported on the discussions at headquarters with the Western powers and gave a survey of the position at the front, which he said was weak. The conversation led to no conclusion, since many factors were still based upon vague information. Opinions were divided in the same manner as before, at the meeting on February 12. The committee decided that, before a final determination should be made, definitive answers to the following questions must be secured:

1. Were auxiliary forces to be had from Sweden? If so, how many, and when?

2. Would Sweden consent to give the Western auxiliary forces the right of passage on the basis of Article 16 of the Covenant of the League of Nations?

3. When could Western auxiliary forces reach their destination?

It was further felt that we must await the return of Professor T. M. Kivimäki and hear what news he brought from Germany. During his visit there he had met various German leaders, among them Hermann Göring.

At once upon the conclusion of the meeting I telephoned Erkko and asked him to present Questions 1 and 2 to the Swedish government.

The next day, February 24, Erkko reported that he had presented the questions to Günther, requesting an early reply. Günther, who had been on the point of leaving for a meeting of Scandinavian foreign ministers at Copenhagen, on this account put off his trip for twenty-four hours. At noon of this day Erkko had been invited by Günther to call in order to receive a written reply to the questions. The Swedish reply had been approved, before its delivery, by the foreign relations committee of the Riksdag. The reply was carefully drafted, but Sweden could merely promise to intensify the existing program of sending volunteers. As for the passage of Western auxiliary forces, the Swedish Cabinet assumed a firmly negative stand.

Since this reply accurately describes Sweden's position, it is well to quote it here in its entirety:

Mr. Chargé d'Affaires:

In reply to the specific questions contained in your letter of the 23d of this month, on the ability of the Swedish government to help Finland, I may inform you as follows.

Being well aware of the solidarity existing between the Swedish and Finnish peoples and being convinced that in proceeding in this fashion it fosters Sweden's vital interests as well, the Swedish government has, since the outbreak of the

Finnish-Russian conflict, tried to assist Finland. In doing so it has had to weigh various differing points of view. On the one hand, the government has been clear regarding the extreme importance of the help it might give Finland—which would be of the greatest benefit to Sweden as well. On the other hand, care must be taken lest the manner of this help result in an extension of the conflict and thus expose Sweden—and Finland as well—to still greater perils. The Swedish government holds that such a peril would exist if Sweden were drawn into the war of the major powers and converted into a theater of war as a consequence of its efforts to aid Finland. For this reason the government has had to regard as an incontrovertible duty the avoidance of such steps as would clearly involve a threat of this kind.

Against this background of its position, to which under present circumstances the Swedish government considers it must adhere, I can furnish you the following as an answer to your questions:

The Swedish government continues to be prepared to afford all such aid in terms of commodities as Sweden can possibly manage. It is hardly feasible to make a precise statement on the quantities of the various commodities.

As for forces composed of volunteers, one may expect with confidence that an increase of the volunteer forces operating in Finland will take place in the near future. Special efforts are being made in this connection. It is nevertheless impossible to indicate in advance the numbers of the new volunteer forces.

At the moment no hope can be held out regarding forces constituted otherwise than as volunteers or regarding transit rights for units pertaining to the nations now at war.

Please accept, etc.,

CHRISTIAN GÜNTHER

The Swedish Minister in Helsinki, Stig Sahlin, came in to see me. I told him about the peace terms offered by the Soviet Union and about the inquiries I had made in Stockholm and their reply. He had not yet received this information from his government.

Sir Paul Dukes of the British Intelligence Service called on me. I knew him for a very intelligent and acute man. He spoke at length regarding his observations in Finland and made a suggestion for the organization of propaganda both in the Soviet Union and abroad. He recommended that we should ask England for some of their fastest planes, which could go even as far as Moscow.

After the meeting of the Cabinet foreign affairs committee, Paasikivi had meditated deeply upon our business, and he now visited me to speak about it. As the fruit of his thought he put forward the following propositions:

1. If we were to enter into a relationship with the Western powers, we must receive binding assurances from them. They must promise to

fight to the last ditch on our fronts and to back us also in the peace negotiations which should follow the war.

2. In negotiations with the Soviet Union, we should assume the position that we would cede Hanko Cape and draw the line on the Isthmus between Suvanto and Seivästö.

3. The press at home should be toned down a good deal. The papers were too confident of victory, and they were not giving really frank accounts of the course of events.

On this day (February 24) we of the Cabinet had an opportunity to meet General Ling, who was visiting here as military representative, and to hear from him more details on the plans being developed in England. First he came during the day to see Ryti and me and presented the same plan as he had earlier at headquarters. We asked him many questions and received the impression that the plans were still very vague. In the course of the same day we called on the President to report this conversation.

In the evening I had a further opportunity to talk to General Ling. This time there was also present at the meeting the new British Minister to Finland, Gordon Vereker. Before I describe this conversation, I should like to relate my first meeting with Vereker.

He had been appointed British Minister at Helsinki to succeed Minister Snow, who in the opinion of his government had not conducted his business with sufficient resolution. Upon Vereker's arrival, agreement had been reached as to when he should visit the President in order to present his credentials. At the appointed time I went to the President's residence, since by reason of my office it was my duty to attend on this occasion. A little before the hour an air raid alert was sounded in the city, and we began to wonder whether our visitor would arrive. We waited for him a fairly long time in the reception chamber. As the warning signals continued to become more and more pressing, we at last thought it best to go into the fairly safe bomb shelter in the courtyard. Back of the more roomy shelter designed for the service personnel of the residence was a narrow compartment, hardly more than four square yards in area, for the President himself. We sat there to await the end of the alert. But after a few moments someone arrived to say that the new British Minister was requesting his audience. President Kallio deemed it best to receive him in the tiny shelter, and Vereker was brought in. He said that he had been driving to the residence in good time when the alert began. The conscientious Helsinki police had insisted on his going into a public bomb shelter, in spite of his protestations of being the representative of a foreign state on important business. When there came a slight lull in the activity of the planes, he had continued his journey and belatedly joined us, once more in a bomb shelter. He delivered his statement and presented his letter of credentials. The President accepted the letter and delivered a statement in reply, which I translated into English. Thereafter our conversation continued for some time, for the raid was a prolonged one. Vereker was delighted with this unusual "state reception" and declared that he would remember it as long as he lived.

The new British Minister requested his first appointment with me the evening of February 24, saying he had important news to communicate. I was at home and it was already late, but I promised to receive him there. He arrived with General Ling and Kenneth Gurney, the Legation secretary. They were conducted by State Councilor Hakkarainen.

Vereker first wished to talk to me alone about politics while the other guests remained in another room. Thereafter General Ling joined us, and we went on to talk about the dispatch of the auxiliary forces planned by England and France. The plan was clarified in greater detail than formerly.

Vereker said that in his own country the interest in helping Finland was great. Public opinion urged the government on, and the government was itself most favorable to the matter. The British government was prepared to help in every possible way, and men, arms, and ships were even now ready. The forces could leave on March 15 and reach here by April 15. First it was thought that British auxiliary forces could take over the defense of the northern portion of our front, at the latitude of Kemi, but at Marshal Mannerheim's suggestion they were prepared to take over the defenses of areas lying farther south, so that Finnish forces could be given a sufficiently free hand on the Isthmus. In this fashion Marshal Mannerheim would be able to carry Finnish and Swedish forces to the southern front up as far as Kuusamo or perhaps Kuhmoniemi. The only obstacle in the way of the arrival of these forces was the transit through Scandinavia. Finland must itself obtain this transit right. The best way would be to inform the Swedish and Norwegian governments about it privately at first, so that they would have time to think the matter over. Thereafter, simultaneously with the dispatch to the Western powers of an official request for aid, the governments of Norway and Sweden should be officially asked for transit rights and informed that the matter was to be made public. In this fashion these countries would be forced to make an affirmative reply.

After this the conversation continued in the following way:

Tanner: I doubt that Norway and Sweden will give transit rights.

They have told us before that they will not consent to this.

Vereker: What are they afraid of? Germany?

Tanner: Partly Germany, but partly they wish to remain neutral. They do not want to become involved in the major war. We have urged them to help us, and in that way they will avoid being drawn into the major war. They fear that this course of action, too, will sweep them into it. We have just recently asked them about this once more on an official basis, even though we had already asked them the same question ten days ago on a private basis.

Vereker: I suppose the subject has come up in the conference of Scandinavian foreign ministers at Copenhagen. Has assistance been asked of Denmark and Norway?

Tanner: Not of Denmark. Norway is even more cautious than Sweden. Denmark is subject to German influence.

Vereker: The matter seems a difficult one to deal with. Do you think it might be profitable if England were to promise to help them in case Germany exerts pressure upon them?

Tanner: I don't think so. But offering a promise of that character would deprive them of that argument in their reply.

Vereker: In any event the matter must be handled in an especially confidential fashion. Finland should make a decision promptly. It should make an official appeal to the Western powers. On this point Finland should reach a decision as early as next week. The appeal should be made by March 5, and so should the official request to Sweden.

Tanner: How many units can the Western powers send?

Vereker listed several units.

Tanner: How many men is that in all?

Vereker: Twenty to twenty-two thousand. But this cannot be computed merely on a basis of manpower. These units are well equipped with automatic weapons. In firing power they correspond to ordinary forces of at least double the number.

Tanner: I promise to bring up the matter in the Cabinet at once. But it must be discussed in the Diet as well, at least in the Foreign Relations Committee.

Ling: It would be possible to make use of a slight prevarication— that the auxiliary forces would come through Scandinavia as private groups. Perhaps in that event those countries would be able to look aside and permit the transit.

Tanner: If we ask the Western powers for auxiliary forces, shall we become involved in the major war? Would we be committed to it until the very end?

Ling: But Finland is not officially at war with Russia. Neither would England be at war with Russia. The British forces on the front would be carrying on an altogether particular war.

Tanner: Could Finland secure guarantees that its independence and frontiers would be underwritten? Can we consider it certain that these matters will be settled at the time of the final great peace conference?

Vereker wrote down some notes. He said he would bring this point to his government's attention.

Ling here added that this aspect of the matter was extremely important.

Tanner: And what about financing a prolonged war? Would England take care of that? If the war goes on for a long time, we can't carry the burden.

Ling: Of course, I'll take that up with our government.

I promised to speed Finland's adoption of a stand. Next week we would try to make a decision and would inform them of the outcome at once.

Both my guests in conclusion emphasized once more the importance of speed in settling this matter. Time was running out, and Finland could not defend itself much longer.

As I had observed that Vereker had read the announcement of the British government from a sheet of paper, I asked for a copy of it. He said he would send one, and I got it on the following day.

The next day, February 25, the same gentlemen wished to see the Prime Minister and me. Our meeting took place in the Bank of Finland. We again went over the details of the plans for the assistance offered by the Western powers, the most important being those concerning the number of men and the time of arrival of the forces. The answers we received still lacked firmness, and in fact they diverged from information we had received earlier.

Professor T. M. Kivimäki, who at the request of the Cabinet had gone to Berlin to meet with certain persons and whose report regarding opinion in German government circles we had decided to await, had first by telephone and today by wire advised us that he could furnish important information. From his telegram it came to light that Germany would interpose no obstacle to Sweden's active participation in the Finnish war if only the Western powers would stay out. Nor would Germany raise objections to the transit of Western volunteers. But if regular forces of those powers should come to Finland, Germany would wage war against them. The people he had met had on the whole, however, urged the making of peace on such terms as could be got. Since he was unable to transmit information freely either by telephone or by

wire, Kivimäki had been urged to return home as soon as possible in
order to furnish a more detailed report on the success of his mission.
He was now on his way.

In the morning a cable arrived from Erkko reporting that Mme.
Kollontai was pressing Finland to accept the Soviet demands without
delay. They were firm and were by no means intended to serve merely
as a basis for negotiation.

The Council of State was invited to assemble at 3:00 P.M. to receive
a report on the situation. President Kallio and General Walden were
also present. First, the Prime Minister gave a fundamental review of
the general situation, dealing for the most part with events at the front.
My task was to report on foreign policy. I told them about the discussions which had taken place with Sweden and with the Western
powers and about the peace inquiries which had been made. The subsequent discussion reflected concern, but no common line could even
now be found. Most of the members wished still to keep open all the
channels to which thought had been given: the assistance requested of
Sweden, the aid offered by the Western powers, and the peace endeavor.
Actually, only Paasikivi, Mauno Pekkala, and I were firmly in favor
of the peace endeavor. Paasikivi now reverted to the thoughts which
he had presented privately the day before. He, too, however, hoped
that the peace terms might yet change for the better and that they would
thus offer room for negotiation. During the course of the discussion
I complained that I had not had the support of the Cabinet foreign affairs
committee when at an earlier stage I had sought its opinion. Possibly
at that juncture it would have been easier to conclude a peace and to
get better terms. Uncompromisingly opposed to peace on the terms
offered were Von Born, Hannula, Heikkinen, Salovaara, and Söderhjelm—thus six members of the Council of State. The President, too,
who some days before had favored the peace line, was now very doubt-
fully disposed toward Swedish mediation. This proved that the activity
displayed by the Western powers during the last few days had considerably affected opinion.

With respect to the heart of the matter, no decision was made upon
this occasion. The one thing it was possible to agree upon was that
I should once more go to Stockholm in order to negotiate on various
questions both with the Swedish Cabinet and, insofar as possible, with
Mme. Kollontai. The undertaking of these journeys seemed for the
time being the one matter on which in the several discussions it was
possible to be of one mind.

In the morning of February 26 I telephoned Erkko in Stockholm and asked him to inquire of Prime Minister Hansson whether he would be able to spare some time for a talk on the following day. At the same time I asked him to say that I also wanted to meet with Mme. Kollontai. Erkko answered a couple of hours later that Prime Minister Hansson would be at his office at 10:00 A.M. on the following day.

During the course of the day I invited in both Vereker and the French Minister, Magny. Referring to my promise to keep them acquainted with the course of events, I conveyed to them the information we had received regarding the Soviet peace terms. This information was also wired to Minister Gripenberg in London and to Minister Holma in Paris.

That evening there was an unofficial meeting of the board of the Social Democratic Party, at which the situation was discussed. A letter from Karl-August Fagerholm was read, expressing serious doubts about making peace on the conditions proposed. The board was nevertheless unanimous that making peace was essential. At least from this quarter I got support for my endeavors.

In the evening of the same day I set out on my third trip to Stockholm.

Ryti had given me two memoranda to take along, in which he set forth his views on how the case should be discussed with the Swedish government and with Mme. Kollontai.

MY THIRD TRIP TO STOCKHOLM

I arrived at Stockholm on February 26 at midnight, Swedish time. Although it was late, Erkko and Professor T. M. Kivimäki came to visit me at my hotel room, where we talked for two hours.

Kivimäki, who had just returned from Germany, told us that everyone he met had urged that we make peace even though on hard terms. In any event, once the major war was over, there would be a chance to get back any ceded areas. Finland would be in a position to say that it had fought to the limit of its powers and then had an opportunity to get out of the war. But when the democratic countries betrayed the confidence reposed in them, Finland had been left alone.

From Kivimäki's report it became clear that Count von der Golz had, on the basis of a letter received from Paasikivi, gone to discuss Finland's case with Hitler. As a consequence of this, the German government had inquired into the possibilities of mediation, but Moscow had rejected the offer.

We agreed that Kivimäki should report to the Cabinet foreign affairs committee on the impressions received from his trip, for which reason I do not set them down in further detail at this point.

The following morning, February 27, General Rappe, chief of the

Swedish general staff, came to see me in my hotel. He wished to secure my views on various matters. I told him in what light we in Finland regarded the situation, and particularly what our attitude was toward the aid which had come from Sweden and what we still hoped for from Sweden.

General Rappe, who did most of the talking, began by explaining the diverse facets of Swedish opinion. In his view, sending volunteers to Finland would produce no results. Sweden ought to join in the war officially. He felt that this opinion was very general in Sweden. He explained that if Finland were obliged to turn to the Western powers, Sweden would be drawn into the major war.

I shared his opinion regarding the sending of volunteers. But I told him that we had never asked Sweden to take part officially in the Finnish war. I also set forth the principal points of the aid plans of the Western powers, with which he did not appear to be familiar.

This conversation lasted for an hour.

At ten o'clock I went to Prime Minister Hansson's office in the Chancellery. I said that I had come to talk with him alone, since our earlier conversation had assumed too official a character through the presence of Ministers Sköld and Günther. For this reason it had turned into an exposition of the official stands of both parties.

Hansson said that I was always welcome and that he was grateful for the opportunity of conversing privately with me.

I began by pointing out that we were now faced with a final decision. In a very few days we must choose the course which we would follow. For this reason it was important for us to examine the situation to its very foundations, so that subsequently we would be able to justify in every detail what we had done. On this account I wished to ask him a number of questions, to which I would desire altogether frank answers. These questions bore upon numerous problems, which are here dealt with separately.

1. *Nature of Aid from Sweden.*—I inquired what the aid offered by Sweden would really amount to. The reply we had received from the Swedish government on February 24 had been vague indeed. It had contained neither figures regarding the scope of this aid nor any indication of the time at which it should reach us. What was meant by the words "under the present circumstances"? Was there anything special back of this?

Hansson answered that everything the Swedish government could say had been said in the Swedish reply. Swedish official participation in the war was impossible, as was the sending of regular forces to Finland. Either measure would automatically involve Sweden in a major war. Germany had told them so directly and officially. However, Sweden would continue to send volunteer forces. To what degree this would be successful, how many of these forces could be sent, and when they would reach Finland—these were matters on which they could say nothing definite in advance. The men in the Swedish armed forces had permission to leave as volunteers for Finland. The earlier top limit of 8,000 men had been raised to 12,000; when Sweden was informed that even this was too little, the limit was again increased by 4,000. Thus a total of 16,000 men were free to separate from their units as volunteers. The Norrbotten forces had permission to detach up to 10 percent of their strength if that many aspirants should come forward. But the government could not force anyone to go. They received varying reports on the attitude of the forces. According to some there were aspirants, according to others there were not. Volunteers who should go were to be fully equipped. The subject had been considered by the foreign relations committee of the Riksdag. Only a single voice (Rickard Sandler) had been raised in advocacy of more extensive aid.

The conversation then passed on to deal with the publicity of a few days before, concerning my previous visit and the statement about it given out by the Swedish government.

Hansson lamented that the matter had been publicized. According to his information it had been revealed to the press by City Councilor Sundberg. Since at the time the children of our Finnish Cabinet Minister J. O. Söderhjelm had been staying with his family, suspicion had been directed toward Söderhjelm, who was thought perhaps to have spoken of my trip to Stockholm. Sundberg had first offered the story to the *Stockholms Tidningen*. This paper, however, had not published the item itself but had passed it on to the *Folkets Dagblad Politiken*.

I remarked that Hansson's communiqué and the subsequently issued royal statement had, as it turned out, cost Finland dear. They had cut the ground from beneath all Swedish activity in aid of Finland and at the same time they had had a seriously crippling effect in Finland. Their significance was plain in the light of the great rejoicing to which they had given rise in Moscow. These official announcements had cost Finland both Viipuri and Sortavala, since up to that time the peace terms had been more modest.

Hansson: What other recourse had I, save to issue the communiqué? Should I have issued a denial or remained silent?

Tanner: Silence would have been best.

2. *Transit of Western Forces.*—I furnished general information regarding the plans of the Western powers without mentioning either figures or dates. As Sweden declined to send auxiliary forces, Finland might be obliged to have recourse to Western aid. It was impossible for such aid to reach us through Petsamo. The only channel was through Scandinavia, using the ports of Narvik and Trondhjem. In such circumstances Sweden would come to hold a key position vis-à-vis Finland. Would Sweden permit the transit passage?

Hansson: The Swedish government has clearly expressed its position on this point. Sweden desires to observe neutrality on this matter as well. No transit passage of forces can be permitted. Volunteers and small groups might be permitted to pass through.

Tanner: How large groups?

Hansson: It is hard to set a figure. Not very large.

Tanner: May they carry their weapons with them?

Hansson: No.

Tanner: In that case transit is impossible. That matter is settled, then. The Western powers will presumably not wish to force their way.

Hansson: It would be dreadful if they tried it. They would force Sweden and Norway to make a difficult decision. If the Western powers should try to come through these countries against their will, Sweden would find itself in the war on the Russian side and against Finland.

3. *The Course of Peace.*—I went on: If both the courses which I had hitherto touched upon were blocked, Finland would be obliged to make peace. Alone we could no longer continue the war. The Soviet terms were now harsher than before. Hansson's communiqué and the royal proclamation had rocked Finland. At the very least Viipuri and Sortavala were now lost. Future defense lines would be much worse than those to date. Peace on such conditions would be a bitter pill to us. The people would hardly be prepared to approve such a peace. Although the Cabinet inclined in that direction, there was no assurance that the Diet could be brought along, and serious dissensions might arise. The structure of the national independence which had thus far been built up might be overthrown on this account.

Hansson replied that it was indeed a terrible business, but it must be looked at realistically. It was easy to go on with the war, but what would the final result be? It could be even worse. Ordinarily much more courage was needed to make peace than to beat the drums of war. To date he had not considered that he might give Finland advice, but now, in this confidential conversation with me, he wanted to say that in his view peace should be made even on hard terms.

4. *Support from Sweden*

Tanner: If we initiate peace negotiations, is Sweden prepared to back them, for instance, by declaring that Sweden will take part in the war officially if Finland is faced with barbarous terms?

Hansson: Impossible. That would be taking part in the war.

Tanner: And diplomatic support?

Hansson: Within the limits of our power.

5. *A Defense Pact*

Tanner: In Finland it is believed that if peace is made now, it will not turn out to be a lasting one. The Soviet party may later present new demands, and the consequence may be a new war. The only chance of warding this off is through a defense pact with Sweden and, we hope, with Norway as well. What is the attitude of the Swedish government toward this idea?

Hansson: The idea is not unfamiliar to the Swedish government. The pact would necessarily have to be made with Norway too. At the meeting of the Committee for Nordic Collaboration I earlier touched upon this matter. If at present there were a defense pact among these countries, the Soviet Union would surely not have attacked Finland.

Tanner: I am quite of the same mind on that point.

Hansson: But the matter is an involved and difficult one. It requires thorough preparation. It would be necessary to coordinate the defense establishment, industry, foreign policy, etc. It would call for extensive ground-laying activity.

Tanner: Of course. But someone would have to advocate it in any case.

Hansson: We'll see about taking the matter up.

6. *Economic Support*

Tanner: So I come to the question which it will be easiest for the Swedish government to answer. After the conclusion of peace, reconstruction work will begin in Finland, and it will be a hard job. We have lost much. May we count on Sweden's help, at least through loans?

Hansson: Definitely. (*With some enthusiasm he added:*) It is our plain duty. We will do everything we can there. You can rely on that.

Having dealt with these questions, we passed on to the meeting of foreign ministers held at Copenhagen on February 24. I lamented that Finland had not been invited to attend, despite the fact that the Finnish question had been the principal subject under discussion. I asked whether observance of a policy of neutrality called for such a line of action. In that case neutrality was a bad program. If a great power attacked a small country, the latter would be like a leper everyone tried to avoid. Third parties would no longer dare to take its case under consideration.

Hansson was startled by my accusation. He did not know how the meeting had been arranged. In any event, he assured me, the fact that Finland was left out had been in no wise deliberate.

The conversation had lasted an hour and a half. We thanked each other for the information given and received, and I departed.

At noon there occurred my third meeting with Mme. Kollontai, at the residence of Baroness Stäel von Holstein on Valhallavägen. The service personnel of the establishment had been sent out, and the house was quite empty.

We talked about the new peace terms. Mme. Kollontai was greatly disturbed by them; she was almost in tears. She lamented that we had not proceeded earlier to negotiations on easier terms, when Hanko Cape would have sufficed as a basis. Now the Soviet forces had met with successes, and this drove up their demands. However, this very fact would make it easier to arrive at workable terms, because Soviet military honor had been vindicated.

I asked her if these terms were perhaps intended as a trial balloon. Would we be able to bargain on them?

Mme. Kollontai did not believe so. They were not a basis for negotiations but firm demands. Possibly some changes could be secured during the course of negotiations.

I described what difficulties a peace of this sort would imply for Finland. There would be great bitterness, and neither good neighborly relations nor a lasting peace would be brought about. I ran over the contents of Ryti's memorandum and promised to give her an abstract of it in writing. I hoped she would send it straight to Stalin. I went on to say that Finland's reply to the Soviet terms could not be given too short a notice. Democracies took more time making their decisions than dictatorships did. It would be necessary to get Diet backing. I asked her to communicate this to Moscow, and also the fact that we would transmit our answer shortly.

Mme. Kollontai promised to do this. She also promised to send Stalin Ryti's memorandum.

I had hardly reached my hotel when Erkko telephoned me and said Günther wished to have him call. Günther had also asked whether I could not drop in at the same time. Erkko had promised he would try to locate me.

We went to Günther's office at 3:00 P.M. I told Erkko beforehand that I knew what Günther wanted to talk about: Finland's having been left out of the Copenhagen conference.

This was the case. He took up this subject at once and described the program of the conference.

I spoke of the matter to him in the same fashion as I had to Prime Minister Hansson.

Günther was quite distressed over what I had to say—he was a poet, and a man of fine feeling. He said that the Danish Foreign Minister, Munch, had organized the meeting and that he had not even advised them of its agenda beforehand. There had been no deliberate purpose in Finland's having been left out.

I continued to express dissatisfaction with the way matters had been arranged. In Finland we had been quite unable to understand it, and the matter had given rise to vexation. Was that what Nordic collaboration turned out to be after all?

I should remark that we had not been entirely forgotten at the Copenhagen conference of foreign ministers. On February 25 I had received from there the following telegram: "In deep sympathy with the sufferings of our brother people, we send you our hearty greetings with hopes for peace and freedom for the Finnish nation. Koht. Günther. Munch."

After this we went on to talk about the difficulties Finland experienced in choosing its course. Should we make peace or rely upon Western aid?

I regretted that after Sweden's decision Finland had been left alone. If we were obliged to apply to the Western powers, Sweden would be in a difficult position. Could it refuse passage? In that case it would be fighting on the Russian side and against Finland.

Günther had feared this possibility might come up. He asked me at least to inform Sweden before we should turn to the Western powers.

I promised to do this, although I did not understand what use it would be. For Sweden had already determined its position, and today I had received a further negative reply from the Prime Minister.

At 4:00 P.M. I left for home by plane. From Turku I continued by car to Helsinki, taking Professor T. M. Kivimäki with me. He was much inclined to talk and decidedly favored making peace. In his opinion there was no other way out if we did not choose to go down to entire destruction.

THE GOVERNMENT DEBATES

On February 28 I was again in my office. Several representatives of foreign powers came in to see me; they were anxious to learn the most recent news. Among them were the American and the British representatives. The latter said he had come to bring important information. I had earlier urged him to find out definitely whether the Western powers could augment their aid in terms of men, for which reason he had cabled his government. In reply the Foreign Office had desired him to inform the Finnish government as follows:

1. According to what the general staff reported, the forces could be in Finland by the third or fourth week of April, that is to say, between the fifteenth and the thirtieth. By the end of the month England and France would have twelve to thirteen thousand fully equipped men in Finland. In addition, they would have considerable forces in Sweden to back this expedition.

2. To my question of how the forces would pass through Scandinavia, whether they might come in units, on the analogy of the Kondor forces, as the Germans had done in the Spanish war, the Foreign Office replied that they did not believe it made any difference whether they came as organized units or as volunteers. Russia and Germany would make no distinction on this point. They would give weight only to the numbers involved and would determine their positions in accordance with that factor, paying no attention to the name under which these forces came. England could not disguise its forces by calling them volunteers, since this would give rise to questions in Parliament and there would have to be a public explanation of the matter. Thus there were technical and legal obstacles to sending these forces under the guise of volunteers.

3. To my question as to what form aid to Sweden would take if Germany should bring pressure to bear upon Sweden, the answer was that this would be taken up with Sweden. The British government could not declare in advance, at least to Finland, anything regarding the number of men involved or regarding the details of such assistance. In any event the Allies would furnish sufficient aid.

I asked Vereker a number of other questions, on the basis of which a further discussion developed.

He again gave assurance that England meant to help Finland and that the aid which it offered would prove sufficient. In any event, the Russians were in a hurry to make peace.

I asked again whether England could give guarantees for our independence and the permanence of our boundaries and whether we might be assured that we would become participants in the final peace settlement.

Vereker: I cannot answer simply in the affirmative. But the Finnish government may rest assured that if England comes in to fight on the Finnish front, England will do everything in its power to guarantee the independence and autonomy of the country.

Tanner: How long does England obligate itself to keep its forces here?

Vereker: If England is asked to fight on Finland's behalf, it will keep its forces here until the conclusion of peace, if they are not indispensably needed elsewhere, and these troops will stand behind Finland's demands to the end. I assure you that England will back Finland a hundred percent. I have sent the Soviet demands to London but as yet have not received an answer on this point.

At 2:00 P.M. I went to see Ryti at the Bank of Finland. It chanced that Erkko telephoned from Stockholm just at that time. He said that at eleven that same morning Mme. Kollontai had informed Foreign Minister Günther that Finland must deliver its reply to the Soviet terms within two days. On this account Erkko had asked Günther whether this declaration signified an ultimatum, since the time limit was precisely specified. To this Günther had answered that he, at least, had not understood it so. The safest thing, however, was to assume that the statement was intended as an ultimatum, so that the time within which a reply might be made ended on March 1 at eleven o'clock. Mme. Kollontai had also said she had cabled Ryti's memorandum to Moscow. She had furthermore inquired whether she could arrange to meet me again. When she learned that I had already left Stockholm, she had not pursued this inquiry.

At 3:00 P.M. the Council of State met in order to continue its consideration of the matter and to hear how my trip had turned out. There were also present President Kallio, Professor T. M. Kivimäki, and General Walden.

I reported in detail both what I had learned in Stockholm and the explanations Minister Vereker and General Ling had given concerning the aid plans of the Western powers. I concluded by observing that the situation was now such that a decision must be made. We had waited for assistance, but we were now alone. Even the auxiliary forces offered by the Western powers had diminished stage by stage. They could not have a decisive effect on the course of the war; they would merely prolong the conflict and sweep us into the major war. In my mind Sweden's position was decisive, because it was plain the Western powers would not come through Sweden by force. Throughout the whole war Sweden had held a key position. It could have helped us on its own or it could have permitted the Western powers to come to our aid. But it did not feel it could do this. Earlier, when many details remained to be cleared up, I had found it difficult to accept the peace terms with which we were confronted. Now there was no longer any choice; it was obligatory to accept the terms offered, burdensome though they were. By cutting a limb from the body of our nation we could save the whole. Russia had won what it was after, but we had won Russia's repudiation of the Kuusinen government.

Kivimäki, who had arrived from Stockholm with me, now described the impressions he had derived from his trip. He had visited in Stockholm, Oslo, and Copenhagen, trying to determine attitudes and to influence the sending of aid. In Sweden much had been done to forward the volunteer movement, but by reason of the reluctance of the Cabinet, and particularly of Prime Minister Hansson, no great results had come of this. The decisive event had occurred when Hansson's negative reply to Finland's official request for assistance had become public. This had given rise to great confusion among groups working to foster this movement. The King's intervention, which was said to have been a consequence of the influence of Markus Wallenberg and contrary to the advice of others, had been a death blow to the aid which had been planned for Finland. At this moment there was no hope that Sweden would join forces with us officially. Sweden would also refuse transit of Western troops. The fundamental reason for the scant results was the unwillingness to make sacrifices, as well as the fear of Germany, which the Cabinet exploited by letting it be understood that Germany had given Sweden a warning.

On his trip to Berlin in order to clarify this point, Kivimäki had been able to ascertain that the statement put out in Sweden was wholly erroneous. The Finnish war was awkward for Germany because it disturbed Germany's importation of goods from Russia and because the judgment of the world with regard to the Finnish war bore indirectly upon Germany as well. The German people were favorably disposed toward Finland. Thus Sweden's joining in the war would not be repugnant to Germany. The statement that Sweden was under pressure must be flatly denied. The only qualification was that the Western powers must not participate in the war in addition to Sweden. If, however, the war remained a local one between Finland and Russia, Sweden might freely determine its own stand. Yet in Germany they were of the view that the inconsiderable Swedish forces would not suffice to bring about a favorable settlement. Kivimäki had been able to determine that Germany had been acquainted with the peace terms at each stage of their development and that it was also familiar with the most recent terms. Germany was indeed prepared to mediate, but evidently only as a mail box, since it had no means of influencing Russia.

Walden then reported on the most recent word from the front, indicating that the situation was very serious. This led to a very anxious discussion, as may be supposed in the light of the fact that the matter had reached a decisive stage.

Prime Minister Ryti associated himself unreservedly with the attitude I had expressed. In his view it would be frivolous to set our hopes upon what might happen in the field of world politics and upon vague wishful thinking about assistance. Consequently, we must make peace even on the most burdensome conditions.

The same stand was taken, for various reasons, by Kotilainen, Paasikivi, Heikkinen, and Koivisto.

Niukkanen and Hannula were rigidly opposed to acceptance of the peace terms offered.

President Kallio declared that the position was dreadfully tragic. The League of Nations had unanimously promised assistance. Sweden and Norway had taken part in this decision, but now they would not even permit aid to be brought to us from other powers. Worst of all was the fact that the government would not have a united nation behind it if it should make peace on these terms. In the President's opinion it was essential that we learn Marshal Mannerheim's view, since there was the danger that he thought differently on the subject. This did not mean that the government would be hiding behind Marshal Mannerheim's back, but the inquiry should be undertaken in order to preserve a spirit of unity.

Several members of the Cabinet were in a position to say that Marshal Mannerheim was familiar with the latest peace terms and that he considered their acceptance unavoidable. Others however, backed President Kallio's idea, asserting that either the Marshal must be brought to the capital or members of the Cabinet should be sent to him in order to ascertain his attitude beyond doubt.

I reminded the Cabinet that, by reason of the time limit set by the Soviet Union I must be in a position on the following morning to present the Cabinet's stand to the Foreign Relations Committee of the Diet. During the evening of that day the matter must be carried to the Diet groups and, on the morning of Friday, March 1, to the Diet as a whole.

On this occasion no decision was reached within the Cabinet. It was only decided that Prime Minister Ryti, Ministers von Born, Fagerholm, Heikkinen, and Söderhjelm, and General Walden should proceed to headquarters as soon as possible to consult with the Commander-in-Chief, after which they should return to Helsinki in the morning.

I should add that, when the President complained of the negative attitude of the Scandinavian countries, Paasikivi inquired whether Sweden had not indicated its attitude at the meeting of the heads of state as far back as last fall. President Kallio replied that the question had not at that time been asked on an official basis because it was feared the reply would be discouraging.

As illustrative of the complicated nature of the situation, there may also be mentioned the fact that while the Cabinet was in session the French Minister, Magny, appeared at the Bank of Finland to express the hope of the French government that an appeal for aid would be made at once. At the same time, in a cable from London, Minister Gripenberg reported that in the opinion of the British government the sending of auxiliary forces depended exclusively on the attitude of the Swedish government. He had been informed by Lord Halifax, the British Foreign Minister, that on February 26 Maisky, the Soviet Ambassador, had asked him to transmit the same peace terms as were later presented to us through Sweden, but Halifax had refused.

At this juncture events began to move at an accelerated pace. The question of peace had to be brought before a wider circle, and on this account it became subjected to more animated consideration than it had previously undergone. The following day, February 29, proved eventful and important.

I had asked the Diet Foreign Relations Committee to assemble at nine in the morning. I supplied it with information on what had happened since the last meeting, on February 21. Headquarters had continued its discussions with representatives of the Western powers concerning their offer of assistance. On February 23 we had received the Soviet announcement of the terms which were to form the basis for peace negotiations. Negotiations with the Swedish government concerning auxiliary forces had led to a negative result. The most recent development was the demand or quasi ultimatum of the Soviet Union to the effect that its terms must be accepted or rejected within two days. The Cabinet had not yet finally determined its position, but despite this fact it desired at this point to acquaint the Foreign Relations Committee with the situation, since it was important that the Diet groups be convened this same evening and that the attitude of the Diet majority be determined.

The members of the committee declared that, even as things stood now, they supported without reservation the making of peace on the terms offered. Only Representative Kekkonen assumed a stand of rigid opposition. Representative Hackzell, while personally supporting our making peace, declared that he could say nothing as to the attitude of the Coalition (conservative) Party. In the meeting of the Diet group a month before, only one of its members had advocated making peace.

Since it had not been possible to declare the Cabinet's position to the committee, the committee decided to meet again at 6:00 P.M. It was decided that the Diet groups should be convened at 7:00 P.M.

I had just left the meeting of the Foreign Relations Committee when the British Minister, Vereker, came in to see me. He had received a cable from his government saying there were rumors that the Finnish government was thinking of asking the German government to mediate for the initiation of peace negotiations. He inquired if he might learn whether there was anything to this. On the basis of earlier discussions, the British government expected that the Finnish government would tell England before it should take such a step.

I assured him there was nothing to it. We had promised to keep the British government advised regarding the course of the matter. After the aid which they had furnished to date, and with further assistance promised, it would be improper to conceal from them a move of this character. Germany had not been asked to take any steps. For a week I had not even seen the local German representative. I read to Vereker the cable we had just received from Gripenberg, indicating that the rumor might have started in Rome.

Vereker: How could that be?

Tanner: I think I understand what happened. Count Bech was on a visit here as a special agent of Ciano, the Italian Foreign Minister. He talked with Ryti about the possibility that Italy might try to get Germany to undertake mediation. Ryti gave him a free hand to work in this sense.

Vereker: That perhaps clears up the source of the rumor.

He also had an interesting story to relate. When Halifax had refused to transmit Russia's peace terms to Finland, Soviet Ambassador Maisky had become angry and threatened that this stand on the part of the British government might bring in its train unexpected consequences with respect to relations between the Soviet Union and England. To this Halifax had replied that it would be difficult to prevent the outbreak of a grim conflict if the Soviet Union were obstinately to continue the war against Finland and present terms which it was difficult to accept.

Vereker went on to say that these latest developments might help us in making our decision. He inquired whether the problem of the appeal to be made to the Western powers had been settled yet.

Tanner: It has not. We are discussing it at the moment. At the same time we are deliberating on the demands made by the Soviet Union. They have given us an ultimatum of two days for the presentation of a reply.

Vereker: That's very important news.

Tanner: If we were sure of the adequacy of the aid offered and of the speed with which it would reach us, a decision would be easy. Since we cannot be sure on these points, the matter becomes difficult.

The members of the Cabinet who had been at headquarters to see the Commander-in-Chief returned to the capital during the course of the morning, so that a new private session of the Cabinet could be held at 4:00 P.M. They reported on the situation at the front, and on the Commander-in-Chief's opinion as to how long the front could hold up. This opinion was quite pessimistic. As one of those who had visited headquarters described it, the situation was "not critical, but disturbing." On the basis of what they had learned, all those who had gone to headquarters were now prepared to accede to Russia's terms. The other members agreed with this stand, except Hannula, who continued to be firmly opposed, and Niukkanen, who was prepared to support our making peace only on the condition that it should not turn out to be another Peace of Nystad. He wanted the line to run south of Viipuri and Jänisjärvi. He, too, was by this time willing to cede Hanko Cape, but he opposed making a treaty of friendship, which many other Cabinet members also found it difficult to approve.

The result of the discussion was to be communicated to the meeting of the Diet Foreign Relations Committee which was shortly to be held.

We further discussed in this meeting the language of the reply to be delivered to the Soviet Union; a draft prepared by the President and the Foreign Minister was taken under consideration. It was to be cleared at a meeting which would be held later on the same day.

There was not much further discussion at the meeting of the Diet Foreign Relations Committee, which was held at 6:00 P.M. Since the members of the committee had heard that the Cabinet had decided to support the delivery of an affirmative reply to the Soviet Union, all members of the committee save Representative Kekkonen associated themselves with this decision.

The meetings of the Diet groups which had been scheduled earlier were held at 7:00 P.M. I set forth the present aspects of the matter before the Social Democratic Diet group, which unanimously approved the stand of the Cabinet. The "bourgeois" (i.e., nonsocialist) groups held a joint meeting at first, and here Prime Minister Ryti furnished them with the necessary information. The discussion which developed as a result was confused, and Ryti was frequently obliged to give further explanations. When the meeting ended, the "bourgeois" groups separated to hold their individual meetings, after which the joint meeting was resumed at 9:00 P.M. At that time I too was present. Again the discussion seemed random, but at length it was possible to discern that almost all those present had approved the Cabinet's stand.

Evidently, despite all precautions, word of these discussions had leaked to outsiders. It was perhaps in consequence of this that the French Minister, Magny, asked at 9:30 P.M. for an audience. I received him in the Diet building, where the meeting of the several groups was even then under way. His business was to announce on behalf of his government that the plan of sending an auxiliary force of only 12,000 men had been abandoned and that there were to come special forces numbering 20,000, made up of Britishers, Frenchmen, and Poles. These forces were at the moment in process of being assembled. He offered this information because Minister Holma in Paris had inquired whether the auxiliary forces might not be increased in number and arrive sooner. Magny continued to believe that the negative attitude of the Swedish government toward transit passage was not final and that neither Sweden nor Norway would undertake to oppose passage when they should get the final detailed information. If only Finnish resistance on the fronts could last a few weeks more, the auxiliary forces would be here in sufficient time. Their arrival would signify only a beginning, as there would be further reinforcements. However, if Finland were to accept a peace, this would be a complete capitulation and the Finnish government would have to bear the responsibility for the mutilation of the country.

When I made reference to the cabled information from Holma to the effect that the arrival of this aid in March was impossible, Magny assured me that the forces would be here in time.

I wished also to hear his views as to whether France could back Finland in peace negotiations with the Soviet Union, so that we might secure more advantageous terms. And, if in these negotiations we could not reach a satisfactory conclusion, could we subsequently return to the question of assistance from the West?

Minister Magny doubted this very much. Sympathy toward Finland in the West would be chilled during the interval. Upon starting negotiations, Finland would move to Germany's side, and this would represent a great success for Germany.

When the Diet groups had finished their meetings, the Cabinet met again at 11:15 P.M. in order to decide upon the language of the reply to be transmitted. On the basis of the earlier discussion the Prime Minister had prepared a new draft, regarding which there was still some further talk. Finally it was approved in the following form:

The Finnish government, which for its part also aspires toward the termination of hostilities and the conclusion of a peace, considers that it can in this sense regard the conditions as a point of departure for negotiations, and accepts them in principle. The comprehensive scope of the proposal and the obscurity of some of its details make clarification and definition necessary, but these points can be cleared up in oral negotiations. The Finnish government awaits a statement as to when and where the Soviet government proposes that the negotiations begin. The Finnish government considers Moscow a suitable meeting place.

The text of the reply was to be sent to Erkko at once, with the additional directive to him that he delay sending it until he had received special instructions to that effect.

Thus ended this day of many shifts and changes, and the matter seemed at last to have been set on a safe course.

THE WESTERN POWERS BECOME ACTIVE

It is rare to be so thoroughly deceived in one's expectations as was the Cabinet in its understanding that everything was settled. The decision merely led to another week of wrestling with the problem, of weighing all the pros and cons.

No sooner had the Cabinet reached its decision than it began to be pressed urgently from without. France and England, which until then had acted rather casually in the matter of furnishing assistance, as soon as word of the Cabinet's most recent decisions had reached them, emerged from their torpor and began to take notice of the necessity to do something definite if they wished to set up a new front in Finland. They had apparently judged that Finland in its need would without further deliberation snatch at their offer. Since this had not happened, they now attempted by all means at their disposal to prevent Finland from engaging in peace negotiations with the Soviet Union. The result was that Gripenberg, our Minister in London, and Holma, our Minister in Paris, telephoned fresh information to the Prime Minister during the night. Ryti called me on the telephone at 1:30 A.M. to give me the gist of these conversations. It was becoming clearer and clearer that Finland was regarded as an important piece in the strategy of the Western powers. To be sure, we ourselves had never imagined that their aid was offered us for the sake of our fine blue eyes.

That night other important cables came in. Holma reported that Premier Daladier had definitely promised the arrival of forces by the end of March. The time of departure would depend on London, which would hardly be prepared to dispatch its forces before March 12. France would be ready earlier. Later that night still another cable from Holma was received, reporting that Daladier had once more promised to insist upon the prompt arrival here of auxiliary forces in sufficient numbers. The information which had come in that night thus afforded much new matter for deliberation.

As the morning of March 1 dawned, it was plain, at least to the Foreign Minister, that the day would be an extremely important one. The Soviet Union had called for a reply by eleven o'clock, and the reply must state whether we accepted or rejected its peace terms. In the light of the vigorous representations the Western powers had made that night, however, it would have been frivolous to disregard their proposals without a thorough analysis. Therefore, I wished to convene the Cabinet at the earliest possible moment to hear its opinion.

The Cabinet session began at 10:30 A.M., an hour and a half before the reply to the Soviet Union must be delivered. (Stockholm clocks were an hour later than Finnish time.) President Kallio also took part, as had been his custom in all the sessions of the past weeks. As a background for discussion I related what had happened since the evening before. According to France's most recent official announcement, the Western powers would send 50,000 men, to arrive in Finland by the end of March. France and England would see to the transit of the auxiliary forces through Norway and Sweden. France asked in addition that discussions with the Soviet Union should not be continued. From London, also, similar news had reached us through our Minister, Gripenberg, who reported urgent preparations for sending off the forces. But in the event that discussions with the Soviet Union should be continued, all preparations would be interrupted and shipments of arms and economic support would cease. Under such circumstances Finland would be powerless to resist new demands on the part of the Soviet Union. England did not regard the Swedish stand on transit rights as final.

I lamented the fact that things had taken such a complicated turn at the last moment and that now, within a few minutes' time, we must decide toward which of the two concentrations of power we should turn. The Soviet offer would perhaps not be renewed if it were not accepted now. On the other hand, it was uncertain whether the Western powers could carry out their endeavor. The Soviet Union was fully aware of the Western intentions, and it was for that reason it was so urgent in its demands. If it was safe to assume the existence of a strong Soviet desire to avoid premature entanglement in a world war (which was what the coming of the Western powers to Finland would mean), it was possible to reply to the Soviet Union neither affirmatively nor negatively but by posing new questions. Thus we might win a few days' time and meanwhile secure clarification of the true intentions of the Western powers. We would have to call upon them for official corroboration of the immediate dispatch of the promised 50,000 men, and thereafter of more as need should arise, and we should urgently request at least a hundred bombing planes with their crews. I reported further that on the previous evening the reply we had approved had been sent to Erkko, but that he had been directed not to forward it until special instructions to that effect should reach him from here.

This time the discussion had an altogether different tone from that of the previous evening, only a few hours before. The size of the aid proffered and the promise that it should be brought rapidly to its destination were factors of such a character that they could not be passed over without further examination. On this account not a single member of the Cabinet now called for the inclusion in the reply of a flat acceptance of the Soviet terms. President Kallio was exceptionally pleased with the new turn matters had taken. After passing a sleepless night because of yesterday's decision, he had concluded that the position prevailing at the front as of March 1 should serve as a basis for negotiations.

The difficulty now lay only in what we should say in reply to the Soviet Union. Erkko telephoned from Stockholm during the session, to ask whether he should forward the reply. I promised him an answer shortly. When the session ended at 11:45, I telephoned Erkko the Cabinet's decision. The reply which had been approved earlier was not to be forwarded, but in its stead the following:

The Finnish government is anxious to bring about a cessation of hostilities and the conclusion of a peace, but since the new frontier contemplated in the proposal is vague, further particulars with regard thereto are requested. Similarly information is desired as to what compensation Finland is to receive.

I asked Erkko to deliver the following message to Minister Günther:

As I promised, I am informing you that by reason of the harsh peace terms of the Soviet Union the Finnish government is seriously considering an approach to the Western powers.

In the Cabinet session it was decided that more detailed information should be sought on the solidity of the Western aid offer. We sent cables to London and Paris requesting urgent information as to whether the Western powers could send at least 50,000 men immediately. They must be here before the end of March. Later we must have more. These forces would engage in battle on all fronts under the orders of the Commander-in-Chief. We also requested 100 bombers with their crews at once. We further asked what guarantees the Western powers could give that the Scandinavian countries would promptly assent to transit passage.

At 2:30 in the afternoon I learned through Ryti that Erkko had telephoned him Günther's greetings from Stockholm. Günther had been at a loss as to our reason for wanting the new frontier settled in advance—surely this would mean a worse point of departure. He thought it would be better to make an affirmative reply now and take care of details later in the negotiations. If we then wanted to break off negotiations, an opportunity would always present itself. Günther did not think that at present we could get any answer on the question of whether we might secure compensation.

Ryti had told Erkko that, as the line suggested was very vague, it might mean fifty percent more or less. For our part we would not want to break off negotiations once we had entered upon them. We had in fact many times declared that we wanted peace.

With reference to the assistance offered by the Western powers, Günther had told Erkko firmly that Sweden would not permit these forces to pass through its territory; to which Ryti had made the comment that the point had not been raised in the present connection.

An hour and a half later Erkko called me to continue the earlier conversation, asking first of all whether I had learned of Günther's attitude through Ryti. When I told him I was aware of it, he said that he had been called in once more to see Günther, who meanwhile had talked with Mme. Kollontai. She had declared that initiation of peace negotiations depended solely upon whether Finland accepted the terms offered "as a basis for discussion." Günther had deemed it best to talk about details during the negotiations, when Stalin would have a chance to make "a grand gesture." On this account Günther had suggested that a sentence be added to our reply, to the effect that "Finland is accordingly prepared in principle to accept the Russian proposal." Among other matters, Günther had inquired whether there was occasion for him to make a proposal that hostilities be suspended. On this point I told Erkko that if Günther felt he could do this on his own initiative, we would be pleased to have him do so.

According to Erkko, Mme. Kollontai had not been told anything by Moscow relative to the cession of Viipuri and Sortavala. This information had come through Sweden's Minister in Moscow, Assarsson.

As Günther had asked us to let him know within a couple of hours whether he might add to our reply the sentence he had suggested, I said that it was impossible to answer this question before the next day.

Erkko went on to say that the Swedish Minister in Helsinki, Sahlin, would shortly call on me to make a statement on the same matter. Sahlin did in fact come in during office hours, making the following statement, which at my request he set down in writing.

Telephoned statement from Foreign Minister Günther to Minister Sahlin in Helsinki, March 1, 1940, 4:15 P.M., for earliest possible delivery to Foreign Minister Tanner:

If the Finnish government's reply to the Soviet Union is intended to be of a positive character, I am obliged to request that there be added a sentence reading as follows: "The Finnish government is accordingly prepared in principle to accept the Russian proposal." (The phrase "in principle" might perhaps be omitted.)

After thorough discussion with the local Soviet Minister I have in fact come to the obvious conclusion that otherwise the reply will be understood in Moscow as a rejection, with the far-reaching consequences which will attend upon that fact.

I should be grateful for the promptest possible reply.

I should consider it most unwise to ask that the frontier be defined, but I am disposed to put forth this suggestion if Finland still holds fast to the idea.

At my invitation the British Minister, Vereker, came to call, and I informed him of the most recent developments. We had not given the Soviet Union its reply within the time specified. Instead we had asked for further information regarding the aid offered by the West. Vereker spoke with enthusiasm of this aid and urged us to request it without delay. If the Scandinavian countries did not permit the Western forces to pass through their territories, so much the worse for them.

With reference to this point, I remarked that this misfortune for them would not save Finland. I promised to keep him informed on developments from then on.

We now judged that the Western powers were exceptionally active with regard to the aid to be dispatched to Finland. Holma telephoned Ryti from Paris in the afternoon to say that there was great activity there in furtherance of the aid in question. General Ironside (the British Commander-in-Chief) had told Finland's military attaché in Paris, Colonel Paasonen, that the figures Generals Ling and Ganeval had given us concerning the assistance to be furnished were wrong. It was the intention of the Western powers to send Finland 50,000 men at once, and subsequently still more. Premier Daladier, too, had told Holma that the Finnish question was the most important political matter of the moment. France was making every effort to help Finland. Daladier had also promised to send fifty bombing planes at once. At this point Holma had not yet received our cable asking for one hundred planes. He went off to ask for fifty more.

During the course of the day, further telegrams came in from the Western nations, dealing with the same subject. Both England and France now promised 50,000 men without delay. The Western powers promised to take care of transit through Norway and Sweden on their own account. Statements received from London, however, were rather more cautious than those from Paris.

March 2.—I considered it necessary to take counsel with the whole Cabinet once more. A session was held at eleven o'clock in the bomb shelter of the Bank of Finland. The President also attended.

I reported the events of the day before, remarking that presumably contact with Moscow had not been broken off despite our passing the time limit. Sweden was trying to get better peace terms for us. We were still considering the merits of the offer of assistance from the Western powers. It appeared, however, that Diet circles were uneasy because we had not replied to the Soviet Union within the time specified; for this reason a meeting of the Diet Foreign Relations Committee had been requested for that evening. I had nevertheless suggested that it be deferred until today, so that the Cabinet might have an opportunity to become acquainted with the most recent developments.

The members of the Cabinet were satisfied to learn that our chances of continuing conversations with Moscow appeared to be still open and that the situation thus was more promising. I received authorization to report the latest developments to the Diet committee.

This report was delivered at a meeting of the committee the same evening at six o'clock. Several committee members took the floor with reference to my report, and the general state of mind appeared easy when I remarked that the peace line had not been lost even though we were simultaneously probing the offer of aid. The members of the committee believed it was possible that by proceeding in this fashion we might bring about an alleviation of the peace terms. Only Representative Kares rigidly opposed peace negotiations on the basis proposed.

All day we awaited a reply from Moscow to our declaration. But none came. This might mean that Moscow considered the exchange broken off. Günther was most uneasy.

The question of the offer of aid from the Western powers engaged our attention that day also. Minister Holma continued to send us urgent cables from Paris. Prime Minister Daladier had talked further to him about the aid, promising to send the bombers at once. From London, Minister Gripenberg cabled word from Foreign Minister Halifax to the effect that the governments of England and France had that day approached the governments at Oslo and Stockholm to ask for their consent to the transit of forces. Halifax had also said that the Allies would send to Finland whatever auxiliary forces the ports and railways could handle. The expedition would begin on March 15 and would be followed up by as many additional troops as possible. This meant, according to Halifax, that both France and England would jointly furnish assistance by every means at their disposal. Despite the negative responses of

Norway and Sweden, the preparations were continuing, and March 15 was set as the target date for departure of the forces. At the same time England and France would exercise the greatest possible pressure upon the governments of Sweden and Norway to secure transit permission. Even rejection of the request need not put a stop to their assistance.

Word of the approach of the Western powers to the Swedish government also reached us from Stockholm via Erkko. Günther had told him that the inquiry had been answered negatively in a preliminary sense. He had also asked Erkko to inform the Finnish government that the final reply would also be negative and that Oslo would proceed in the same fashion.

At 11:45 P.M. the Swedish Minister, Sahlin, telephoned me at home. He was instructed to present the following declaration:

1. The governments of Great Britain and France have today made a démarche at the request of the Finnish government. [Here I interjected that, for the time being, we had made no request.] The Swedish government has replied that permission for transit passage cannot be granted. If the question is brought up again, the reply will be the same.

2. With reference to the endeavor to secure elucidation of the peace terms, no reply has been received thus far. It is indeed conceivable that no reply may come in. Wish to know whether we can get a reply from the Finnish government with regard to our proposal to add sentence. Appreciate an answer.

The day ended without bringing the clarification we were awaiting.

March 3.—At a meeting of the Council of State at 11:30 I spoke of the effect which the pressure of England and France had produced upon the Swedish and Norwegian governments. According to information which Erkko had reported by cable and in letters, Foreign Minister Günther had spoken to him in exceptionally severe fashion. Günther had started out by telling him that he had had some conversation with the Germans; they still were hoping for a termination of the conflict between Finland and the Soviet Union but they had regretfully declared that there was nothing they could do about the matter. He then had gone on to say that he had heard the Russian terms included the demand that Kuusinen be taken into the Finnish Cabinet. He had advised the Soviet government that if this was true and if the Soviet Union was thus coming forward with fresh demands, Sweden would have to reconsider the entire question and its attitude toward the conflict in all its amplitude. To this Molotov had replied that all Russian demands had already been communicated to the Swedish government.

Günther had then discussed the approach of the British and French governments to the governments of the Scandinavian countries in the matter of the transit problem. If subjected to pressure, Sweden would become a theater of war, because Germany would in that event attack Sweden. His most important duty, Günther had told Erkko, was to prevent such a contingency. He had wondered what attitude the Swedish people would assume if they learned that Finland was prepared to see Sweden converted into a battlefield in order to save the cities of Viipuri and Sortavala. Neither city was a matter of vital interest to Finland, and their loss did not mean Finland's ruin. Finland could surely liberate them once more when favorable circumstances should present themselves. The Swedish people would be unable to comprehend how even Hanko could be a matter of life and death to Finland. In any event, it was not a matter over which the Swedish people would go to war. If Sweden was being swept into war, it would be obliged to think of itself and its own needs, and to retain for itself all materials of war. He also said that he might be obliged to declare to the Riksdag that an opportunity to make peace existed, but that Finland was not altogether disposed to take advantage of it.

In reply Erkko observed that it would be a great mistake to bring these questions up at this stage. The fact that the cities of Viipuri and Sortavala were now included among the Soviet demands was attributable to Prime Minister Hansson's communiqué, which had been catastrophic in its effect upon Finland's situation. It had conspicuously reinforced the diplomatic position of the USSR and increased its demands.

During the conversation it had also come to light that Mme. Kollontai had not referred to the cession of Viipuri and Sortavala as being among the terms. These had been specified by Molotov when he announced the Soviet terms to Minister Assarsson in Moscow.

The information thus received showed that in conducting its mediatory mission Sweden was devoting great attention to Sweden's own position and security.

I went on to tell the Council of State that before the session began the ministers of Great Britain and France in Helsinki had come to call on me. The British Minister had been the first to tell me of the representations of the Western powers, referred to above, in Oslo and Stockholm. He declared that the Western powers expected our request for aid by March 5 at the latest. When they received it, they would on March 11 again address Norway and Sweden to demand the right of transit. On March 15 the first force would be ready to depart. During the first and second weeks of April some six thousand men would reach their destination. To my observation that the main problem seemed to consist of transit through the Scandinavian countries, the ministers had been unable to give any answer save that they put their faith in the pressure being brought to bear. To the question whether they intended to come even against the will of the Scandinavian countries, they again replied by referring to the pressure. When I observed that this was precisely the main question, Magny, the French Minister, answered that it was no question at all but a matter of strategy.

Finally I remarked that, so far as I could see, we had come to the end of our rope. We had exceeded the time limit set by the Soviet Union, and now the Western powers too had set a time limit—March 5. We were thus in as tight a squeeze as before. We could of course let the Western powers try to exercise pressure upon the Scandinavian countries, but I could not believe that they would have recourse to direct measures of force. We could not follow this line any further, so our only recourse was a return to the peace line. We had still received no reply from Moscow. This was part of Molotov's customary tactics. There now seemed no other expedient than to send on the first answer which we had already approved. The only change I would make would be to omit the suggestion that Moscow be the place of negotiation. At the present stage of developments I regarded all side excursions as superfluous, and I recommended that we swallow the bitter pill.

This recommendation was supported by three members of the Cabinet—Von Fieandt, Kotilainen, and Pekkala. In the opinion of the others there was no need to come to a final decision, particularly since we had no way of knowing definitely whether or not Mme. Kollontai had sent our reply to its destination officially. Hannula, consistent with his earlier position, suggested that we ought now to turn to the Western powers with an appeal for aid.

Since my first recommendation had not been approved, I asked whether I might inform Moscow that we agreed to negotiations on the basis proposed if Viipuri and Sortavala were left out of the demands. Even this they did not wish to accept at once but instead postponed the discussion until the following session, to be held at six o'clock that afternoon. I was in the meantime to secure further elucidation and to determine whether our reply had been transmitted to Moscow.

After the session Prime Minister Ryti, Paasikivi, General Walden, and I stayed behind to discuss what steps we should take. The upshot was that, accepting Günther's idea, we decided to assure the Soviet government that we were prepared to negotiate if Viipuri and Sortavala were left out of the demands.

Upon the conclusion of this discussion I telephoned Foreign Minister Günther in Stockholm at 1:45 P.M., Ryti being at my side. I told Günther that I could well understand his troubles and that we did not wish to add to them, but that we too must think of ourselves, and this consideration would in the last analysis determine our choice. I said that we had not transmitted to the Western powers the appeal they were hoping for, contrary to what the Western powers had told the Swedes yesterday. Their deadline of March 5 seemed to have been determined by technical considerations.

Günther: Interesting news. Thanks.

Tanner: I should like to ask what you have told Moscow on our behalf. Has the reply we proposed been transmitted to its destination?

Günther: It has not. Mme. Kollontai and I have been debating whether it might not be interpreted as negative.

Tanner: Just what is it, then, that you are awaiting a reply to?

Günther: The cable inquiring about easier terms.

Tanner: Is there occasion to doubt that a reply will be received?

Günther: Mme. Kollontai is very pessimistic. She does not believe there will be a reply.

Tanner: The extra sentence Mme. Kollontai suggested would bind us to the whole program.

Günther: Indeed it would.

Tanner: In his letter Erkko refers to your idea: "If Russia were to make its terms easier, Finland would give its answer at once." Where does this idea come from? Is there any basis for it?

Günther: I had brought this idea up on Mme. Kollontai's suggestion. She was pessimistic about it, to be sure, but favored it nevertheless.

Tanner: I could promise that Finland would undertake negotiations at once if Viipuri and Sortavala were left out of the terms. In that case we would conclude the bargain immediately.

Günther: I promise to make a try in that direction.

Tanner: Is the discussion with Moscow still holding, or is it to be regarded as having been broken off because the deadline, March 1, has passed?

Günther: I judge that despite the deadline the discussion is still holding, particularly if an answer could be given today.

Tanner: Is there any good advice you can give us as a third party?

Günther: It would be best to seek negotiations.

Tanner: What should be done to that end?

Günther: Perhaps it would be best to bring up the question we have been referring to—leaving out Viipuri and Sortavala.

Tanner: What can be said on Sweden's part regarding the chances of concluding a defense league with Sweden? Hansson and I had some talk of this the last time I was there.

Günther: The groundwork would take months. It would not fit this emergency. Yet there is great sympathy for the idea insofar as it concerns economic problems.

In the course of the day the ministers of the Western powers in Helsinki were invited to call at the Bank of Finland, where Ryti and I received them.

Vereker arrived first, accompanied by his military attaché. He had been instructed to inform us officially that a démarche for the purpose of securing transit rights for the forces had been made in Stockholm. If the British government should by March 5 receive Finland's request for aid, the forces could depart on March 11, be in Narvik on March 20, and reach Finland in the first or second week of April. The number of the forces which he declared would arrive was again smaller than that most recently cited. From England perhaps some six thousand men would come. England would again approach the Scandinavian countries on March 11. The forces could reach Finland only through the cooperation of the Scandinavian countries. They would have to arrive here before the ice broke up in the Gulf of Bothnia; otherwise the German fleet would be able to obstruct the transfer and would even be able to breach the railroad at Haaparanta. Vereker said the number of forces was the maximum the harbors and communications of Scandinavia could handle and the means of Finland could maintain. Yet England was prepared to augment these forces as much as possible and as much as military experience should warrant. British and French forces would jointly back the success of this operation. He hoped that Finland would soon present the appeal referred to.

Ryti asked what would happen if Norway and Sweden did not assent to their passage.

Vereker did not know. He trusted that internal tension within those countries would make it necessary to give permission. Possibly there would even have to be a change of government.

I then inquired if the forces could reach their destination against the will of the Swedish government.

Vereker could not say. If the appeal was made by March 5 at the latest, there was a week's time to cultivate a favorable attitude in Scandinavia before March 11.

Magny came in after Vereker. He wished to confirm what Vereker had said about the démarche made in Stockholm. He had nothing to offer on the size of the forces or the time they would arrive. He asserted that France was prepared to send forces the minute Finland presented its appeal. The Scandinavian countries would be assured they had nothing to fear. He now wished to know whether Finland was prepared to appeal to France for aid on the basis of Article 16 of the Covenant of the League of Nations. He declared that France and England were ready to follow to the end their course of furnishing aid. If the appeal were not presented soon, there was a danger that the aid contemplated would no longer be quite certain, since the Germans would be able to take steps to obstruct the dispatch of the auxiliary forces.

Ryti then asked the same question he had asked of Vereker: how would the forces pass through Scandinavia?

Magny: That depends on Finland's reply.

Tanner: The transit question is the heart of the matter.

Magny: It is not a question. It is a matter of strategy.

Ryti: Could the arrival of the forces take place right now, in March?

Magny: The longer we wait, the longer the forces will be delayed. The amount of the forces is dependent on the need.

The Swedish Minister, Sahlin, telephoned me at home at 4:00 P.M.

I told him I had just been informing his people that we could not give our answer that day. I told him I had only just now been talking by telephone with Minister Günther.

Sahlin: I know. I have just received from Foreign Minister Günther the following declaration for you: "Minister Günther confirms that the proposal has been forwarded and that the proper person has sent a cable to Moscow. This cable asks that the Commissar be informed at once that Hanko Cape will be ceded; the terms are accepted with the exception of the two cities."

I thanked him for the information.

When the meeting of the Council of State was resumed at 6:00 P.M., I related the additional information I had received in the course of the day. General Enckell had tried to secure from London further data on the assistance of the Western powers. On the basis of what he had learned, he had sent the following telegram to Marshal Mannerheim:

Answer received. Officials confirm there has been no alteration in the figures Vereker cited to the Finnish government February 27, namely, a well-armed force of twelve to thirteen thousand men, to be supported by considerable forces in Sweden. Confirmed that forces can arrive in Scandinavian ports March 20 and proceed shortly toward Finland, depending on communications. Higher figure mentioned corresponds to forces ordered to Sweden and Finland together.

General Walden had interpreted the sense of this cable to be that the forces would come to twelve or thirteen thousand in all but that part of them would remain in Sweden. Of the whole, a detachment of perhaps some six thousand men would proceed to Finland.

Since the information concerning the size of the forces varied in this fashion from day to day, Hannula called upon me to approach the ministers of the Western powers once more to secure definitive statements. This, however, I declined to do.

Paasikivi was now prepared to define his stand, subject to change in the light of later information. Since the aid offered by the Western powers was not sufficient and would not arrive in time, since this aid was uncertain because of the attitude assumed by Sweden, and since the danger of our becoming involved in an incident with Germany as a result of this aid was increased, he declared that we must work for peace negotiations and set aside all other suggestions. We should seek negotiations through the intermediary of Stockholm. Paasikivi further proposed that we turn to Germany with the plea that it endeavor to influence the peace terms in such fashion that they should satisfy Russian requirements without imposing too heavy a burden on Finland. This approach to Germany should be made independently of what we might do about the Stockholm matter. This proposal was supported by Von Born and Pekkala.

Marshal Mannerheim had, through the Prime Minister, advanced the idea that we should try to secure as intermediary some country other than Sweden, which was principally concerned with saving itself. He had thought of the United States as such a disinterested intermediary. In order to put pressure on the Scandinavian countries to help us more effectively, he thought we should offer the Russians an exchange of territories in which they would receive tracts in northern Finland and also the Aaland Islands.

I opposed approaching Germany. We had tried that course twice already and had failed. Clearly Moscow did not wish to permit Germany to operate on Finland's behalf. Moreover, our playing a double game of this kind was a repugnant thought: to be negotiating with the Western powers for aid and at the same time to approach their enemy. As the discussion seemed once again to be dragging on, I complained of the Cabinet's indecisiveness. In the present situation we had to act rapidly, but there was no getting a decision out of the Cabinet.

To conclude the discussion, the President declared that the suggestion of an approach to Germany was rejected. We decided to wait on the other points till we got our reply from Moscow.

In the evening I telephoned Erkko to tell him what had taken place in the conversations with Günther and Sahlin. I urged Erkko to get the text of the telegram which had come from Moscow.

Erkko said that the Swedish Consul General in Paris, Nordling, had come to Stockholm the day before on a special mission for Daladier. He had delivered a letter to the King, in the presence of the Crown Prince and of Foreign Minister Günther, which stated that the Western powers had decided to send military aid to Finland through Norway and Sweden. The letter inquired regarding Sweden's attitude. The King and the Crown

Prince had been ready to permit the transit without objection, but Günther had been doubtful. The King's reply to Premier Daladier's letter
was still awaited.

March 4.—This day was tense and uneasy. We waited for the reply
from Moscow all day. First of all, we did not know whether the road
toward peace discussions was still open to us, and second, we did not
know what answer to give the Western powers on the appeal for aid. I
had hardly slept the night before, racking my brains for a solution; nor
did a course become clear for us during the day.

As no answer had come from Moscow, no Cabinet meeting was held.
In the evening I went to the Diet. The representatives were uneasy regarding the turn matters had taken. Minister Niukkanen was privately
lobbying with vigor in favor of appealing to the Western powers for aid.

Late in the evening the French military representative, Colonel Ganeval, once more visited Prime Minister Ryti for a discussion. General
Walden was also present. Ganeval said that if Finland asked for assistance and continued to fight, the first Western forces would be ready
to leave England in a week. The French forces would also be sent off
via England. In this event the Western powers would regard the Finnish
front as a part of their own major front. Transport would take place
through three Norwegian ports. The first installment would include
fifteen thousand French troops, so strong in fire power that they would
correspond to one and a half of our divisions. There would be eighteen
thousand British troops, bringing the total to thirty-three thousand men.
This would be only a beginning; these forces could be expanded as much
as necessary. By orders of Gamelin, the French Commander-in-Chief,
fifty British and twelve French bombers were to arrive here in the next
few days. By reason of the bad condition of Finnish airfields, it was
not possible to send more. England and France were also planning a
naval operation in Petsamo. It would be total war so far as France and
England were concerned. The aid to be given Finland was being organized specially, independent of other operations. If it should become
necessary to help Sweden and Norway, this would not diminish the assistance to be given Finland. The forces would come fully armed and
equipped, but under the designation of volunteers. The entire contingent
would arrive under a British leader but would place itself under the
command of Marshal Mannerheim. The French forces, at least, might
by Mannerheim's order go anywhere, but the Western powers would prefer to see them fighting on the eastern frontier. There was no corresponding clarification regarding the British troops. The forces would be in
Finland between April 10 and 15. England and France would consider

the Soviet Union an enemy state the moment their forces set out on their expedition, but they would not issue a declaration of war. Colonel Ganeval complained that we had wasted time. If we had made our appeal a month earlier, aid would be much closer at hand. He further said he had learned that Sweden would not oppose transit by force of arms.

In the course of the day various representatives of foreign powers came in for information. When Schoenfeld, the American Minister, came in to see me, I asked him whether he thought the United States could support Finland if negotiations in Moscow should start.

Schoenfeld replied that the United States was certainly prepared to give Finland all possible support. Finland ought to define its program more precisely, but, in any event, it should make peace. Perhaps peace would be possible after the Russians had taken Viipuri.

The Rumanian Minister, Lecca, also came in for information. He too urged us to make peace, and he referred to Rumania's experience during the First World War, when Rumania, left alone, had made peace, trusting that the areas ceded in the settlement would be returned to it later, as indeed they were. He, too, believed that the Russians would be ready for peace once they had taken Viipuri and thus saved face.

A number of cables were sent to Paris and London during the day. They expressed surprise at the continuing disparities in the information on the size of the auxiliary forces.

March 5.—Since on this day the final decision must be made regarding assistance from the West, I had made up the following program for the day:

Erkko must be called in Stockholm early in the morning and asked whether a reply had come from Moscow. If not, he was to send on through Günther our new statement accepting Moscow's terms, to cover the eventuality that our offer might still be considered. He must then inform the Swedish government that we were making this sacrifice to save the situation and also with a view to the best interests of Sweden. The statement to go to Moscow should be filled out with a proposal that during the negotiations an armistice should be arranged on the basis of the *status quo* at the front.

If these actions did not bring results that same day, or at the latest within a day or two, then: (1) we should turn to the Western powers and ask their armed intervention; (2) we should request assent of the Scandinavian countries to the transit of Western forces; and (3) we should send out an SOS to the whole world for help.

I telephoned these ideas to Prime Minister Ryti early in the morning.

He had not slept well and was in ill humor. He questioned the whole program, particularly in the light of the new information on Western aid which he had received through Colonel Ganeval the evening before. This information had made him hesitate. I nevertheless asked for a meeting of the Cabinet at ten that morning and promised meanwhile to call Günther in Stockholm and ask whether there had been an answer.

The call to Günther was put through at 9:00 A.M.

Tanner: Have you a reply from Moscow?

Günther: No. I am expecting one any minute. I am afraid it will not be favorable. There ought at least to be some word from Assarsson (the Swedish Minister in Moscow).

Tanner: We have to make a decision today on the Western aid offer.

Günther: I know.

Tanner: If the question of Sweden's approaching Germany for support of Sweden's mediation comes up, I can say Finland will have no objections to interpose if this is done in Sweden's name and without mention of Finland.

Günther: We have investigated the possibilities of such an approach. But Germany is not willing, because Moscow is against it. Of course there is a chance this may be a more propitious moment.

Tanner: I have nothing more to say for the moment. Erkko will call on you to deliver a document at ten today.

The meeting of the Council of State was held at ten o'clock. It was attended by the President and by General Walden.

At the outset, I acquainted the Council with what had happened since the last meeting—not much to be sure. No reply had been received from Moscow. The Western powers, on the other hand, were more eager to furnish aid than before, and to that end they were raising their offers and working hard in other ways. It was reported this morning that Daladier had addressed the King of Sweden directly to inquire regarding the right of transit through Swedish territory. The King had replied that he hoped France would not compromise Sweden's position. An official of the Swedish Foreign Ministry, Söderblom, had declared Sweden would not fight if the troops came through. A cable from Erkko reported that, according to the King, the British had asked Norway for four ports as landing points. Sweden did not propose to fight yet, but if Germany pressed Sweden on this account, it would fight. It was further said Sweden planned to obstruct the transit by withdrawing all its rolling stock from the railways. Moreover, Holma had cabled from Paris that Koht, the Norwegian Foreign Minister, intended to put the question of the passage of Western forces up to the Storting for decision and that even Sweden's attitude, although negative, did not mean armed resistance. In Paris both replies were viewed as relatively favorable. All they were waiting for there was Finland's official request.

Then I asked Walden, who had talked to Colonel Ganeval, to report on the military side of the matter. Walden described his meeting with Colonel Ganeval, which has been discussed above. In his opinion the aid offered was not enough, nor could it arrive in time. Walden also related news from the war fronts. On telephoning headquarters he had learned that the Marshal was ill—he had a fever and was worn out—but the Marshal had nevertheless taken the phone. He had talked with General Airo, who said the situation was critical. The enemy was established at some points on the western shore of Viipuri Bay. Headquarters had hoped to push them back last night, but the operation had failed. There were not many enemy beachheads yet, but their number might increase. In other respects, the line on the Isthmus was as before. The front had been comparatively quiet except around Pölläkkälä. The enemy's amphibious operation was difficult to analyze. It might be a diversion to entice our forces away from the main objective, but it might also be quite in earnest. It was possible our divisions could hold their positions, but just at this moment it was difficult to gauge the situation.

The Marshal had said briefly, "Anyone can understand the significance of Viipuri Bay, and the even greater significance of its western shore. We must be prepared for unpleasant surprises. The situation on the ice of Viipuri Bay is impossible, since we are short of men on every hand." Regarding Western auxiliary forces, the Marshal had declared in advance that they would be too few and too late.

Resuming the floor after this, I said that the situation gave ground for concern. The state of affairs at the front was critical, and the whole Viipuri sector was threatened. Consequently the case was urgent. We had made a mistake last Friday when we had not sent our reply on to Moscow. Now we had been given to understand that the time limit had lapsed. I nevertheless proposed that we state acceptance of the Soviet terms. Therefore, I recommended that we at once have Erkko hand to Foreign Minister Günther the statement which had been ready since last Friday. The statement should be delivered if no reply had been received from Moscow or if the reply was negative. Erkko should tell Günther we were faced with a forced decision and on that account should request a reply that very day. If Moscow turned down this proposal, we had no recourse but to appeal to the Western powers. Their assistance would afford us but scant support, as our army might have been pushed back into Bothnia before the promised assistance reached us. Yet the appeal should be made, since this was the deadline they themselves had set. At the same time we should make an effort to arrange transit through Scandinavia. I hoped there would be no more arguing about the matter but finally a decision.

Prime Minister Ryti at once seconded this proposal of mine. He suggested, however, that a sentence regarding an armistice should be added to our reply. Doubting that this course would eventually lead to any result, however, he also suggested that I get in touch with the French and British ministers in Helsinki that same day and request through them confirmation of the data furnished by the military. They should also be asked to keep preparations for the auxiliary expedition under way. They should further be informed we were seeking peace and were awaiting a reply from Moscow which would bear upon that issue. If the reply was unsatisfactory, we would submit a formal appeal for aid.

Hannula, however, briefly recommended that we accept the Western offer of aid out of hand.

Niukkanen was of the opinion that the Soviet terms could be accepted only if our army was beaten. For this reason we should keep up the fight, and we should ask for Western aid even though we should start to talk peace. Finally, however, he associated himself with my proposal, plus the addition suggested by the Prime Minister.

After the discussion, the President summarized our position as follows: All members of the Cabinet had taken the floor. All save Hannula believed that we should pursue the peace course and that, if it failed, we should present our appeal for aid to the Western powers, who should be asked to continue their preparations. I was obliged to associate myself with these conclusions, but I deeply regretted that our inquiry had not been sent on to Moscow the preceding Friday.

At 11:30 I called Foreign Minister Günther in Stockholm, who had been trying to get in touch with me during the session. Erkko was with him.

Günther: Now a reply from Moscow has come in. Assarsson called on Molotov. Molotov inflexibly persisted in his demand that both cities, Viipuri and Sortavala, be ceded. The Soviet government has consented to await Finland's answer for a few days. The Red Army demands that it be permitted to advance. Molotov during the conversation wondered whether it would not be most advantageous for them to negotiate and reach an agreement with Kuusinen. If the Soviet government's terms are not accepted now, the demands will increase and the Soviet Union will make a final treaty with Kuusinen.

Günther then told me that the Western powers had asked the Swedish government for transit rights and had received a definitive and negative reply.

Tanner: We have been given to understand otherwise. The refusal is supposed to have been for form's sake only.

Günther: Where could you have got that from? The Cabinet is altogether unanimous.

Tanner: From various sources. They have it that the frame of mind in Scandinavia is changing and that quarters higher up hold a different view from the Cabinet.

Günther went on to criticize *in extenso* the aid activities of the Western powers. They would bring Finland no assistance but would drag the whole North into the war. "The whole plan is childish. We won't leave a single rail in our ports or on our railways."

Tanner: I don't want to go into that. Over here we are currently thrashing out the plans of the Western powers with their military representatives. It is the business of our military to weigh and judge them.

Günther: Has the Finnish government made a decision on the Moscow proposal yet?

Tanner: It has. I can tell you that we are accepting the Moscow terms. Matters of detail are indeed obscure, but they can be cleared up in negotiations. We are proposing that during the negotiations there be an armistice on the basis of the *status quo*. Erkko will give you my answer in writing. Will you give Erkko the text of the Moscow reply, so that we shall have everything clear for the future?

Günther promised to do so, after which Erkko took the telephone.

I asked him to deliver our answer in accordance with our earlier cable, plus certain alterations, of which the proposal on the armistice was the most important. In delivering the answer he should make the following statement to Günther: "Even at this last minute we are doing all we can to save the situation by means of great sacrifices. I should appreciate it if I might learn from you no later than today whether this settles the matter."

Erkko wrote down these points and went directly to the Legation to draw up the papers.

Several cables arrived from Erkko in the course of the day. The Finnish reply had been delivered to the Soviet representative, Mme. Kollontai, at 11:55 A.M. Swedish time. The Soviet Union consented to wait a few days more for final acceptance, but the Red Army was demanding permission to march forward. The demands would be more burdensome if we delayed. If the terms were not accepted now, the requirements would increase, and the Soviet Union would make the final treaty with Kuusinen.

In the evening President Kallio telephoned to ask for the latest news. I said that Moscow had granted a few days' delay, and I reported the contents of the answer which had been received. Instead of being gratified by this news the President grumbled, "The scoundrels, demanding Sortavala when they're nowhere near it yet!"

At four o'clock Magny, who was leaving the country, came in to present his successor, Carra de Vaux.

We began to discuss the aid offer of the Western powers. I explained to him again that we were hoping for peace first and that we were awaiting a decisive answer from Moscow. If it was negative, we should be glad to receive aid and to present our appeal to the Western powers.

Magny was not greatly satisfied with this statement. He had hoped for a decision on this matter before his departure.

At 4:30 P.M. Vereker called. He said he had reported to Halifax that there might be a decision in Helsinki on March 5. In this connection Halifax had cabled him, "Time is getting short; try your best to secure a decision."

I explained our situation to him from the Finnish point of view, just as I had earlier to the French representative. Vereker understood our position and the far-reaching character of the decision to be made.

At 5:45 the Swedish Minister, Sahlin, called, saying that he had received the following notice from Stockholm: "We have advised Moscow that Finland has accepted the terms, and in this connection the Swedish government has suggested that hostilities be terminated on Wednesday, March 6, at 11:00 A.M. Russian time. If this proposal is accepted, we hope to secure acceptance from the Finns."

Sahlin also left with me the text of Assarsson's cable of March 4.

At 9:00 P.M. Sahlin telephoned that no reply had yet come from Moscow. It would probably arrive in the night.

At 11:00 P.M. I had a further talk with Günther. He had not yet received a reply from Moscow. These cables usually came late. He asked and received permission to telephone during the night if it was necessary to take action before morning—for example, in connection with the armistice.

THE FINAL HARD DECISION

On March 6 matters had developed to such a point that it was at last essential to come to a final decision. Before dawn, events started to happen fast. At 4:45 A.M. Erkko telephoned from Stockholm to report that the Swedish Foreign Ministry had handed him the following statement: "At 10:30 in the evening the Finnish reply was presented in Moscow. Molotov remarked that it was not precise enough. The Soviet

government could not accept an armistice before Viipuri and Viipuri
Bay were evacuated. He promised to tell his government and to return
to the matter during the night."

At 7:00 A.M. came a telephone call from Sahlin. He started off with
the same report as Erkko. He added that Assarsson had observed to
Molotov that there was no ambiguity in the Finnish reply. Everything
was covered quite as precisely as it had been in Moscow's terms. Assarsson had further emphasized the danger attendant upon Moscow's delay
and had remarked that it would be wisest to follow the previous line.
Molotov had said he would consult his government and make a reply
the same night.

At 8:45 A.M. Sahlin telephoned again with more details on his earlier
report, which had come in at 8:30 from Stockholm:

"At one o'clock last night Molotov informed Assarsson as follows:
'Having regard to the fact that the Finnish government has accepted the
terms which the Russians offered, the government of the Soviet Union
is agreeable to initiating negotiations with the Finnish government to
the end of making peace and terminating hostilities. It is suggested the
negotiations be carried on in Moscow, where a Finnish delegation is
awaited.'

"Assarsson asked why an armistice could not be accepted. Molotov
replied that the situation at the front was very uncertain. For that
reason Russia must define its attitude toward an armistice during the
negotiations. When Assarsson referred to the dangers inherent in delay
and to the fact that other powers might intervene, Molotov said that there
was no need to fear such a development if Finland itself did not wish it.
The Finnish delegation could come at once. The security of Leningrad
was to remain outside the discussions. The terms offered were the Soviet
Union's minimal demands.

"Günther says he is expecting an immediate reply."

Erkko called in from Stockholm at the same time, interrupting
Sahlin's call. He made the same report as Sahlin, adding that Sweden
could arrange direct airplane communication from Stockholm to Mos-
cow. The Soviet Union did not believe in the Western aid offer. He said
Sweden congratulated itself in that it had received new evidence of the
Soviet Union's friendship toward Sweden.

At 10:30 I called Günther in Stockholm. "Molotov's reply," I told
him, "shows up the Russians for what they are. They are ready to negotiate, but they will not agree to an armistice during the negotiations.
On this account the situation becomes altogether confused. If we accept
the Moscow invitation to negotiate, the Western powers will throw us
over, the aid offer will collapse, and they will not even furnish arms.

Meanwhile the Russians can go on attacking. Thus we shall be entirely in their hands. Could Sweden promise to come to our aid if peace is not made?"

Günther urged us to go to Moscow. Peace could be completed in two days. He did not believe Sweden could alter its attitude toward aid for Finland even if the quest for peace failed. He urged us to set out at once. His government could at a moment's notice arrange the trip from Stockholm on.

At eleven o'clock the Cabinet assembled again. President Kallio and General Walden were also present. At this session I related in detail the events of the past few hours. I reported that Moscow was disposed to negotiate, so that the road to Moscow was open, but that the Soviet government did not consent to an armistice. "Thus, on the one hand, we have received good news to the effect that the deadline was not absolutely immutable—that is to say, that Russia wants peace—but, on the other hand, the unpleasant news that there can be no armistice." I said that for this reason I had been uncertain at first what to do, but I had finally come to the conclusion that we would lose nothing by sending a delegation to Moscow. The course of the Western powers was just as dangerous as before. If we followed it, the fate of Poland might await us. In case of need, the Western powers might come to our assistance even at a future date, since what they wanted was to open a new front against Germany. So, in bringing my report to an end, I suggested that a delegation depart that very day, if at all possible, for Moscow.

Prime Minister Ryti supported my proposal. He further said that he had talked to the ministers of the Western powers here and learned that they could wait for our answer until March 12, but that we had to make our appeal for aid by then at the very latest, for after that date the forces would be required elsewhere.

Hannula, as usual, demanded that we seek Western aid. In no event could he accept the Russian terms as a basis for negotiations.

In Niukkanen's view, the armistice question was of secondary importance. He believed that the Russians would have to sacrifice at least a hundred thousand men before they could occupy Viipuri. Yet if it was believed that an acceptable treaty could be secured in Moscow, he would go along with that proposal. It would be well to find out quickly whether acceptable terms could be had or not. He proposed that the new line should run south of Viipuri and east of Sortavala.

All the other members of the Cabinet supported without reservation the proposal that a delegation be sent.

Next we discussed the composition of the delegation to be sent to

Moscow. Various persons were suggested, including Prime Minister Ryti, whom many favored, whereas others considered that his presence in the capital was more important. Since there was no agreement regarding the candidates, a decision was postponed until later that day.

Before the end of the session, I asked for authority to report our most recent information to the Foreign Relations Committee of the Diet. As no one opposed this, I asked the committee to assemble at noon.

At the meeting of the Diet Foreign Relations Committee, I gave my report and announced that the Cabinet had decided to send a delegation and at the same time had asked the Western powers to grant us an extension of time until March 12. I said I had asked the committee to meet in order to ascertain whether it was prepared to accept the peace conditions laid down by the Soviet Union.

Of the committee members who took the floor, all supported acceptance of the conditions except Representative Kares. He did not approve the Cabinet's stand and inquired what it was that had changed the committee's attitude since last fall.

At 1:30 P.M. Günther reported by telephone that he had talked with Mme. Kollontai, telling her his regret at the negative response regarding the armistice. She had thought that an armistice might be arranged as soon as the delegation left, and had even sent to Moscow a suggestion along these lines.

The Cabinet met again at 3:00 P.M. to decide who should be sent as members of the delegation. President Kallio was present this time, too. The principal discussion centered around whether Prime Minister Ryti should be among those to go. Paasikivi, in particular, emphasized the importance of his accompanying the group. In Moscow it would be necessary to handle a very difficult matter which would affect the destinies of our people for a long time. His presence was important not only as a matter of foreign policy but also from the point of view of domestic policy. The Prime Minister enjoyed confidence at home, and his going along would also make an impression on the Russians, since they would see that we were taking the negotiations seriously.

Ryti himself felt that his presence in Helsinki was more important, but he consented to go since this was generally considered desirable.

General Walden's presence was also felt to be important, because of his experience in military affairs and of his thorough knowledge of the Russian language. Marshal Mannerheim had opposed his going, but it was not considered possible to take this into account.

It finally was decided that the delegation should consist of Ryti, Paasikivi, Walden, and Voionmaa. The Cabinet did not think it was

possible to give the delegation a set of regular instructions. The group
was to leave that same day at 7:00 P.M., first by car for Turku, then by
plane to Stockholm. There a direct plane for Moscow would be reserved.
The trip was to be completely secret.

At 6:00 P.M. I telephoned Erkko in Stockholm, asking him to inform
Günther of the trip and of the identity of the delegates. Passports issued
under assumed names were to be delivered to the delegation members
in Stockholm, and visas should be obtained there. The Swedish government was to arrange for a plane direct to Moscow.

Now that the decision had been made, I instructed Ministers Gripenberg and Holma to notify the authorities in London and Paris that negotiations were to begin. They were also to ask for an extension of time
until March 12 for the making of our appeal regarding aid, since we
were not convinced we would be successful in making peace.

In thus weighing against each other for weeks the two alternatives—
making peace with the Soviet Union on the hard terms offered or turning
to the Western powers with an appeal for aid—the Cabinet had had in
its hands a decision of importance to the history of the whole world.
The Cabinet was then dealing with heavier responsibilities than it could
even have guessed. If Finland had presented to the Western powers an
appeal for aid, the war between the major powers would obviously have
taken a different turn. The Western powers would have been at war
with the Soviet Union in the spring of 1940, and that country would
presumably in such a case have had recourse to its ally, Germany. Thus
the fronts would have sprung up in an altogether different fashion than
they actually did as the war progressed. The Scandinavian countries
would clearly also have become a theater of war. Would Germany in
that event have anticipated England and France in occupying Norway,
or would England and France have been able to get there first and thus
secure so powerful a foothold that the German attack on Norway would
have failed? One may well ask! And would the Western powers have
succeeded in defeating a Germany backed by the Soviet Union? It is
all speculation, but beneath there lies a certain basis of fact. Presumably the history of the world would have been written somewhat
differently if at that fateful moment Finland had chosen the other course.

CHAPTER 10

THE PEACE TERMS DICTATED

Although an effort had been made to arrange the trip of our delegation in complete secrecy and although the members of the Cabinet had been sworn to keep it to themselves, it soon became clear that word had been spread in Helsinki, at least to a restricted circle. This time suspicion fell upon the chauffeur who had driven the delegation; he was supposed to be a supporter of the Patriotic People's Movement (the IKL). But at the start the public in general was unaware of the trip.

March 7.—Erkko reported from Stockholm by telephone that the delegation had arrived there safely the evening before and had left that morning at 8:30 by plane, planning to arrive at Moscow about four or five o'clock Swedish time. It had not yet been possible to arrange an armistice, for which reason a final agreement had to be brought about without delay.

Our military attaché in Paris, Colonel Paasonen, had arrived in Helsinki, and he came in to see me. He had come by way of London with important information on Western aid plans to deliver. This information had originated with Premier Daladier of France, and the more recent part with Ironside, the British Commander-in-Chief, as of March 4.

According to this information the aggregate figure of those who would make up the expeditionary force would come to 57,000; of these, at least 15,500 men would depart in a first echelon on March 15.

Paasonen spoke strongly in favor of Western aid. Premier Daladier had told him that, if Finland made peace now, the major war would be over. Thus the Western powers appeared to want little Finland to fight on their behalf. There was also a great deal of talk in Paris about a

Baku front. Plans for one were ready, and the Western powers could initiate action there in a month and a half.

I knew Paasonen had called on the President the day before and had transmitted this information to him. As I considered his presence in Helsinki at this moment less than desirable, particularly since his opinion was heard with pleasure at the President's residence, I thought it best that he should leave the capital. For this reason I urged him to go to headquarters with his news at once.

A moment after Paasonen had left, I was on the telephone to the President. He sighed and asked whether Paasonen's information affected my stand.

Tanner: Not in the least. I regret only that we are behind time in our peace endeavor. A month ago we would have gotten off with the loss of Hanko Cape alone.

The President (*sighing again*): I suppose everyone has done his best in this business.

Tanner: That's no consolation if the result is bad.

We hung up.

At 12:30 I sent Ryti in Moscow the following notice via Erkko: "Situation worse. Further forces over the bay. Necessary work fast and resolutely. Paasonen here; busy on the aid line."

At 4:00 P.M. I telephoned Marshal Mannerheim at headquarters and asked for news of the front. He summed it up as follows:

"The situation is serious. New units are coming across Viipuri Bay. They are large, with artillery, infantry, and hundreds of tanks. We can't throw them back. We're trying to localize the infection, but I can't say whether we'll succeed. There is no trouble yet from ski troops on the Finnish Gulf. Since our front is long, with the ice still so firm, our line is threatened. It is our last line. In summertime it would be a different matter. The Russians are still concentrating their forces. Their troops are pushing ahead as vigorously as ever.

"Ganeval is at headquarters now. I have asked France for bombers to resist the attack and have told them that if they do not send them, the whole world will say that France and England have not done their best."

I told Mannerheim about Paasonen's visit and the information he had furnished. He recommended that I send Paasonen to headquarters, which I had already done.

At 5:30 P.M., during a session of the Cabinet, held in the Bank of Finland, the American Minister, Schoenfeld, arrived, desiring to see me urgently. He showed me a wire he had received from Steinhardt, the American Ambassador in Moscow, inquiring whether he could do anything to help Finland in the matter of peace. He also asked what Finland's program was. Schoenfeld asked me whether Finland wanted the United States to take a hand in the business, and what we would suggest. He would rather cable Washington than Moscow.

I told him that we would be glad to see the United States support our peace negotiations, and set forth my own program of action. We were prepared to cede Hanko Cape and, on the Isthmus, the areas east of the Suvanto-Koivisto line. Confidentially I told him that we could increase our offer if need be. I said Sweden had replied in the negative to the request of Finland for further aid as well as to the request of the Western powers for transit rights. We were prepared to make sacrifices to prevent the major war from spreading.

Schoenfeld promised to cable my reply to his government that same evening.

Mannerheim telephoned from headquarters at 10:30 P.M., confirming what he had said before. The situation was unchanged. Russian troops were holding the positions they had won, a foothold on two capes, and it had not been possible to throw them back. The situation had become more serious. He doubted whether Moscow would want an immediate settlement in the negotiations. Perhaps the Soviet government wished to prolong the negotiations, now that their forces were making progress.

During the night Erkko again telephoned, having received word that the delegation had reached Moscow safely.

MOSCOW MAKES ADDITIONAL DEMANDS

March 8.—Further word from Erkko advised me that Günther had heard from Moscow that our delegation had paid a courtesy call on Molotov. The first meeting was planned for 4:00 P.M. that day.

I communicated this to headquarters, whereupon Mannerheim said that developments at the front were continuing unfavorable. Russian reinforcements had crossed the ice at Viipuri Bay. There was nothing further to report on other fronts.

I at once telephoned Erkko in Stockholm to transmit the following information to our delegates in Moscow: "Developments same course. Further forces cross ice. Otherwise as before. Delay till twelfth authorized."

Half an hour later a new call came from Mannerheim at headquarters. He inquired whether anything had been heard about the bomber

planes requested of the Western powers. I told him that twelve planes
had left France and appeared to be in Narvik. Halifax had said that
England was sending fifty planes. Mannerheim asked that they be delivered at once, and I promised to speed the matter.

At 3:00 P.M. Schoenfeld came in to show me a cable he had just
received from Washington in answer to the one sent from Helsinki on
March 7, which had asked for support in possible peace negotiations.
The reply indicated that the United States was "deeply interested" in
the Finnish case and would do all it could to back Finland. Ambassador
Steinhardt had been instructed to advise Molotov that the United States
was very anxious to see Finland treated equitably by the Soviet Union.
At the same time he was to state that the United States was considering
the stimulation of commercial interchange with the Soviet Union. Its
decision might be greatly influenced by the Soviet course of action in
the Finnish matter.

At 4:30 Mr. Pakaslahti, a bureau chief in the Foreign Office, told
me that Mannerheim was insisting through a liaison officer, Melander,
that to be on the safe side an appeal must be made to the Western
powers. This might facilitate negotiations.

I said this was impossible, but I promised to telephone Mannerheim
at eleven that evening.

But at 7:00 P.M. Mannerheim called me. He had read Colonel
Paasonen's memorandum, which made the situation look more promising. Could not the appeal to the Western powers be made simultaneously with the Moscow negotiations? He feared that we had risen to a
Russian bait. The Russians were offering us impossible terms, and the
appeal might modify their demands.

Tanner: If we make the appeal, we can no longer check the coming
of the Western forces. The appeal would surely break off the negotiations in Moscow.

Mannerheim: It ought to be possible to make the appeal, since the
war is still going on and an armistice has not been granted. The bombing planes are actually coming from the Western powers in the midst
of the negotiations.

Tanner: It will be a month before the auxiliary forces reach us.
Will the front last that long?

Mannerheim: Nothing is certain in war. The coming weeks are
critical.

Tanner: It will be best to inform the delegation in Moscow of this
idea and then decide.

At 10:00, in a further telephone conversation, Mannerheim repeated the same ideas. "Time is running out."

At 10:30 Erkko reported from Stockholm that a cable had come in from Moscow advising that the meeting had been postponed three hours, until 7:00 P.M.

During the evening I sent our delegation the report on the situation at the front.

At 11:00 P.M. our Minister, Procopé, telephoned from Washington that in a press conference President Roosevelt had referred to possible peace negotiations on the part of Finland. Asked whether the United States would come forward as a mediator, Roosevelt had replied that this had not been requested. In Procopé's opinion there was no reason to request it, since it would be of no help. To his query as to whether Steinhardt was being kept up to date on the course of the matter, I replied that he was.

Procopé added that there were rumors in Washington that Paasikivi and Tanner were in Moscow already.

From Minister Holma in Paris a long cable arrived with a pronouncement from Premier Daladier, lamenting that Finland had not yet made its appeal. It agreed, however, to an extension of the time limit until March 12. It asserted that the Soviet Union was dealing treacherously with Finland. If Finland did not wish the aid of the West now, it was futile to suppose that in the final peace settlement the Western powers would guarantee Finnish territory.

Rumors of peace feelers had begun to spread throughout the world. The journalists with their constant inquiries and telephone calls were a nuisance, particularly one in New York who many times called between two and three o'clock in the morning. Yet I could not cut off my telephone for fear of missing an important call. Even in my office I did not have a secretary who might have screened the calls, much less at home.

In order to prepare the public for what was in store, I had that day given the papers the first brief notice regarding the possibility of peace. It was printed under large headlines: "So far as the Finnish government has been able to ascertain, it appears that the Soviet Union plans to present to Finland more far-reaching demands than last fall. There is, however, as yet no information regarding details."

At 7:00 P.M. a short Cabinet session was held, primarily for the purpose of briefing its members. I reported the new items I had received, mentioning also the uneasy reports of the Marshal from the front. At this point Niukkanen remarked that he was in constant touch with General Airo, whose view was that the situation was unchanged. The enemy had indeed gained a foothold on certain capes, but General Airo judged that they could not advance from there. At Uuras pressure was heavy, but nothing worthy of mention was heard from other sectors.

It was noted at the meeting that the Russian peace terms had been published that day in the press throughout the world. I said there was nothing strange about that when two hundred Diet representatives knew of them. Also, the absence of several people from Helsinki had been noticed; Svinhufvud had gone off on a trip without telling anybody and had been seen in Stockholm. So had Paasikivi.

Several members indulged in some more wishful thinking. Niukkanen thought that the Russians would not take over Viipuri quickly; the President added that the present line would be good if only it were summer. But now . . .

Concerning the Svinhufvud trip referred to above, I may remark that not even the Cabinet had been informed of it. Ex-President Svinhufvud had left for Germany, together with P. H. Norrmen, a bank director, and Erkki Räikkönen, a journalist, in order to persuade Hitler to use his influence for honorable peace terms. But he did not succeed in seeing Hitler or even Ribbentrop and had to content himself with expressing his hopes to people in subaltern capacities. The only official person who received him appears to have been the Undersecretary of State, Weizsäcker. Apparently the delicate relationship between Germany and the Soviet Union prevented most German officials from listening to what Svinhufvud had to say. From Berlin Svinhufvud went on to Rome. The trip was wholly fruitless. At the time the general belief was it had been undertaken on a commission from the Cabinet. However, the Cabinet heard of it only after the trip was already begun.

March 9.—The Cabinet was tensely awaiting news from Moscow. Even the President called me at frequent intervals to ask if there were any news. It was only at noon that the delegation's cable No. 4 arrived (No. 3 had not yet come in). It advised us that the Soviet representatives in the negotiations were Molotov, Zhdanov, and General Vasilevski. It appeared to be a bad omen that Zhdanov, who had attacked Finland in the most violent fashion, was among them. Fortunately, however, Kuusinen was not one of the group; his presence would have been a great humiliation.

The cable said that both Molotov and Zhdanov had assumed a very harsh and accusatory attitude. The discussion had lasted more than two hours, during which the Russians had paid not the least heed to the counterassertions made. The Soviet Union had announced that it did not seek to intervene in the internal politics of our country. Our delegation had promised to consider the demands presented and to give an answer at the next meeting.

Cable No. 3, delayed because of its length, arrived only at 3:30 P.M. It contained the demands made by the Russians:

First meeting today 7:00 P.M. Russians represented by Molotov, Zhdanov, General Vasilevski. Stalin not present. Molotov curtly presented Russian demands: first, Hanko Cape including Lappohja harbor and surrounding islands. Second, whole area south of line beginning between Virolahti church and Paatio and running through Vainikkala, Nuijamaa, Enso, Koitsanlahti, Uukuniemi, Värtsilä, and Korpiselkä to Salmijärvi, where border forms a bend; whole line generally very straight and without enclaves, approximately Peter the Great's line. Third, by reason of proximity to Murmansk Railway, southern part of Kuusamo and, south of Salla, a line running from Virmajoki bend through Joukamojärvi to Paanajärvi (western end), turning northeast at point west of Salla church, and joining present line southeast of Nuortetunturi. Fourth, Rybachi Peninsula, both capes. Rest of Petsamo saved.

Most of the demands were familiar, but the one for the cession of the Salla area was an addition. We must give up both capes of the Rybachi Peninsula at Petsamo, the remainder staying with Finland.

Meanwhile Marshal Mannerheim had already inquired by telephone for news from Moscow. I promised to tell him as soon as the coded cables were deciphered. At 4:15 P.M. I called him and read the contents of the cables. I remarked that things looked bad.

Mannerheim wondered if Western aid was still available now that it was known that the delegation had gone to Moscow, and I promised to ask the representatives of the Western powers to come in and discuss matters at once.

At 4:40 P.M. Sahlin, the Swedish Minister, came at my invitation to the Bank of Finland. I told him of the fresh demands just received from the Soviet Union and described their significance. Areas important industrially and in other ways must be ceded. Moscow was increasing its demands although it had promised that no new demands would be presented; Mme. Kollontai had even spoken of Stalin's making a "grand gesture." Then we had been promised an armistice when the delegation should set off. Now the truth had come out, and the Scandinavian countries must define their attitude. I asked him to bring this new information to the knowledge of the Swedish government, which had come forward as mediator. I promised to telephone Günther at 8:00 P.M. to learn what Sweden would say about the matter.

In order that I might communicate the sense of the cables received to the Cabinet, I had convened it for 5:00 P.M. The President attended as he had earlier.

I related what was known regarding the Moscow negotiations and also Mannerheim's idea of making our appeal to the Western powers simultaneously with these negotiations. The members of the Cabinet were astounded at the harshness of the terms offered. The thought that Finland should be altogether shut off from Lake Ladoga, that two important cities and several important industrial regions should be lost, and that the wholly new demand had been presented for the cession of the Salla area was so novel that at first they all found it difficult to determine their stand. The discussion was prolonged and sporadic. An appeal to the Western powers was mentioned by several members. Hannula called for it now, as he had before, and this time Niukkanen agreed with him completely. It was again necessary for me to describe the ineffectiveness of Western aid and the difficulties of obtaining transit through Sweden.

While the session was in progress, Mannerheim telephoned to say he was momentarily awaiting word of the situation at the front and to ask that no final decision be made before we had received these data and his own conclusions that same evening. We agreed to delay decision until that evening, since the information from the Commander-in-Chief was important and everyone needed time for reflection.

Between the meetings I invited the British and French ministers, Vereker and De Vaux, to talk with me. I frankly reported to them the trip of our delegation to Moscow and the demands presented by the Russians. I also told them of Svinhufvud's trip to Germany and Italy, which was an entirely private venture.

Both were grateful for the frankness exhibited and acknowledged that fair play was important to both sides. At the same time they pointed out that Finland had still time, up to March 12, to present its appeal. Vereker read further reports received from London, to the effect that England was waiting but, after the twelfth, would use the forces for other purposes. I spoke to them about securing bombers. I also referred to the Commander-in-Chief's idea that we should present our appeal despite the fact that negotiations were under way. The idea did not please them in the least. It was their impression that it would be difficult to cancel the aid endeavor if a peace should be brought about.

The Cabinet meeting resumed at 8:00 P.M., and I read the Commander-in-Chief's report, which had been received in the meanwhile. It ran as follows:

Following up what I have already communicated to the Prime Minister and the Foreign Minister, I am sending you this statement on the present combat fitness of his army from Lieutenant General Heinrichs, commander of the Isthmus Army, which is our principal force:

"To the Commander-in-Chief:

"As commander of the Isthmus Army I consider it my duty to report that the present state of the army is such that continued military operations can lead to nothing but further debilitation and fresh losses of territory. In support of my view I set forth the loss of personnel which has occurred and which is still going on. The battle strength of battalions is reported now generally to be below 250 men, with the aggregate daily casualties rising into the thousands. As a consequence of physical and spiritual exhaustion, the battle fitness of those who remain is not what it was when the war started. Considerable losses of officers further reduce the utility of these diminished units. Through enemy artillery fire and air bombing our machine gun and antitank weapons have been demolished to such an extent that a sensible lack is generally perceptible on critical fronts. Since, in addition, events on the right wing have made indispensable fresh expenditures of troops on unprepared terrain and at the expense of the present front, the permanence of our defense has been critically weakened. Enemy air activity frequently makes the transfer and maintenance of forces decidedly difficult. Lieutenant General Oesch, the commander of the Coast Corps, has emphasized to me the scanty numbers and the moral exhaustion of his forces, and does not seem to believe he can succeed with them. Lieutenant General Öhqvist, commander of the Second Army Corps, has expressed the opinion that if no surprises take place, his present front may last a week, but no longer, by reason of the expenditure of personnel, particularly officers. Major General Talvela, commander of the Third Army Corps, expresses his view by saying that everything is hanging by a thread."

After I had read this report I went on: "This is the Commander-in-Chief's view. Our situation is such that we are faced by a forced peace. We must make haste before the collapse occurs. After that our views would not be asked. I have deliberated upon the matter and have come to the conclusion that we must give our representatives authority to conclude such a peace as may be possible and at the same time to propose that an immediate armistice be agreed upon. We do indeed have reason to object to the terms presented, inasmuch as they are not the same as those which were exhibited to us before our representatives departed. The new line would deprive us of our central industrial area on the Isthmus and also of parts of Kuusamo and Salla."

As the meeting went on, I finally got through a call to Foreign Minister Günther in Stockholm. The following conversation took place:

Tanner: You have by now received through Sahlin information on the present demands of the Russians. The demands have been raised, contrary to what we were told beforehand. In the original proposal they spoke of the Isthmus, including Viipuri, and the north shore of Lake Ladoga, including Sortavala. Now the line runs much farther west. This is very hard on Finland. They are demanding vital areas. Entirely new requirements are the additional ones relating to Kuusamo and Salla and to the railway to Kemijärvi. Hitherto they had promised an armistice as soon as our representatives left for Moscow. Nothing has come of it. The Russians promised to negotiate in good faith. What do you say to this? What is Sweden's attitude?

Günther: The demands must be brought back to what they originally were. I think myself that they can be lightened. I have told the representative of the Soviet Union [Mme. Kollontai] that no government can undertake, in the midst of negotiations, to demand more than at the beginning of the negotiations. I have been discussing this matter with Mme. Kollontai, who promised to send on my views.

Tanner: Can this development change the attitude of the Swedish government?

Günther: That is difficult to answer. I don't believe so.

Tanner: I would point out that through the new line Finland loses important industrial areas such as Enso and Värtsilä. The new line encroaches far beyond the line of Peter the Great. The negotiations in Moscow must be concluded within two days. Tuesday is the fatal day for us, as we must then give our answer to the Western powers.

Günther: I promise I will point out to Assarsson and to Mme. Kollontai that the matter is urgent. What will Finland's reply be?

Tanner: We stay with what was agreed upon before our delegation left.

Günther: It is indeed important that you stick to the earlier terms.

After I came back to the Cabinet meeting, there was a discussion of the Commander-in-Chief's report on the situation and of the answer which should be sent to our delegation. All the members of the Cabinet who took the floor, except Hannula and Niukkanen, supported my proposal that our representatives in Moscow be given a free hand. Hannula strove to minimize the significance of the Commander-in-Chief's report by saying that we had at all times received pessimistic reports from headquarters. Moreover, the information in the report was limited to a description of the situation on the Isthmus and nothing was said about the eastern front. He took this to mean that the situation there was unchanged, thus satisfactory at some points, good at others. The army was still unbroken. The peace terms were so severe that it was impossible to accept them. He once more reverted to the proposal he had made many times before, that Western aid should be sought without delay.

Niukkanen also, who thus far had been prepared to support acceptance of the terms offered, now changed his stand. The new line now demanded involved his home town of Kirvu. He said that no matter how pessimistically one might regard the situation, it was more advantageous to continue the struggle than to submit. Now they were demanding the cession of densely settled centers of population and of channels of communication. If this came to pass without our fighting for them, they were lost forever. But if we continued the struggle, it would be possible to get them back in the final settlement of accounts. For this reason he joined with Hannula in proposing that aid be sought of the Western powers. The news of its arrival would raise morale. In this way Finland would be saved.

The President remarked that when he had heard of the additional demands presented, he had been of the view that the delegates should be called home from Moscow, that aid should be sought of the Western powers, and that the war should be continued. Yet the report of the generals on the situation was so grave that it must be given weight.

Tanner: Officers are usually more inclined than civilians to continue fighting, but when even they become pessimistic, what of the civilians then?

The President: The new demands go further than what has been told the Diet. It ought to be informed of this change in the situation.

Tanner: There is not time. Moreover, it might be dangerous at this stage. On Monday [March 11] I must present the matter to the Foreign Relations Committee of the Diet.

Several speakers still doubted whether the people could be brought to submit to the inevitable. They feared that a difficult crisis in domestic policy would arise. In the end, however, they concluded that they were faced with a forced decision, for which reason even these new demands must be accepted.

Now that the position of the Cabinet had become clear, we went on to discuss just how the Commander-in-Chief's report should be transmitted to our delegates. Some considered it dangerous to trust such bad news to the telegraph.

We finally decided to send to our delegates in Moscow a cable of the following tenor:

We have communicated Soviet demands to Sweden and Western powers. Sweden seems to maintain its past attitude regarding aid and transit. The Western powers continue to be prepared to assist. They expect our reply by March 12. Headquarters has furnished written situation report; not sanguine about chances of carrying on. The Cabinet considers terms presented as shocking, particularly as line carries into vital centers and as numerous new demands are made—Hanko islands, Enso, Värtsilä, Kuusamo, and Salla—despite the fact that we were informed via Sweden that all demands were covered in advance terms. Also line of Peter the Great crossed in central Karelia. We have told Swedish Foreign Minister we cannot accept terms as broadened. Such procedure is without example in discussions of this character. Günther agrees. He has communicated this to the Soviet Union and has demanded that it return to its original program. As continuation of the war on the basis of the aid promised is difficult and as contact with you is slow, we authorize you to decide the matter in all respects, provided you are unanimous. Armistice must also be brought about at once. When is next meeting? On twelfth we must without fail reply to the Western powers. When does the Prime Minister plan to return?

Having made these decisions, we broke up well after midnight.

All over the world there began to appear ever more insistent reports that something was afoot between Finland and the Soviet Union. For this reason I had brought up in the Cabinet meeting the question of whether some sort of soothing communiqué should be issued. But it was considered dangerous to take such a step, as it might give rise to the impression that the peace terms were reasonable. On the other hand, it was considered necessary to send to Minister Gripenberg in London and to Minister Holma in Paris detailed information regarding the trip of our delegation. Ministers to other nations were informed briefly that for reasons of policy we were unable to brief them on the situation at present. The journalists, who continued to press with their inquiries, could not be told anything new, and they gave vigorous expression to their discontent. Yet the nature of many delicate political events is such that their premature coming to light may endanger the goal itself. After a decision has been reached, however, it is no longer news in the view of the journalists. This gives rise to constant conflict between news sources and newspapermen.

This time the situation was further complicated by the fact that Svinhufvud was on his way to Germany and Italy. This bit of news aroused certain suspicions on the part of the Western powers.

TENSE DAYS

March 10.—I had not yet fallen asleep when at 1:00 A.M. Foreign Minister Günther telephoned from Stockholm. He had again talked to Mme. Kollontai and had pointed out that, by reason of the new demands of the Soviet Union, the situation had gone past the breaking point. He did not believe the Finnish government could accept the demands in their augmented version, particularly since the boundary would run far north of Viipuri. He had asked what might follow upon rejection. Was the Soviet Union prepared to assume responsibility for the consequences of rejection of its terms, and thus to go on with the war? Was it not informed of England's plans?

Mme. Kollontai had been upset by the conversation. She had promised to cable Moscow at once.

Günther was of the opinion that Molotov had not realized that England was in earnest in planning the dispatch of aid.

When I remarked that both in Sweden and in Norway the attitude toward Finland was changing for the better, Günther replied that the stand of the Riksdag was unanimously against sending aid, as before.

At 10:40 A.M. Marshal Mannerheim called. He inquired whether I had received the telegram containing the report of the generals on the situation at the front. I said that I had received it and had shown it to the Cabinet.

"There is no exaggeration in the telegram," Mannerheim replied. "If the war must go on, large reinforcements are needed. There are many breaches in the front already. We are not in a position to train the troops. The lack of officers is increasing. The quality is getting worse. If aid came at once, so that the forces could get a rest and some training, it would be another matter. But the auxiliary forces, even if they lived up to their promise, would be here only after a month. And you can't count on a change in the weather. Then, too, the aid is conditional, depending on the attitude of Norway and Sweden. Formerly the Western powers promised to take care of that themselves. What is certain is that Norway and Sweden will not give transit rights of their own free will."

I explained the stand taken by the Cabinet. We had given full authority to the delegates in Moscow. He would soon get a copy of the cable sent them.

Mannerheim then asked what was happening in Moscow.

I read him cable No. 5, which had come in that morning:

We are trying to find out promptly and with complete certainty what the Soviet Union can be brought to assent to. If the terms are not satisfactory and if it is considered that the military and civilian fronts will hold out for a longer war, we can break off and try the other line. The American Ambassador recommends peace.

Mannerheim inquired by what route the wire had come.

I explained to him the course taken by the cables, from Moscow to the Foreign Ministry in Stockholm and thence to me. I further told him about the conversation of the previous night between Günther and Mme. Kollontai.

From this conversation it was quite plain that Mannerheim hoped peace would be made before the front crumbled.

At 5:00 P.M. Mannerheim called again. He had meanwhile received a copy of the Cabinet's cable to Moscow and was dissatisfied that his report containing the statements of the generals had been communicated to Moscow in such abbreviated form. He went on to describe the situation as follows: Viipuri must be abandoned the next day or the day after. Then we would be faced with a general rectification of the front, which would be difficult to carry out.

I explained that I had suggested sending a more extensive extract from the Commander-in-Chief's description of the situation at the front, but the Cabinet had considered it dangerous to trust such a description to the telegraph. On this account his extensive description had been cut down to the information: "Headquarters not sanguine about chances of carrying on."

Mannerheim asked that a more complete description be sent to Moscow. This was in fact sent to the delegates that same day.

At 5:30 P.M. censorship officials headed by Dr. Kustaa Vilkuna came to my home seeking directives. Thus far it had been their task to supervise the dissemination of military news, but now diplomatic and political items were becoming more important. There was a whirlwind of cables and expressions of opinion coming in from abroad, and local and foreign journalists were trying to send out news items. What should be their attitude toward these?

I told them confidentially of the negotiations which had started in Moscow. I also informed them that a communiqué regarding these negotiations would be given to the press that day. They might permit factual information to be printed, but nothing which might harm the country. They must guard against the publication in local papers of editorials either for or against peace.

At 5:45 Dr. Numelin, who served as liaison officer between the Foreign Ministry and the press, informed me that the newspapermen wanted some more precise information; Moscow had already given out official news concerning the negotiations. I gave him the communiqué which I had drafted and held ready and which was to be published in the press the next day.

During the day further information had come in regarding the plans and actions of the Western powers. Evidently we were not, after all, to get from England the bombers we had requested until an appeal was made for the aid offered.

The British Minister, Mr. Vereker, delivered a four-point memorandum setting forth England's stand. The most notable point in it was to the effect that the departure of the British auxiliary forces would naturally depend on the positions of Norway and Sweden. If these countries opposed the transit of the forces, either actively or passively, it might become impossible for the forces to reach us. Yet the British government promised to do everything within its power to oblige these countries to cooperate with it.

This confirmed our fear of the difficulties involved. It was at this point that hope of receiving aid finally collapsed. One may speculate what would have been our fate if we had trusted the earlier lavishly extended assurances that opposition on the part of Norway and Sweden would not affect the arrival of the forces.

March 11.—Because of the current peace rumors, the government communiqué was published on this day. It mentioned the composition of the delegation which had been sent to Moscow and stated that no decision had been reached thus far. The communiqué, which was printed under banner headlines, was of the following tenor:

So far as the Finnish News Agency has been able to determine, there has now for some time been contact between the Finnish government and the government of the Soviet Union. This contact has occurred through the mediation of the Swedish government. The purpose has been to determine whether a possibility of terminating hostilities and bringing about a peace might be found. The result was that both sides considered it practicable to initiate direct conversations. At the invitation of the Soviet government to the effect that representatives of the Finnish government come to Moscow for negotiations, last Wednesday evening a delegation left here, composed of Prime Minister Ryti, Minister Paasikivi, General Walden, and Representative Voionmaa. The delegation has had two meetings with representatives of the Soviet government. On these occasions they have familiarized themselves with the peace terms presented by the Soviet Union. No decision has thus far been reached.

The communiqué aroused lively interest in the country. The papers furthermore began cautiously to publish information received from abroad.

The Cabinet again convened at 8:00 A.M. The President appeared, as was his custom, and led the discussion. I gave my usual report on events since the last meeting. I told them of my telephone conversations with the Commander-in-Chief and with Foreign Minister Günther. I also said that it had been necessary to give to the press in the name of the Cabinet a communiqué regarding the negotiations in Moscow.

I then read a telegram, received that morning, from our delegates in Moscow:

Second meeting held the 10th, 2:00 P.M. Meeting lasted two hours; participants as before. We set forth Finnish views *in extenso*, also all views set forth in cipher cable which arrived later in day. Soviet representatives yielded on no point. We now add that in an earlier meeting they presented demands for transit rights from the boundary between the two countries to Kemijärvi via a railway which is to be built by Finland, and from there to Tornio and Sweden. As the Soviet Union does not demand any special privileges with respect to this railway, in our view this is not dangerous. The Soviet Union will pay no compensation even for property of private individuals. In the Soviet view, this concerns the Finnish state. Foreign Commissar Molotov declared he had communicated all Soviet peace terms, part orally and part in writing, to the Swedish Minister in Moscow and to Mme. Kollontai. Molotov said several times that, if we do not accept the terms, negotiations will be broken off. If the government thinks peace and an armistice must be brought about rapidly, the only course is through acceptance of these terms. We do not think any alterations, save perhaps a few minor ones, can be won. Since we believe it would be better for us to meet the 11th rather than the 12th, we await a prompt reply.

I called attention to the time lapse. This cable had been twelve hours on the way before it reached our hands. As the Cabinet had determined its position in our previous meeting and as the state of affairs was as before, I believed the case was clear and that we need send off only a word or so in confirmation of our earlier cable.

Hannula requested that the peace question now be dealt with in official session and entered in the minutes. The world was aware that a delegation had been sent to Moscow. The Soviet Union's terms were known, and it was plain that they were final. Thus there could be no danger in treating the matter in official session, with minutes being taken.

Up to this time, because of the delicacy of the matter, the peace question had been discussed on all occasions in unofficial meetings of the Cabinet, at which the President had been present. Hannula's demand won no support.

Hannula went on to renew his demand that aid be sought of the Western powers without delay. His stand was supported by Niukkanen, in whose view the situation was by no means hopeless. The army had not been beaten. It could withdraw to a new defensive position along the line Virolahti-Luumäki-Saimaa-Joensuu. To be sure, the line was not entirely ready, as there was need for barbed-wire entanglements and dugouts, but antitank defenses were in readiness. Perhaps there would soon be further protection when the ice thawed.

The President was disposed to go on with the fight if the Cabinet agreed unanimously. However, as the ministers did not consider it possible to continue the war, he must adopt the same stand, even though the terms were disastrous. He could not run the country through an imposed war cabinet.

Söderhjelm was also ready to go on with the struggle if the Cabinet was agreed. It was dangerous to the nation's morale to give up before the army was beaten. Yet he was prepared to submit to the will of the majority, because now the most important thing was to stick together.

In this meeting, as in preceding ones, I received the most powerful support from Kotilainen and from Pekkala. The other ministers also gave their support to the proposal for making peace. In the opinion of some, the decision should be left to the Commander-in-Chief. I opposed this idea sharply, as it was not the business of the Commander-in-Chief to intervene in a political decision. I said, however, that in our telephone conversation I had received the impression that he hoped peace would be made. He had emphasized that the army was not beaten and that he had tried to preserve it by retreating. Yet it was his opinion that if the army were beaten, everything would be over.

President Kallio brought up the further point that, upon arrangement of an armistice, the troops should be allowed to remain for the time being in their present positions. If they were required to withdraw at once behind the new line, fresh difficulties would arise. We must have time in which to evacuate the ceded areas in good order. In order to avert criticism at a later date, he desired us to secure from the Swedish government an official reply to the effect that it would not permit passage of the Western forces. We must be in a position to show the world that we had not submitted through faintheartedness.

Toward the end of the meeting I suggested that a telegram be sent to Moscow stating that the government was prepared, if no other course was left, to accept the terms offered and that it hoped for an armistice on the basis of the *status quo*, so that it should be possible to evacuate the ceded areas. This proposal was accepted.

I had asked the Foreign Relations Committee of the Diet to meet at 9:30 A.M., as the terms presented had altered substantially since the matter was debated in the committee and it was important to get the broadest possible support behind the stand adopted by the Cabinet. At that meeting I reported on the most recent political events and on the information which had come in from our delegation in Moscow, and I told them that the Cabinet had decided to accept the peace terms offered despite their harshness.

A rather lively discussion ensued. Representatives Kekkonen and Kares rigidly opposed acceptance of the peace terms. In the opinions of both, the war must be continued. Kekkonen felt that Western aid should be sought, whereas Kares felt that Finland's present situation was the result of its pro-British policy. He further thought the composition of the delegation sent to Moscow was unfortunate. In favor of accepting the peace terms were representatives Reinikainen, Vesterinen, Cajander (who asked a number of questions), Kukkonen, Sillanpää, and Hackzell. In Hackzell's opinion, the situation had been ripe for peace for the past two months. He placed no trust in the aid of the Western powers, which would only bring about Germany's intervention in the game.

This time a vote was taken on the subject, so that the attitude of the committee should be made clear. In favor of the Cabinet's proposal were thirteen members and opposed were four — Kares, Kekkonen, Komu, and Kämäräinen. Representative Ikola was also opposed, but in his capacity as an alternate on the committee he was not entitled to vote.

At 10:00 Mannerheim called. The second telegram I had sent to Moscow on the situation at the front had this time been too pessimistic. He wanted it corrected and dictated his own draft to me. In the correction, however, there was nothing which affected the facts. I asked for his correction in writing and promised I would send it on when it arrived.

At 10:30 Vereker and De Vaux, the British and French ministers, came in at my invitation. I told them that we must secure complete clarification regarding the attitude of Norway and Sweden toward the transit of forces. I inquired whether the Western powers could make a final attempt to clear up this matter, now that our business was in its decisive phase.

Both were doubtful, since Finland had made no appeal to the Western powers. They nevertheless promised to communicate the matter to their governments.

At 11:00 Michelet, the Norwegian Minister, came in and asked if anything had been decided yet.

I told him no. We for our part would like a clear answer from Norway on two points: What was Norway's final, official attitude toward the matter of transit for the Western forces? Was Norway definitely prepared to investigate the possibilities of a defense league among the countries of the North in the event we should make peace with the Soviet Union? He promised to take steps toward this end.

At 11:20 Marshal Mannerheim was on the telephone again. He asked whether we might not make a counterproposal to the Russians and offer to cede areas in northern Finland and Petsamo—the so-called "Heel." By sacrificing these we could perhaps save Hanko Cape and a certain amount of territory in southeast Finland.

I told him I thought this would hardly tempt the Soviet Union. In addition, it would be an unpleasant irritant to Sweden and Norway.

Mannerheim replied: "Everybody must think for himself. That's what Sweden and Norway have done."

I promised to present the suggestion to our delegates for their consideration.

The President, too, telephoned several times during the day to ask for news. I told him what I had learned.

At 1:10 Hjelt, our press attaché in the Stockholm Legation, told me by telephone that the Swedish news bureau TT had received a cable from Helsinki to the effect that the Foreign Relations Committee of the Diet had accepted the Soviet Union's peace terms.

This thoroughly angered me. With the peace negotiations in their most critical stage, someone had blurted out a piece of news like this. It was irresponsible. Who had sent the wire, and how had the censorship conceivably passed it? I told Hjelt to demand that the TT not disseminate the news the telegram contained.

Hjelt told me that the TT had already given the news to the papers.

I categorically insisted that the TT should prevent its being published, but in Hjelt's opinion this would be possible only if the report were categorically denied. I told him to deny it.

This measure succeeded only in part. Most of the Swedish papers did indeed loyally refrain from printing the item, but the sensation-seeking afternoon papers nevertheless published it as a rumor. The consequence was that the same evening it was being discussed in all the cafés and restaurants of Stockholm. And naturally the news was cabled at once to Moscow, where our representatives found it coming up to face them in that day's negotiations.

I was profoundly agitated by this incident, and took steps to determine through what channels such a leak could conceivably have occurred. Dr. Vilkuna, the censorship head, reported that A. E. Berg, director of the Finnish News Bureau (STT), had sent the wire to Sweden. However, when I tried to locate him, Berg seemed to have disappeared completely. I demanded that the STT take every possible measure to prevent the story from spreading. Simultaneously I reported the matter to the police authorities so that they might take the necessary steps.

When Berg was found, he came to the Ministry to report his part in the matter. He acknowledged that he had seen the cable before it went out but said that he had thought it innocuous and had given permission for its dispatch. Such exceptional naïveté irked me so that I dare say I have rarely barked at any man as I did at the sinner before me at that moment.

The way in which the leak had occurred was later cleared up. A couple of members of the Diet Foreign Relations Committee, sitting in the Diet café, had talked too loudly about the decision the committee had reached. An STT reporter, Viljo Heinämies, had overheard a part of this conversation as he walked by, and, considering what he had picked up to be newsworthy, he had written the unfortunate cable, which STT Director Berg had marked "urgent" and sent to Stockholm. Naturally an action was brought against both these men, and they were sentenced to terms of imprisonment. If I recall rightly, Berg served his sentence, but Heinämies contrived to secure a pardon. Consequently, none of the members of the Foreign Relations Committee seem to have violated their obligations of secrecy on this occasion, but unnecessarily loose-jawed these two members certainly were. The journalists in question, on the other hand, behaved in downright criminal fashion toward their country.

At 2:30 P.M. Sahlin, the Swedish Minister, came in at my request. In compliance with the wish of the Cabinet I sought of the Swedish government through him the same information as I had just desired of the Norwegian government through Michelet. In order to avoid any misunderstanding, I presented my questions in writing: (1) What was the attitude of Sweden toward a possible march-through of British and French forces? (2) Was the Swedish government prepared to examine the possibilities of a defense league after the war?

Sahlin promised to secure from his government an answer to these questions. He returned, in fact, on the following the day, and delivered a written reply to the effect that, as to the first question, the Swedish government must as before reply in the negative, since it considered that the result would be the involvement of the North in the major war, with unfortunate consequences to the whole North; as to the second question, the Swedish government was prepared to examine the possibilities of a defense league.

On the same day Michelet brought the reply of the Norwegian government: "The Norwegian government continues in its refusal relative to transit of British and French forces, but it is prepared to examine the possibilities for a defense league."

The answers were clear. They eliminated all remaining doubt as to whether the transit of forces of the Western powers would encounter resistance on the part of Sweden and Norway.

At 4:00 P.M. Mannerheim called. He asked whether inquiry had been made of the British and French governments concerning permission for their forces to pass through the Scandinavian countries.

Tanner: The British and French ministers have been here. I asked them to present this question to their governments. They were doubtful, but promised to do so.

Mannerheim: Everything is so ambiguous on that score. If they cannot secure transit rights, the whole question of auxiliary forces is very doubtful. Has the Cabinet assumed any stand on accepting the peace terms?

Tanner: It has. Early this morning. Hasn't the telegram I sent reached you?

Mannerheim: No. Did the Cabinet hear of my idea that the "Heel" be exchanged for areas in southern Finland?

Tanner: That proposal reached here only after the Cabinet session. I have sent it on to our delegates in Moscow.

At 5:00 P.M. the British Prime Minister, Chamberlain, and the French Premier, Daladier, issued simultaneous communiqués concerning the aid promised to Finland. The communiqués were read over the foreign radio. Both promised on behalf of their nations to come to our aid, if only Finland made an appeal to them.

The following day, March 12, I received a written copy of the British communiqué. Vereker called to deliver a memorandum on behalf of his government, which stated that Prime Minister Chamberlain had on March 11 in the House of Commons replied to a question of the Leader of the Opposition in the following words:

The House will be aware that both the French and British Governments have sent and are continuing to send material assistance to Finland. This has been of considerable value to the Finnish Forces. As His Majesty's Government and the French Government have already informed the Finnish Government, they are prepared, in response to an appeal from them for further aid, to proceed immediately and jointly to the help of Finland, using all available resources at their disposal.

This communication was the last effort of the Western powers to influence the attitude of the Finnish government, one day before the expiration of the time limit granted Finland. At the same time its purpose may well have been to calm public opinion in the Western countries. It was no longer possible to affect the stand of the Finnish government.

In the course of the day, word was received that the next discussion in Moscow would be held at 6:00 P.M. local time.

Günther telephoned later in the evening and asked what had been heard from Moscow. I told him what had come of the last meeting. All the demands put forward by the Soviet representatives seemed harsh. I said I presumed the dispute which had arisen was susceptible of elimination. The demands earlier presented by the Soviet Union and those made at the Moscow negotiations differed in many points. When our representatives had remarked upon this in the negotiations, Molotov had said he had communicated all the requirements, both orally and in writing, to the Swedish Minister, Assarsson, as well as to Mme. Kollontai. We, however, had not been informed of them in the earlier phase of the conversations. This conflict must be cleared up without fail.

Günther: Molotov's statement is a fabrication.

Tanner: As for Western transit rights, does the Swedish government maintain its earlier stand?

Günther: Yes. The matter was up in the Foreign Relations Committee of the Riksdag today. The committee approved the Cabinet's stand.

Tanner: May we have that information today in writing?

Günther: You shall. There are rumors here that the [Finnish] Diet Foreign Relations Committee has accepted the Soviet terms.

Tanner: The report is without foundation. It has been officially denied.

I had to stick by my false denial even with Günther. It was necessary to undo the effects of that unfortunate telegram, even though I knew it was in vain.

March 12.—In the course of the night several important telegrams from our delegation in Moscow had been received. On this account I asked the Cabinet members to assemble at 9:00 A.M.

At the meeting I undertook to deal with the most important part of the business by relating the contents of the telegrams. The day before, at 4:55 P.M., a cable from the delegation had arrived, calling for information of a technical military nature. It ran as follows:

To cover the eventuality of an armistice, wish guidance from Commander-in-Chief on interval between moment of signing and moment of taking effect, separately for various sectors of the front. Desire written reply.

This was answered, on the Commander-in-Chief's instructions, to the effect that twenty-four hours was sufficient time south of the latitude of Lieksa and forty-eight hours from there northward, assuming that transmission time from Moscow to headquarters should not be more than four hours.

That morning at 5:25 the following report had come in on the session of the previous evening:

Session March 11 lasted from 6:00 to 7:30. Soviet representatives made no concessions and required that their terms be accepted. For tomorrow, however, they promised three minor concessions. We get final treaty draft Tuesday (March 12). They have not agreed to an armistice but will terminate hostilities when the treaty is signed. We hasten this by all means in our power.

In a second telegram within the hour, they asked that full powers to sign the treaty be sent them without delay.

I went on to speak of the communiqués issued by the prime ministers of the Western powers, which were reported in the morning press. Gripenberg had cabled from London that Prime Minister Chamberlain had declared that twelve bombers would fly to Finland on March 12, and forty-two more as soon as possible, but that they would return to England if peace was made. Holma had cabled from Paris that Premier Daladier had been authorized to tell him that on receiving the appeal for aid the Cabinet would respond without the least delay. I added that the attitude of the Swedish and Norwegian governments on the question of transit of forces was unchanged. Finally, I described to them the Commander-in-Chief's idea of offering the "Heel" as ransom.

My report gave rise to further discussion of various questions. It will be well to record the statements relating to the main decision.

Niukkanen: I should like to inquire what the Foreign Minister proposes to do about British and French aid. Is the idea to refrain from requesting aid, thus leaving us at Russia's mercy?

Tanner: Once we conclude an armistice and make peace, we may thank the Western powers for their good intentions.

Niukkanen: With the situation such as it was, I did not oppose our opening negotiations in order to get a clear idea of the peace terms. Now it becomes clear that it is more advantageous to go on with the fighting than to accept a peace on these terms. For this reason aid should be sought of the Western powers at once. I have pondered the matter in all its aspects, and I have come to the conclusion that to make peace would leave us at Russia's mercy, since the Western powers are withdrawing and Sweden offers no help. I cannot go on as Defense Minister if the majority of the Cabinet and the Commander-in-Chief hold another view.

Hannula: I agree completely with Niukkanen. I have reached the same conclusion.

Tanner: I can well understand that there should be divergent opinions in the light of the harshness of the terms. Yet I hope we shall try to hold together to the end. It would be unfortunate if we should split; it would merely weaken the country. It is my feeling that, once peace is concluded, the Cabinet's duty is done, and it should then report to the Diet. If the Diet gives it a vote of confidence, the Cabinet should remain in power; if it is voted down, it should resign. New men could then take over. But it would be regrettable if before that time some of us withdrew from our posts.

Niukkanen: I admit that it is difficult to settle upon a final stand, for I will confess that the views presented by the majority also have their logic. It is for that reason I did not oppose negotiations. But the peace terms give Russia a vantage point assaulting us. Therefore we should go on fighting. I should in no way criticize the stand of the majority; yet I do not wish to remain if the views of the military command and the Cabinet differ from mine.

President Kallio: This is a distressing situation. We know nothing of the fate of half a million of our fellow citizens whose homes will be on the other side of the new line. There is no telling what will happen to them. I shudder at these terms. I should be ready to go on with the war if I had support from the Diet and the Cabinet, but we have come to this pass by slow degrees. It is sad that feeble Sweden became the mediator.

These statements show what was in the minds of some Cabinet members even at the moment of final decision. What they had to say reflected despair as to the future of the country and as to the fate of our fellow citizens who would lose their homes. Yet harsh actualities drove us to continue upon the course already chosen.

The Cabinet went on to inquire how the matter had been handled in the Diet Foreign Relations Committee. I told them about this and about the leak of the decision made by the committee, which had obviously reached Moscow before the final settlement. Letting out this information was treason, for which reason I had reported the matter to the police.

Some of the Cabinet members still desired that the Prime Minister be asked to return to Helsinki to report on the Moscow negotiations before full, definitive powers were granted. I remarked that this was impossible, since it would take at least two days, and we must make our final decision now. The time limit of the Western powers lapsed on that day, and, furthermore, the Moscow negotiations might be broken off if there were such a delay.

I was asked in what order the evacuation of the ceded areas was to take place. I had to answer that, unfortunately, no information had yet been received on this point, though I assumed we would be granted a reasonable period. Here, however, I was utterly mistaken, as experience showed a few days later.

Niukkanen then demanded that before the ceded areas were abandoned, they should be thoroughly evacuated and laid waste. In these areas there were vast amounts of goods, cattle, fodder, grain, etc., which must not be left to the Russians. Nor did the inhabitants wish to leave their houses to the Russians; they would burn them down. Our forces should not leave bridges, railways, or factories intact behind them. It would be unthinkable to let the Russians move half a million to a million people into areas all set up for them.

Fortunately, as it turned out, no action was taken on this proposal. Many arguments arose later with the Russians over destroyed property, which they called upon us to make good. They even demanded the return of property which had been removed.

At the end of the discussion I presented a French text of the full powers to be assigned:

Through these presents I authorize Prime Minister Risto Ryti, Minister Without Portfolio J. K. Paasikivi, General Rudolf Walden, and Representative Väinö Voionmaa to represent the Republic of Finland in negotiations in progress at Moscow with delegates of the Union of Soviet Socialist Republics, to the end of bringing about a termination of hostilities and the conclusion of a peace between the two countries, and on behalf of the Republic of Finland to sign agreements which may be reached at the said negotiations. Given at Helsinki this twelfth day of March, 1940.

This was to be signed by the President and the Foreign Minister. The credentials were to be cabled to Moscow.

"This is the most disgraceful document I have ever signed," President Kallio said.

Immediately upon the conclusion of this private session, the official presentation to the President was arranged at 9:00 A.M.

As Foreign Minister I offered to the President for signature the credentials to be delivered to the members of our delegation in Moscow.

This gave rise to the following discussion:

Niukkanen: In my opinion it would have been better to continue armed resistance rather than to submit to wholly disgraceful terms.

I do not advocate signature of the treaty but rather an appeal for the assistance of the Western powers.

Hannula: As this problem now comes up for the first time in official session, I wish it to be recorded in the minutes that in meetings both of the foreign affairs committee and of the Cabinet I have steadfastly been of the opinion that there should be no peace negotiations with the Russians but that instead the aid offered by the Western powers should be accepted. I continue to hold the same view, and with all the more reason since the peace terms are frightfully severe.

Bureau Chief Aaro Pakaslahti: I wish to declare that if I had had to report on this question in a general session of the Council of State, I should have said that, in my opinion, such terms should not be accepted.

Von Born: As I have come to the conclusion that the speedy signing of a peace is a military necessity, I cannot but associate myself with the proposal advanced.

The President decided to approve the proposal in question.

Now that the decision had been made, Niukkanen asked whether his resignation might be made public at once.

The President asked: "May it not remain a matter known only to the Cabinet until the business is done? A resignation must be presented to the Prime Minister; this can take place only after his return."

On signing the credentials President Kallio declared in Old Testament language, "May the hand wither, that is forced to sign such a paper as this."

This imprecation was answered in fateful fashion. Some months later the President suffered a stroke which paralyzed his right arm. Before a year was out he was dead.

Upon the conclusion of the meeting, the credentials were cabled to Moscow in clear. We also instructed the delegates to allow adequate time in the cession of territories for the population and property in the ceded areas to be evacuated in good order.

At 11:45, Marshal Mannerheim called, asking for news from Moscow. He planned to destroy at once the factories in the area to be ceded. In particular, he wanted to blow up the Enso factories and the Rouhiala power plant. I strictly forbade this. Their fate was yet to be settled.

Mannerheim agreed to wait a while longer on these but said that in any event he would destroy the Waldhof factories in Kexholm. This I did not flatly oppose, an omission I had occasion to regret later, because they were indeed blown up and Finland subsequently had to pay for this destruction.

I told Mannerheim that the Cabinet had sent the credentials to Moscow for the signing of the peace treaty.

At 3:00 P.M. Minister Vereker visited me, bringing the memorandum of his government and the statement Prime Minister Chamberlain had made in Parliament, referred to earlier. He advised me that, on the previous day, Finland's request that the British and French governments ask for the reactions of Norway and Sweden to the passage of Western forces through their territory had been acted upon.

Erkko confirmed this from Stockholm.

At 4:00 P.M. I learned from an informant that the Moscow radio had announced the signing of the peace terms and of an armistice, and that the armistice would become effective the following day at 3:00 P.M.

At 4:30 Holma telephoned from Paris, saying that he and Colonel Paasonen had called on Premier Daladier. Daladier had strongly emphasized the importance of dispatching the auxiliary forces and promised immediate aid if requested. In the British ports all preparations for sending the forces had been concluded. If Finland requested aid, the governments of France and England would notify Oslo and Stockholm and would proceed to march through. Holma added, as an important news item, that not only would aid be sent at once but France would immediately break off diplomatic relations with the Soviet Union.

I thanked Holma for his call and said I was at the moment awaiting final word from Moscow.

These Paris calls came by way of Germany and were of course recorded on tape there. We heard much about them from the Germans later.

At 4:45 Günther called. The Swedish Riksdag was meeting the next day, and he planned to report on the outcome of the peace negotiations.

Tanner: I'm not sure at all it will be settled. Thus far there has been no word of it.

Günther: But the Finnish government sent authority to Moscow today?

Tanner: It was sent so we should be ready, but there is no word on the final outcome yet.

Günther: As for the conversations on the defense league, I should like to know whether the Finnish government intends to publish a statement on the matter.

Tanner: We should be glad to announce that if the Swedish government has nothing against the idea.

Günther: We have nothing against it. We should only wish to make our announcements simultaneous.

Tanner: Good. We're agreed on that. I'll call you later in the evening.

Günther: The British and French ministers today inquired further about transit. That's a mere formality, I suppose?

Tanner: We asked them to do it. Even at the last minute we wanted to get the matter absolutely clear.

A further meeting of the Council of State was held at 5:00 P.M., primarily to inform the Cabinet of the latest developments. But no news had come from Moscow.

I took the floor first, remarking that we must deal with a major problem to which passing reference had been made in the morning, namely, what should be done in the areas beyond the new frontier. The Commander-in-Chief wished to destroy all plants, including the Enso factories and the Rouhiala power installations. I thought the Cabinet should take a stand on this point. I then mentioned the information I had received an hour before, that the Moscow radio had announced the signing of the armistice and the peace terms, to go into effect at 3:00 P.M., but my informant had been unable to say whether it was this day or the next. We were not too familiar with the new line. In any case, we ought to destroy nothing which could possibly remain on our side. Generally I considered that factories should not be destroyed, even though they were beyond the line. They would be purchasers of Finnish lumber. Moreover, if the armistice was signed, we could no longer undertake to destroy anything. In principle, too, I was opposed to destruction. The Great War had not really begun yet, and we knew nothing of how it would end. This peace of ours was an interlude, and we did not know how the final peace settlement would look. When he learned of the radio broadcast I had referred to, the Commander-in-Chief was inclined to abandon any further idea of demolitions.

Talk of peace as an interlude may sound queer at this writing. An endeavor has been made to interpret it as plotting a war of revenge, which we were supposed to have had in mind even as we made the Moscow peace. At that time, however, it was imagined that the Great War would end in a grand peace conference at which the affairs of Europe would again be put into order, as had occurred a couple of decades before at the Paris Peace Conference. It was expected that Finland's fate would then be settled once and for all. The Moscow peace would in that event have the character of an interlude and would last only until the end of the Great War, after which any talk of security guarantees for Leningrad would become superfluous. For this reason the representatives of the Western powers in Helsinki were on numerous occasions informed of our hope that their governments would back Finland in the final peace conference; for in the spring of 1940 it was generally believed in our country that the Western powers would win the war as they had won the First World War. Later, by reason of Germany's great victories, the belief for a time favored Germany, here as elsewhere. In any case there was no Paris Peace Conference.

Regarding the problem of whether to demolish the property in the ceded areas, a brief discussion ensued at the meeting of the Council of State. It came out that a letter had been sent earlier to the Commander-in-Chief by the Defense Ministry in which a plan had been set forth for the destruction of industrial plants on three alternative lines, each far-reaching, but reserving the final decision for the Cabinet.

Niukkanen proposed that the Commander-in-Chief be authorized to carry out demolition in accordance with the maximum plan. The areas should be devastated and not left to the Russians as they stood.

Heikkinen protested: "We cannot decide the matter, as we are not acquainted with the boundary and do not know what has been agreed to in Moscow. It would be a sad story if we were to destroy anything contrary to the treaty. In that event we should have to pay for the destruction in cash."

I added: "Even if there had been no agreement, destruction would be vandalism. The thought of the Cabinet's sanctioning a work of destruction is intolerable. The idea is even worse when applied to industry. Why, all the Saimaa lake basin wants to sell wood."

The majority of the Cabinet favored waiting.

Next there came up the question of what should be done with the population of the ceded areas.

Niukkanen demanded that the Cabinet take a stand at least with regard to the population. The Cabinet could not assume responsibility for leaving Finns on the Russian side. He felt it was clear that the population in its entirety should be moved to the Finnish side. It would be criminal to leave our fellow nationals under Kuusinen.

Tanner: The inhabitants should be allowed to choose for themselves where they wish to live.

Pekkala: I have an idea the people themselves know what they want.

Kotilainen: We have just decided to evacuate the areas we shall cede. I do not believe people can be forced to leave if they want to stay where they are. But they can be urged to move this side of the line.

Söderhjelm: Surely arrangements must be made so that all may leave.

I went on to propose that the decision reached should be communicated to the nation, which had no notion of the point matters had reached.

I thought the Cabinet should issue a communiqué and that the matter should be broadcast over the radio. It was also indispensable that the Commander-in-Chief issue his own communiqué to the army and to the people.

This was agreed upon. I undertook to draft the communiqué and the radio statement, which were to be cleared with the Cabinet.

At this session of the Council of State, Niukkanen and Hannula handed in their official resignation.

At 5:30 Erkko telephoned from Stockholm to say that "Aunty on Valhallavägen" (Mme. Kollontai) had asked whether I could come to Stockholm at once. She appeared to have some very important business, and she would be available the next day.

I said I was so busy I could by no means manage to leave.

At 5:35, Marshal Mannerheim called. He pointed out that it was essential to reserve sufficient time for the evacuation of the areas to be ceded. In his opinion it would take a month for the removal of all property. I replied that I had mentioned this fact to the delegation in Moscow.

At 8:15, for the second time that day, Vereker came to my home to say that he had something urgent and important to communicate. He declared on behalf of his government that despite the negative attitude of the Norwegian and Swedish governments toward transit, the Western powers would not abandon their plan, which was now entirely in readiness, but would assist the Finnish government with sufficient and rapid aid in the form of troops. This, however, was not to be communicated to the Norwegian and Swedish governments. He asked that instead I communicate it to the Finnish Cabinet, to Marshal Mannerheim, and to the delegation in Moscow.

The day had been full of tensions and of discussions leading in various directions. As it happened to be my birthday, I shall surely recall it with distaste all the days of my life.

CHAPTER 11

WE BOW TO SUPERIOR FORCE

If March 12 had been a restless and involved day, the night which followed upon it was no more peaceful, at least it was not for me. I did not have a single moment to close my eyes. I waited all night for news concerning the final outcome of the Moscow negotiations. Would they make peace, or would the war continue? And in the latter event would we present our appeal to the Western powers, thus sweeping along into the World War?

Immediately after midnight the German radio announced that agreements had been signed in Moscow, but no details as to their content were given. We had no confirmation of this from our own delegates. This occasioned no surprise, as we were aware how slow the devious route of the cables via Stockholm had proved to be. The newspapermen kept calling all night and asking for news. These calls were partly local ones, but most were from abroad. That night I had to answer telephone calls from the capitals of at least six nations.

All through the night important cables were also coming in, and these were read to me over the telephone at once.

THE PEACE IS SIGNED

March 13.—The morning papers were in a position to report under large headlines that "according to radio announcements by stations in many foreign countries" peace had been concluded and that hostilities would be terminated at 11:00 A.M. No officials had confirmed this news. There was no information on the peace terms.

Among other news items was the report that Premier Daladier had informed the French Parliament that as far back as February 5 the Supreme Council of the Allies had decided to aid Finland, and that a French army of 50,000 men had been ready to leave since February 26, awaiting only the Finnish appeal for aid. From London it was reported that the Finnish government had been advised, before its delegation had departed for Moscow, that the Allied army was ready and that its strength was 100,000 men.

All this was indeed news to the Finnish people.

I had summoned the Council of State for a private session at 9:00
A.M. This time the President was absent.

I referred to the most recent reports: In a telegram which had
arrived at 11:00 the evening before, it was announced that the next
discussion of peace terms had been set for 6:00 P.M. (March 12). A
little later a telegram came in saying that evacuation of Hanko within
three days was being demanded and that the evacuation schedules for
other areas also allowed for little time. This was to be communicated
to the residents of the areas to be ceded. At 2:00 A.M. a telegram had
arrived to inform us that the Russians had not during the negotiations
made any concessions whatsoever and that another meeting, at which
the treaty was to be signed, would be held that same evening. At 2:30
A.M. we received from Stockholm by telephone the text of a protocol
to the peace treaty, containing directives for the cessation of military
activities and for the withdrawal of armed forces.* This was transmitted
urgently to headquarters. At 6:00 A.M. an incoming telegram had announced that the peace treaty and the protocol had gone into effect. Ten
days were granted us for handing over Hanko.

I asked that Ministers Fagerholm, Heikkinen, and Söderhjelm assist
me in drafting a communiqué to be issued by the Cabinet. Once prepared, it should be scrutinized in general session. I also announced that
at noon I should make a statement over the national radio in which the
principal features of the peace treaty would be announced.

At 11:00 A.M. Vereker and De Vaux, the ministers of Great Britain
and France, called in response to my invitation. I explained to them
the course of events of the last few hours and thanked them for all their
trouble and the sympathy they had shown in connection with the problem
of sending the auxiliary forces of the Western powers.

A similar statement was sent to our envoys in London and Paris.
They were instructed to present our thanks to the governments of Great
Britain and France.

At noon I read the peace terms over the radio, and in my statement
which followed I set forth the reasoning which had led to the peace.
Within an hour the newspapers were selling special editions announcing
the peace terms.

At 5:00 P.M. another meeting of the Council of State was held, this
time with the President in attendance. On this occasion I presented the
draft which I had prepared for the Cabinet's proclamation. It was
printed in the papers the following day. These papers also published

---

* The texts of the peace treaty and of the protocol are translated in the Appendix,
pp. 263–67.

the eloquent order of the day from the Commander-in-Chief to his troops.

The discussion at this Cabinet meeting was primarily concerned with the most urgent tasks imposed upon us by the peace treaty. It was indicated that the soldiers were eager to go home and that public officials and others who had been removed from the capital wished to return as soon as possible. However, since our most urgent duty was to see to the evacuation of the ceded and leased territory, this was put in first place, in order that those who lived there might be moved out with their property in good time. Trains and buses were reserved for this purpose. Everything else had to wait for the time being.

At 8:00 P.M. a press conference was arranged at the Hotel Kämp. It was attended by representatives of the domestic press and by a large group of foreign correspondents, some of whom had settled down in the Hotel Kämp press room during the entire period of the war, and particularly during the recent critical days. This meeting was arranged by Laurin Zilliacus, who had seen to the needs of the foreign correspondents during the war period. After he had explained the contents of the peace treaty, I gave some details on the negotiations which had led to the treaty. These statements were made in English, which most of the journalists understood. They gave rise to numerous questions, to which we replied.

As I left this gathering, I met at the door of the Kämp the Swedish minister, Sahlin, who had waited for me there. He wished to suggest on behalf of his government a slight change in our communiqué regarding the defense league. I had used language according to which the matter was to be deliberated upon "promptly." He proposed that this word "promptly" be eliminated. Evidently the Swedish desire was to proceed cautiously. Naturally I agreed to his suggestion.

The harsh provisions of the peace treaty were a great surprise to the country. The general feeling was that our army had carried out its duties successfully and that, accordingly, honorable peace terms were to be expected. When the harshness of the terms became known and when it was observed that the Soviet Union had demanded areas much greater than those it had been able to conquer, our people were astounded. Grief and tears were to be seen among the civilian population of the capital; what then must have been the sentiments of the army and of that part of the population which was under the necessity of finding new homes? Flags were everywhere flown at half-mast. On the other hand, there were indications of relief that we had really come through and that it was all over now. I received an abundance of telegrams containing congratulations upon the return of peace. However, there also were some severely critical ones. The bitterest of them was one which came from Aavasaksa; the signers appeared to be members of the Lotta Svärd organization, among them the wife of a distinguished general. Its criticism culminated in the words, "A swinish, disgraceful peace we shall never submit to."

March 14.—Our Moscow delegation having returned at four o'clock during the night, a Cabinet meeting was held at 11:30 A.M. The members of the Cabinet who were in Helsinki could now for the first time see the peace treaty, only the principal provisions of which had been cabled to Helsinki, along with the protocols. The documents were read in their entirety. The returning delegates reported on the course of the negotiations, on the counterproposals they had made, and on the coldness with which they had been treated.

For instance, the question of the relationship of the new treaty to the peace treaty made at Tartu in 1920 had been of importance. In the view of the Finnish delegation, the provisions of the peace of Tartu should have been regarded as still in effect insofar as the directives of the new treaty did not specifically nullify them. The Russians, however, considered that the outbreak of war had annulled the treaty of Tartu in its entirety. Accordingly, the provisions relating to economic and other matters had to be considered anew. In the course of the negotiations the Finns had brought up a number of problems of a commercial character, such as freedom of navigation in Viipuri Bay and on the Saimaa Canal and the use of the Uuras loading facilities and of the fisheries in the Gulf of Finland and in the waters of the Rybachi Peninsula at Petsamo. All these questions had to be left for settlement later.

Similarly, the timetable according to which the Finnish army was to be withdrawn had given rise to a difference of opinion between the negotiators. The Russians had demanded a rate of ten kilometers a day but had at length consented to seven kilometers. At first they had demanded that Hanko be evacuated in three days, but later they had extended the period to ten days. There had been no mention of overland transit traffic to Hanko, an important point that should have been cleared up, in the light of subsequent pretensions advanced by the Soviet Union.

Demarcation of the new boundary must be undertaken with dispatch. A mixed committee for the purpose of carrying out this assignment was to be set up within ten days. Professor Ilmari Bonsdorff, who was experienced in work of this sort, was suggested as chairman.

Some questions having to do with property in the area to be ceded were also cleared up. We had the right to remove personal property, but the Russians seemed to have their own idea of what constituted personal property. The Prime Minister explained that the directives in the protocol meant that nonmilitary installations of importance should by no means be destroyed, burned, or blown up. Fixed artillery must be left in position, but mobile artillery and ammunition might be removed.

Since a very short period had been left for ratification of the peace treaty—this had to be done by March 22 at the latest—it was decided that a proposal to the Diet for approval of ratification should be prepared with all speed. At first there was uncertainty as to whether this approval should be signified in the form of a law or of a simple resolution of the Diet. When on examination it was determined that the treaty contained nothing which affected existing laws, it became clear that the approval could be signified through a Diet resolution. C. G. Möller, assistant to the Chancellor of Justice, was of the same view.

As we were now in open waters, we set to work urgently on every hand. Our principal concern was naturally the fate of the residents and of their property in the ceded and leased areas. All available resources were used to evacuate them. The Cabinet set up a special committee to take charge of this and named Dr. U. K. Kekkonen as its chairman. In the work of evacuation we received exceptionally valuable help from Sweden, which sent over hundreds of buses and trucks. As a result of the limited time, however, much damage was suffered.

In the ensuing days the Foreign Ministry, too, was the scene of a whirlwind of activity. The proposal for the Diet had to be drafted and maps drawn to set forth the new boundaries, which the treaty defined in terms of degrees of longitude and latitude. Professor E. A. Piponius labored assiduously in the Ministry during these days.

March 15.—At ten o'clock in the morning there was a Cabinet session, which the President attended. The Foreign Ministry's draft proposal for approval of the peace treaty between Finland and the Soviet Union was introduced.

The proponent, Bureau Chief Aaro Pakaslahti, hereupon made reference to the adverse opinion he had voiced in the session of March 12, when he had opposed the acceptance of the peace treaty. As Foreign Minister I recommended that the Cabinet advise the President that the proposal be presented to the Diet. This recommendation was approved.

Immediately thereafter this recommendation was made to the President. Thereupon Hannula referred to his dissenting opinion pronounced in the meeting of March 12. Niukkanen was not present at this session.

The proposal was transmitted to the Diet that same day.

At 10:30 Sahlin, the Swedish Minister, called on me to inquire on behalf of his government how we thought the groundwork for the defense league might be laid.

I told him that we had not yet had a chance to plan the matter in detail, though I had requested opinions from experts in international law and from the general staff. I would ask, in turn, that the Swedish and Norwegian governments make corresponding inquiries. Perhaps after that it would be practicable to hold a consultation of foreign ministers, at which lines could be plotted along which the work should proceed. We had no idea of Denmark's attitude toward this problem, so I hoped Sweden might act as go-between.

Since my radio statement had given rise to some displeasure in Sweden, in that it had contained no special mention of the aid that country had furnished during the war period, I asked Sahlin to convey my explanation to the Swedish government. The statement had been most hastily prepared, and its purpose had been to explain to our own people the reasons why Finland had had to make peace. In that connection it would not have been altogether fitting to speak of other considerations. There had not been the least intention of offending the Swedish government or the Swedish public, and the highly valuable assistance which they had given was acknowledged with gratitude in Finland.

At eleven o'clock Von Blücher, the German Minister, came to speak to me at the Foreign Ministry. He made a fine statement, not as the official representative of his government but "als Mensch zu Mensch." He praised Finland's heroic defense and expressed his regret over our great losses, territorial and otherwise. He felt, however, that he could give assurance that everything would be made right in time. Next he brought up several matters: What would happen to German property in the ceded areas, for instance the Waldhof factories in Kexholm? When could commercial exchange with Germany be resumed? Finally, there came a vigorous criticism of the French and British offer of aid. In Von Blücher's view it had been a very selfish scheme, aimed chiefly at securing possession of the ore deposits in northern Sweden.

At 3:30 P.M. I took part in a meeting of the Social Democratic Party, which was attended by its press and by its regional secretaries. I gave a detailed report on how things had gone. Those present were glad to get clarification on many points which had remained obscure to them.

At 6:45 P.M. I spoke over the national radio to the United States on our war with Russia and on the factors which had led to the peace treaty.

RATIFICATION

The principal scene of events now shifted to the Diet, which had its first chance to deal with the peace treaty officially. In general, questions of war and peace had not come before the Diet since that dark evening of November 30 in the Vallila Labor Center, when the Diet had given its vote of confidence to Cajander's government. Now, in a way, it was a question of confidence in Ryti's government. Ryti and I attended a meeting of the Diet Foreign Relations Committee at noon in order to furnish information on the considerations which had led to the making of peace. An extensive discussion developed, in the course of which numerous questions were asked. A decision was deferred till the Cabinet's proposal should be sent to the committee.

It was possible to deliver the Cabinet's proposal for confirmation of the peace treaty to the Diet at the session which began at 2:00 P.M. that day. In accordance with the provisions of the rules of procedure, the proposal was first tabled. In another session held a few minutes later, a general discussion took place. On account of the delicacy of the matter the session was declared closed, which meant that the discussion could not be published.

Prime Minister Ryti began by reporting on the measures undertaken by the Cabinet during the whole period of its activity. The Cabinet had considered its prime task to be the restoration of peace. While all the power and resources of the nation were being devoted to the most vigorous possible conduct of the war, all chances of peace were being explored, and peace was being sought. When the unjustified attack had occurred, we had been ill prepared for war. We had trusted in the justice of our cause and had been confident that Russia would not attack us lawlessly. We had had no promises of aid from any quarter. Contrary to what was said, no one had incited us to oppose the Soviet Union's demands during the phase of negotiation.

The whole world had at first considered Finland's cause to be hopeless. Of sympathy we received an abundance, but no effective aid from any quarter. Only when it turned out that Finland was capable of effective defense was humanitarian and material aid furnished in ample measure, particularly by Sweden and by the countries of the West. In contradistinction, no aid worth mentioning had come in the form of manpower. What had come was so limited and reached the front so late that its significance, in relation to the character and extent of the war, had been small. Consequently, with respect to manpower we had fought the war virtually alone. When it proved beyond our power to go on, the Cabinet had after serious deliberation come to the conclusion that, despite the burdensome nature of the peace terms, we must pull out of the war while it was still possible. The future would show whether we had acted rightly and wisely.

Even during this introductory discussion, voices opposed to peace were heard. They came from the direction of the Patriotic People's

Movement (the IKL). Representative Annala spoke in opposition to the Prime Minister's statement. As the Prime Minister had asserted that making peace often called for more courage and more initiative than starting a war, Annala declared that making peace can also prove to be the fruit of cowardice. "There are many of us here in this country who despite all assurances do not see that there was any compelling reason for putting up with such a peace." He laid the blame on the diplomacy of earlier years. Our whole foreign policy had been full of sentimentality. We had felt boundless sympathy toward the so-called democracies and equal distaste for the so-called dictatorships, especially Germany and Italy. If our relations with Germany had been conducted in another way, Finland would not be in its present unfortunate plight. He did not think it necessary to go into details regarding the peace treaty, since it was of such a character that he could not approve it.

Representative Salmiala, another IKL member, took his stand on the basis of formal legality. In his view the Cabinet was not entitled to bring about a peace treaty before the Diet had reached a decision on the matter. For this reason he would have expected the Cabinet, before making this decision, to seek the opinion of the Diet. What significance did a Diet decision have at this point? A mere formality.

Prime Minister Ryti replied to these accusations by remarking that it had been an indispensable prerequisite to our getting an armistice that we should accept the provision whereby the peace treaty came into effect. As cession of territory would begin only on March 15—that very day—the Diet theoretically had an opportunity to reject the treaty; so the franchises of the Diet had not been abused. It was much more important to stop as quickly as possible the shedding of blood than to hold fast to the forms of law.

At the end of the discussion the Cabinet's proposal was sent to the Foreign Relations Committee, which acted swiftly. It met at 3:30 P.M., twenty-five minutes after the Diet session had ended.

By five o'clock the committee was able to distribute its mimeographed opinion at the new session of the Diet. In this memorandum the committee declared unanimously that it supported the Cabinet's proposal. The memorandum was at once tabled. Regular debate upon it was begun at a closed session of the Diet starting at 5:30.

In accordance with established custom, Väinö Voionmaa, chairman of the committee, took the floor first. His moving speech accorded well with the sadness of the occasion:

The Diet has now assembled to carry out a task the like of which for grievousness and bitterness the history of our country has hardly known. Much though we have lost, we still retain what is more important and valuable to our country than all the territories of which it is shorn—the independence of our nation and the freedom of our people. Of this we have not been deprived; nor can we be. . . . Was it in vain that Finland's army has fought, and our fearless young soldiers have reddened with their blood the wintry drifts at our borders? No; for they have fought victoriously for indestructible values.

The speech continued in this style, concluding with the declaration that the committee had unanimously supported approval of the peace treaty. He added that the Social Democratic Diet group, too, was of the same view, without dissenting opinion.

The Minister of Education, Hannula, declared to the Diet that within the Cabinet he had most consistently opposed the making of peace and had demanded that we place our reliance upon Western aid. However, now he no longer undertook to defend his point of view or to criticize the treaty, since the Diet was no longer in a position to affect the course of events. Instead he concentrated upon words of appreciation for the soldiers who had defended their country. "The soldiers of Europe's most heroic army now return to their homes, downcast in heart. We must be able to tell them that their battle has not been in vain. Had it not been for their boundless sacrifice, our liberties would have perished as have those of so many other countries." Referring to the uncertain future he remarked, "We must grit our teeth and go forward, and show the world that Finland lives and intends to go on living. . . . Just as during the war there was above everything the fatherland which united us, now that peace has come we can have no other striving than conjointly to work for our fatherland."

Representative Estlander, a member of the Swedish People's Party group and a sworn defender of attitudes of formal legality, reproached the Cabinet for having infringed upon the prerogatives of the Diet in signing the peace treaty. With respect to the content of the treaty, he was dissatisfied that Hanko and Lappohja had been leased; they should not under any circumstances have been handed over for exploitation. In his opinion the Diet ought unanimously to refuse approval to the pact. With a view to entering his protest against what had taken place, he proposed that the peace treaty be rejected.

Representative Kares, a member of the IKL group, spoke at length. In earlier meetings of the Diet Foreign Relations Committee he had most severely opposed the move toward peace. He had just now proposed in the committee that the following passage be included in the preamble of its report:

One member of the committee is indeed of the opinion that peace with Russia on the terms offered has been concluded too hastily and that the text of the treaty is decidedly vague on several important points, thus readily offering occasion for renewed dissensions. But in view of the fact that developments have proceeded, in part through violation of our constitution, so far as to be almost irretrievable, and that in consequence the combat effectiveness of the army is at the moment greatly reduced, he does not consider that he can vote against ratification.

The committee, however, had rejected the addition which he advocated. He was thoroughly dissatisfied with the way the situation had developed. "Gentlemen of the Cabinet, it is not the war, but your proceedings, which have faced us with an impasse from which there is no escape—if escape it may be called—other than ratification of this paper."

While I am on the subject of the Reverend Mr. Kares' statement, I wish to add a small personal memoir. Some months later we happened to meet in a corridor of the Diet building. He fell into conversation with me and frankly acknowledged that he had been mistaken in opposing the peace. "You were right, and I was wrong all along the line." In the meantime we had received a little demonstration of what the Western aid, offered for arrival in April, would really have meant. Not a month after we had made peace, Germany attacked both Denmark and Norway, and in a couple of months the British forces which had been landed in Norway were driven out altogether. The aid which was to have come through Norway would never have reached its destination. Even though he was a vehement party man, Kares' judgment was basically sound and he was prepared to recognize facts.

Representative Furuhjelm said the Swedish People's Party group would submit to what had occurred, since to continue the struggle might lead to an even harder fate.

Representative Kukkonen declared on behalf of the Agrarian Party that it would also bow to the inevitable, as represented in the peace treaty.

Representative Pennanen, chairman of the Coalition (conservative) Party Diet group, said, though indeed with a heavy heart, that his group would support the Cabinet's proposal. He could wish that the treaty might have been approved by the Diet in silence, with no effort to differentiate the feelings of the various members by speeches. In a few eloquent words, he, too, gave his tribute to the heroic soldiers who had defended their country.

Representative Kekkonen then spoke:

The present Cabinet has been faced with a more difficult decision than any other Finnish governmental entity bearing responsibility for Finland's destinies. One may well imagine how difficult it has been to choose the course whose approval the Diet and the Finnish people now helplessly witness. But it would not have been easy to choose its alternative either—that of continuing the war. And yet I venture to believe that the Finnish people would still have chosen the latter course, if their opinion had been decisive, rough though that road might have proved. . . .

My position has been that a peace dictated by Moscow should not be suffered, but that the fight for independence should go on. Nothing has happened these days to change my stand. . . . And yet one cannot recommend rejection of this treaty. . . . The position is now such that although the Diet is formally entitled to reject the peace treaty, I can nevertheless not suppose that any responsible representative of the people could seriously propose that it be rejected.

Representative Kallia, of the IKL, said that he could not be associated with the approval of the Cabinet proposal. Yet he could not support Representative Estlander's recommendation that it be rejected. To vote for the peace treaty would be dishonorable, and to vote against it would be unreasonable. On this account, abstention in the present instance would not represent indifference, but a protest against the Cabinet's proceedings.

Representative Rytinki, of the Small Farmers, and Representative Heiniö, Progressive, said their groups would approve the Cabinet's proposal.

Representative Schildt, of the IKL, aggressively disputed the statement of his party colleague Kares:

We have not fought in vain; our armed forces have saved the country from complete conquest. When Russia, violating diplomatic custom, had recourse to acts of war without an ultimatum, this was a sure sign that they feared that we in this chamber would assent to the conditions contained in the ultimatum— in other words, that they would get what they wanted. But this would have been merely an appearance, since Russia's purpose was not only to get those areas it had asked for but to conquer the whole country. It was to that end that they violated diplomatic forms and started the war and forced us to this. As to Russia's plans to take over Finland, of that we have documentary proof from the Russian units crushed at Suomussalmi and Salla. These papers show unmistakably that the divisions in question had clear directives as to their mission and designate their future garrison cities on the shores of the Gulf of Bothnia. The obstinate resistance which the Finnish army put up made this Russian plan impossible of realization.

At the conclusion of the debate it was apparent that only Representative Estlander had proposed rejection of the peace treaty. A few speakers had declared that they could not accept it, and one had said that he would abstain from voting. The result of the balloting through the voting machines was that the peace treaty was approved by 145 votes, with only three Representatives voting against it. In addition, nine Representatives had abstained. Forty-two Representatives were absent. As they had been absent at the roll call despite the importance of the occasion, it may be assumed that they wished to signify their unwillingness to participate in the heavy task which the forced approval of the treaty constituted.

On March 16 the President confirmed the decision of the Diet and ratified the peace treaty. Paasikivi and Voionmaa left for Moscow on March 18 in order to exchange the instruments of ratification.

The same day, at 11:45 A.M., Michelet, the Norwegian Minister, called on me to deliver a statement of Halvdan Koht, the Norwegian Foreign Minister, to the effect that Finland had not officially requested auxiliary forces of Norway. I expressed great surprise that this declaration should be deemed necessary so far after events. As to its content, I pointed out that we had many times presented to Norway requests bearing upon auxiliary forces. Furthermore, I had frequently emphasized to Michelet himself Finland's need for aid in the form of troops and had suggested that Norway assume responsibility for the defense of the Petsamo area. It was strange that Norway should now wish to take refuge in the allegation that no official request had been made in the matter.

Michelet acknowledged that representations of this character had been made to him and that the question of the defense of Petsamo had arisen, but in his view no regular official request had been made.

I replied that the request had been made a number of times, and each time in a sufficiently official fashion.

The instruments of ratification of the peace treaty were exchanged in Moscow on March 20. Our delegates, Paasikivi and Voionmaa, remained there many days longer to discuss a variety of most urgent steps made necessary by the peace treaty. More detailed agreements were made on the exact location of the border and on the exchange of prisoners. Information was exchanged regarding the location of mine fields laid down by both sides, and ways of making them harmless were determined. It was as early as this that the first disagreement regarding the Enso area arose. According to the map annexed to the peace treaty, it clearly remained Finnish territory, but the Russians demanded it for themselves. Later the map was altered in favor of the Russians by introducing the necessary bulge at the locality of Enso.

The Russians expressed the hope that two prisoners, Antikainen and Taimi, would be freed and be permitted to go to Russia. Our delegates declared that this was altogether a Finnish domestic concern, since the persons in question were not prisoners of war but spies arrested in time of peace. They were later freed.

Molotov then raised the question of the planned defensive alliance of the Northern countries. He made a protest against the plan, asserting that it was aimed against the Soviet Union and that it harbored a design of revenge. The Finnish delegates set forth a contrary opinion on this point, which, however, made no impression on the opposing party. Subsequently, nothing came of this defensive alliance, precisely by reason of the Soviet Union's opposition.

In a private session of the Council of State held on this day, March 20, we agreed unanimously that, after the exchange of instruments of ratification, the Cabinet should place its portfolios at the disposal of the President. The Cabinet had entered office in December with the sole assignment of bringing about a peace.

It was resolved, however, that no official announcement concerning the resignation should be made until the composition of a new Cabinet was agreed upon. With the intervention of the Easter holidays, the matter remained pending for some days. On March 27, the first day of business after Easter, the Cabinet requested the President to accept its collective resignation. The President approved the request and simultanously appointed a new government.

My task as Foreign Minister was done.

APPENDIX

THE TREATY OF PEACE BETWEEN THE REPUBLIC OF FINLAND AND THE UNION OF SOVIET SOCIALIST REPUBLICS

The government of the Republic of Finland on the one hand and

The Presidium of the Supreme Soviet of the Union of Soviet Socialist Republics on the other hand,

Desiring to put an end to the hostilities which have arisen between the two countries and to create lasting peaceful relations between them,

And being convinced that the creation of precise conditions for reciprocal security, including the security of the cities of Leningrad and Murmansk and of the Murmansk Railway, corresponds to the interest of both contracting parties,

Have to this end found it necessary to conclude a peace treaty and have appointed as their representatives for this purpose

The government of the Republic of Finland:

Risto Ryti, Prime Minister of the Republic of Finland,
Juho Kusti Paasikivi, Minister,
General Rudolf Walden, and
Professor Väinö Voionmaa.

The Presidium of the Supreme Soviet of the Union of Soviet Socialist Republics:

Vyacheslav Mikhailovich Molotov, chairman of the Council of People's Commissars of the Union of Soviet Socialist Republics and People's Commissar for Foreign Affairs,

Andrei Aleksandrovich Zhdanov, member of the Presidium of the Supreme Soviet of the Union of Soviet Socialist Republics,

Aleksandr Mikhailovich Vasilevski, brigade commander.

The above-mentioned representatives, after exchange of credentials, which were found to be in due form and good order, have agreed upon the following:

Article 1

Hostilities between Finland and the U.S.S.R. shall cease immediately in accordance with procedure laid down in the protocol appended to this treaty.

Article 2

The national frontier between the Republic of Finland and the U.S.S.R. shall run along a new line in such fashion that there shall be included in the territory of the U.S.S.R. the entire Karelian Isthmus with the city of Viipuri and Viipuri Bay with its islands, the western and northern shores of Lake Ladoga with the cities of Kexholm and Sortavala and the town of Suojärvi, a number of islands in the Gulf of Finland, the area east of Märkäjärvi with the town of Kuolajärvi, and part of the Rybachi and Sredni peninsulas, all in accordance with the map appended to this treaty.

A more detailed determination and establishment of the frontier line shall be carried out by a mixed commission made up of representatives of the contracting powers, which commission shall be named within ten days from the date of the signing of this treaty.

Article 3

Both contracting parties undertake each to refrain from any attack upon the other and to make no alliance and to participate in no coalition directed against either of the contracting parties.

Article 4

The Republic of Finland agrees to lease to the Soviet Union for thirty years, against an annual rental of eight million Finnish marks to be paid by the Soviet Union, Hanko Cape and the waters surrounding it in a radius of five miles to the south and east and three miles to the north and west, and also the several islands falling within that area, in accordance with the map appended to this treaty, for the establishment of a naval base capable of defending the mouth of the Gulf of Finland against attack; in addition to which, for the purpose of protecting the naval base, the Soviet Union is granted the right of maintaining there at its own expense the necessary number of armed land and air forces.

Within ten days from the date this treaty enters into effect, the government of Finland shall withdraw all its military forces from Hanko Cape, which together with its adjoining islands shall be transferred to the jurisdiction of the U.S.S.R. in accordance with this article of the treaty.

Article 5

The U.S.S.R. undertakes to withdraw its troops from the Petsamo area which the Soviet state voluntarily ceded to Finland under the peace treaty of 1920.

Finland undertakes, as provided in the peace treaty of 1920, to refrain from maintaining in the waters running along its coast of the Arctic Ocean warships and other armed ships, excluding armed ships of less than one hundred tons displacement, which Finland shall be entitled to maintain without restriction, and also at most fifteen warships or other armed ships, the displacement of none of which shall exceed four hundred tons.

Finland undertakes, as was provided in the same treaty, not to maintain in the said waters any submarines or armed aircraft.

Finland similarly undertakes, as was provided in the same treaty, not to establish on that coast military ports, naval bases, or naval repair shops of greater capacity than is necessary for the above-mentioned ships and their armament.

Article 6

As provided in the treaty of 1920, the Soviet Union and its citizens are granted the right of free transit across the Petsamo area to Norway and back, in addition to which the Soviet Union is granted the right to establish a consulate in the Petsamo area.

Merchandise shipped through the Petsamo area from the Soviet Union to Norway, and likewise merchandise shipped through the same area from Norway to the Soviet Union, is exempted from inspection and control, with the exception of such control as is necessary for the regulation of transit traffic; neither customs duties nor transit or other charges shall be assessed.

The above-mentioned control of transit merchandise shall be permitted only in the form usual in such cases in accordance with established practice in international communications.

Citizens of the Soviet Union who travel through the Petsamo area to Norway and from Norway back to the Soviet Union shall be entitled to free transit passage on the basis of passports issued by the appropriate officials of the Soviet Union.

Observing general directives in effect, unarmed Soviet aircraft shall be entitled to maintain air service between the Soviet Union and Norway via the Petsamo area.

Article 7

The government of Finland grants to the Soviet Union the right of transit for goods between the Soviet Union and Sweden, and, with a view to developing this traffic along the shortest railway route, the Soviet Union and Finland consider it necessary to build, each upon its own territory and insofar as possible in the year 1940, a railway which shall connect Kantalahti (Kandalaksha) with Kemijärvi.

Article 8

Upon the coming into force of this treaty economic relations between the contracting parties shall be restored, and with this end in view the contracting parties shall enter into negotiations for the conclusion of a trade agreement.

Article 9

This treaty of peace shall enter into effect immediately upon being signed, and shall be subject to subsequent ratification.

The exchange of instruments of ratification shall take place within ten days in the city of Moscow.

This treaty has been prepared in two original instruments, in the Finnish and Swedish languages and in Russian, at Moscow this twelfth day of March, 1940.

RISTO RYTI   V. MOLOTOV
J. K. PAASIKIVI   A. ZHDANOV
R. WALDEN   A. VASILEVSKI
VÄINÖ VOIONMAA

PROTOCOL APPENDED TO THE TREATY OF PEACE CONCLUDED
BETWEEN FINLAND AND THE UNION OF SOVIET SOCIALIST
REPUBLICS ON MARCH 12, 1940

The contracting parties confirm the following arrangement for cessation of
hostilities and the withdrawal of troops beyond the national boundary established by the peace treaty:

1. Both sides shall cease hostilities on March 13, 1940, at 12:00 noon
Leningrad time.

2. As from the hour fixed for the cessation of hostilities there shall be established a neutral zone, one kilometer in depth, between the positions of advanced
units, whereupon within the course of the first day forces of that party to the
treaty which under the new national boundary find themselves in territory pertaining to the other party to the treaty shall withdraw one kilometer's distance.

3. Withdrawal of troops beyond the new national boundary and advance
of the troops of the other party to this national boundary shall commence on
March 15 from 10:00 A.M. along the whole frontier from the Gulf of Finland
to Lieksa, and on March 16 from 10:00 A.M. at points north of Lieksa. Withdrawal shall be effected through daily marches of not less than seven kilometers,
the advance of troops of the other party taking place in such fashion that there
shall be maintained between the rear guard of the withdrawing troops and the
advance units of the other party to the treaty an interval of not less than seven
kilometers.

4. The following time limits are established for withdrawal, on various
sectors of the national boundary, in accordance with Paragraph 3:

a) In the sector comprising the upper course of the Tuntsajoki River,
Kuolajärvi, Takala, and the eastern shore of Lake Joukamojärvi the movement
of troops of both parties to the treaty shall be completed on March 20, 1940,
at 8:00 P.M.

b) In the Latva sector south of Kuhmoniemi, troop movements shall be
completed on March 22, 1940, at 8:00 P.M.

c) In the Lonkavaara, Värtsilä, and Matkaselkä station sector, troop movements of both parties shall be completed on March 22, 1940, at 8:00 P.M.

d) In the Koitsanlahti sector at Matkaselkä station, troop movements shall
be completed on March 25, 1940, at 8:00 P.M.

e) In the Enso station sector at Koitsanlahti, troop movements shall be
completed on March 25, 1940, at 8:00 P.M.

f) In the Paationsaari sector at Enso station, troop movements shall be
completed on March 19, 1940, at 8:00 P.M.

5. Evacuation of troops of the Red Army from the Petsamo area shall be
completed by April 10, 1940.

6. The command of each party to the treaty undertakes, while troops are
withdrawing to the other side of the national boundary, to put into effect in the
cities and localities to be ceded to the other party necessary measures for their
preservation undamaged, and to put into effect measures necessary to the end

that cities, localities, and establishments of defensive and economic importance (bridges, dams, airfields, barracks, storehouses, railway communications, industrial plants, telegraphs, electric power plants) shall be preserved from damage and destruction.

7. All questions which may arise upon the cession by one contracting party to the other of the areas, localities, cities, or other objectives referred to in Paragraph 6 of this protocol shall be settled on the spot by representatives of both parties to the treaty, for which purpose the command shall appoint special delegates for each main route of movement of both armies.

8. The exchange of prisoners of war shall be carried out in the briefest possible time after the cessation of hostilities on the basis of a special agreement.

March 12, 1940

Risto Ryti	V. Molotov
J. K. Paasikivi	A. Zhdanov
R. Walden	A. Vasilevski
Väinö Voionmaa	

INDEX

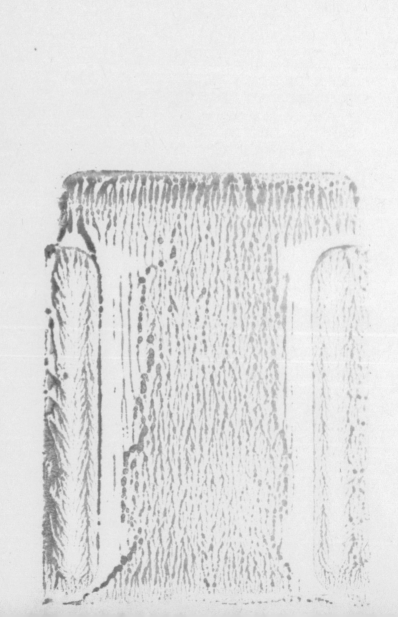